Queer Beirut

Queer Beirut

BY SOFIAN MERABET

University of Texas Press *Austin*

The University of Texas Press and the author gratefully acknowledge financial assistance provided for the publication of this book from the President's Office at The University of Texas at Austin.

Copyright © 2014 by the University of Texas Press
All rights reserved
Printed in the United States of America
First edition, 2014
First paperback edition, 2015

Requests for permission to reproduce material from this work should be sent to:
Permissions
University of Texas Press
P.O. Box 7819
Austin, TX 78713-7819
http://utpress.utexas.edu/index.php/rp-form

♾ The paper used in this book meets the minimum requirements of ANSI/NISO Z39.48-1992 (R1997) (Permanence of Paper).

Library of Congress Cataloging-in-Publication Data
Merabet, Sofian
Queer Beirut / by Sofian Merabet.
pages cm
ISBN 978-0-292-76096-7 (hardback)
1. Gay men—Lebanon—Beirut. 2. Gender identity—Lebanon—Beirut.
3. Homosexuality—Lebanon—Beirut. I. Title.
HQ76.2.L42B456 2014
306.76′620956925—dc23

2014013809

doi:10.7560/760967

978-1-4773-0991-9 (pbk.)

عيوني

Für meinen Neffen Jules und meine Patentochter Widad.

Mögen sie im Strudel der Identitäten stets zahlreiche Querverbindungen finden.

Contents

Illustrations

Acknowledgments

Queer Beirut has been inspired and shaped by countless people, places, and encounters. Yet, this book would not exist without the constant reassurances of a host of individuals. To thank them here is the least I can do. I express my heartfelt gratitude to all of them, named and unnamed. Even though most of my interlocutors, whose lives form the central part of this book, shall remain anonymous through the systematic use of pseudonyms, my first "thank you" goes to them.

A city that since 1995 has turned into a place full of personal twists and turns, Beirut has also become a home. Helping me to feel at home there were dear friends, such as the most hospitable and always receptive Iman Humaydan, Wissam Hojaiban, Nisrine Maktabi, Dia Abou-Mousleh, Ghassan Makarem, Haydar Sadek, Amale Abi-Saab, Sami and Ynesse Abdel-Malak, Pierre Azar, Sami Khalife, Vicky Abboud, and the two Pascales, Fakhry and Féghali.

First as an associate researcher, then as a full-time instructor in the social sciences, I spent three years in the early 2000s affiliated with the American University of Beirut (AUB). I am indebted to the indefatigable Samir Khalaf for his generosity and his unfailing professional support. In Lebanon, I found sources of intellectual inspiration and mentorship in Abbas Beydoun, Elias Khoury, Franck Mermier, Lucine Taminian, Jean Hannoyer, Mona Harb, George Arbid, and Nizar Saghieh. Straddling the transnational community of "glocal" scholars, artists, and thinkers who nourished my mind with their respective projects were the late Ulla Klaes, Monika Borgmann, Paola Yaqoub, Akram Zaatari, and, especially, Friederike Stolleis, whose dear friendship I could not value more.

Some of the people I cannot thank enough for their camaraderie and motivation "commuted" between Lebanon and the United States. They include academics like Lara Deeb, Ramzi Kassem, Aseel Sawalha, Randa Serhan, Yasser Munif, and Nadya Sbaiti. Others were freer spirits and not bound by the constraints of academia, namely Laure Bjawi-Levine and Rabih Alameddine. Rabih's unshakable appreciation made him endure the countless stories of love and trepidation I imposed on him. He still listens, or so I hope. I initially met my friend and fellow academic Markus Schmitz on a gloomy Beirut day in early March 2002. He cleared the clouds for me and has continued to do so.

Nothing would have been possible without the caring reassurance of my peers on the western side of the Atlantic. The Columbia connection included Sonali Pahwa, Ruchi Chaturvedi, Yukiko Koga, Nadia Latif, and Munira Khayyat, whose human qualities shaped me in more ways than I am aware of. I thank my soul mate Max Krämer for being there whenever I need him. What I share with Max is much more than specific languages and cultures; it is also anecdotal humor and the idiosyncrasies of unusual lives. Entirely outside of the academic loop is Bosko Boskovic. I owe Bosko so much that I need more than just a sentence or two to acknowledge his relentless commitment to what unites both of us.

Books of this kind are rarely written without long-lasting academic support and mentorship. I must, therefore, thank my teachers Brinkley Messick and Lila Abu-Lughod for their unending encouragement and intellectual stimulation. Nick DeGenova, Peter Awn, Lynn Meskell, and Elaine Combs-Schilling provided me with invaluable advice at an earlier stage. So did Julie Peteet, to whom I also owe an unforgettable year in lovely Lu'ville, Kentucky.

First as a graduate student, then as a junior faculty member, I had the opportunity to spend almost eight years in New York City, a period during which many minds made an irrevocable impact on me. I extend my deepest gratitude to Sylvère Lotringer and Andreas Huyssen at Columbia University, Michael Gilsenan and Ella Shohat at New York University, Vincent Crapanzano and Talal Asad at the Graduate Center, City University of New York, and Alan Bass at the New School for Social Research.

In the mid-1990s, I boarded a westbound plane and crossed the North Atlantic for the first time. I met a fine and humble gentleman in upstate New York. Without him, any academic achievement of mine is unthinkable, for it was he who took the inexperienced international student under his mentoring wings. Although our first conversation had to be conducted in Arabic because my English was abysmal at the time, for some reason, he did not give up on me. Richard Antoun, you are dearly missed!

I must thank many of my colleagues at the University of Texas at Austin, both in and out of the Department of Anthropology, for their relentless support. I am especially indebted to Kamran Ali, Elizabeth Keating, Ward Keeler, Shannon Speed, Katie Stewart, Polly Strong, Tony di Fiore, and Fátima Wade. Kamala Visweswaran read an early draft of this book and gave me vital feedback. The members of my writing group, Craig Campbell, Heather Hindman, and Kaushik Ghosh know the work they have done, and I cannot thank them enough. Beyond my department, Ann Cvetkovich, the queen of Texas Queer Studies, has been instrumental in fomenting that "critical mass" at and around UT that keeps me going. Thanks also to Lisa Moore, Sue Heinzelman, Arturo Arias, Jill Robbins, David Quinto-Pozos, Tarek El-Ariss, Karin Wilkins, Doug Biow, Akbar Hyder, Karen Engle, and my dear fellow Algerian(ist), Ben Brower. Their respective contributions to the battle of ideas on and around campus have been crucial to my intellectual well-being. My two sisters-in-arms, Barbara Bullock and Almeida Toribio, keep reminding me that collegiality can also include a heartfelt friendship.

Segments of this book benefited from questions asked and comments made during various panels at meetings of the Middle East Association of North America (MESA) and the American Anthropological Association (AAA) that were sponsored by the Association for Queer Anthropology (AQA), the Society for Cultural Anthropology, and the Middle East Section (MES). I also presented parts of some chapters at a number of institutions, including the American University of Beirut; the École des Hautes Études en Sciences Sociales (EHESS) in Paris; the University of Massachusetts, Amherst; the University of Denver; the College of Wooster; the University of Saskatchewan; the University of California, Los Angeles; the University of Münster; Amherst College; Hunter College in the City University of New York; the University of Maryland, Baltimore County; and the Zentrum Moderner Orient (ZMO) in Berlin. I must, therefore, thank colleagues such as Naisargi Dave, Cymene Howe, Shaka McGlotten, Michelle Obeid, Sami Hermez, Mona Fawaz, Svati Shah, Maria das Dores Cruz, Jimmy Noriega, Ahmet Atay, Gil Hochberg, Maya Boutaghou, Janell Rothenberg, Olivia Harrison, Monica Ringer, and Anja Peleikis for their helpful remarks and criticisms. At my own institution, the University of Texas at Austin, I have been fortunate to be part of numerous stimulating dialogues around "zones of intellectual encounter" that include, but are not limited to, the Humanities Institute Faculty Seminar, the Center for Women's and Gender Studies, and the LGBT/Sexualities Research Cluster.

Beyond Texas, I am thankful for the support of my former colleague,

Lok Siu, and for her incisive appreciation of all things anthropological. Susan Slyomovics and Steve Caton, although living on the shores of two different oceans, have been a source of constant inspiration. In Paris, I am indebted to Jocelyne Dakhlia, Sonia Dayan-Herzbrun, Gianfranco Rebucini, Tassadit Yacine, Mira Younes, and Ludovic Zahed for the many transatlantic and transdisciplinary dialogues we have had over the years. In Buenos Aires, I must thank four generations of the Barreyra family, *mi familia argentina*, especially the brothers Sergio and Facundo, as well as Lisa Franz, for their heartfelt friendship that has survived the decades, and for the moral support they gave me when, sitting at my *porteña* kitchen table, I was putting the final touches to this book. And back in Central Texas, I am very grateful to my University of Texas Press editor, the unflagging Jim Burr, whose backing and patience I have put to the test more than I should have. The same applies to Lynne Chapman, the manuscript editor, and Sally Furgeson, the copyeditor, who demonstrated utmost bravery on the battlefield of wordiness and verbiage. I am also indebted to Matthew LaFevor, who designed from scratch both of the maps included in this book.

No acknowledgment of mine would be complete without paying tribute to my family. After all, it is they who, full of love and support, waited patiently year after year, "pushing their thumbs" across ocean and sea so that I would finally finish this book. My mother, Doris Merabet, never failed to provide me with everything only the most fortunate of sons can hope for. Always interested in what I was doing, be it in the Americas, in the Arab world, or back in Europe, she taught me how to discover and gain access to new horizons, even if they seemed unattainable. My sister Miriam followed all my experiences closely and never withheld words and acts of endorsement and love, especially when her older brother had major doubts about the ground he was standing on.

It is to new generations to make decisions about how to shape the various worlds they inhabit. It is thus to my nephew Jules and my goddaughter Widad, two prime examples of individuals living at the intersection of several cultures and languages, that I dedicate *Queer Beirut*. May they always find connections beyond the maelstrom of conventional identities.

PROLOGUE

Itinerant Journeys

I grew up at the time of the Lebanese civil war, not on the eastern shore of the Mediterranean, but in the southwest of the mare nostrum. While parallels exist between post-civil-war Lebanon and the Algeria of my childhood, numerous differences between the two countries color respectively a complex socio-historical picture. The child in Algeria had almost grown accustomed to daily television news bulletins that depicted the violence of a civil war raging some three thousand kilometers (1,860 miles) to the east. However, some twenty years later, the adult, who had moved to the Levant, was horror-struck whenever he read in the local press about the human slaughtering that, by then, was taking place on a regular basis in the North African country of his upbringing.[1]

Although circumlocutory in nature, my first concrete encounter with Lebanon was in 1982. I will never forget the bizarre month of June of that year. On the fourteenth, Argentina had surrendered to Britain after a seventy-four-day military conflict over what the former called Las Islas Malvinas, and the latter, the Falklands. Meanwhile, the world championship of what some referred to as *le foot* and others, as I would find out much later, soccer, was under way in Spain, capturing the undivided attention of countless fans from Rio to Recklinghausen. Cynics would later say that it was the perfect moment to divert attention from another event taking place at the exact same time at the opposite end of the Mediterranean from where the world worshipped the black-and-white leather ball.

I remember being horrified by images of thousands of Lebanese and Palestinians, of all ages, trying to leave Beirut in order to flee from the approaching Israeli troops. The Israeli commanders had timed their invasion in a way that, in a soccer-crazed world, could not have been better. This was my very first encounter with Lebanon. The underlying tenor of violence and pain continued throughout my childhood, with the regular news briefings of this and that massacre, the numerous car bombs, and the unanticipated word *masīḥī* that I kept hearing later on Algerian state television.

I was not yet ten when the Arabic word for "Christian"—*masīḥī*—all of a sudden made sense to me. So did the discovery of why Madame Giselle Yaghmour, my strict Arabic teacher from Aleppo, had the first name she had and why she did not fast during the month of Ramadan: she was Christian. At the same time, Madame Yaghmour was not "foreign" but Arab, if not to say "very Arab," at least as compared to us Maghrebi "mongrels" who had the post-colonial privilege of going to one of the elite French schools in Algiers.[2]

For the remaining years of the 1980s, *lubnān* (Lebanon) was the setting of daily news items about fights and struggles that had become a fixture for everybody around me.[3] However, when my family and I left Algeria in 1988, the overall situation seemed to have changed altogether. Now I was watching what would turn out to be the last battles of the Lebanese civil war, traumatized by the unanticipated dreadful news of the October riots in Algiers. From the comfortable living room of my German grandparents, I saw the collapse of the city I had grown up in, whose seemingly peaceful atmosphere I had left just three months earlier. What marked me considerably at the time was a sentence uttered by an eyewitness on the French channel Antenne 2: "Alger est devenue un deuxième Beyrouth!" (Algiers has become a second Beirut!)

My formal introduction to Beirut happened seven years later, and the city's capacity to harbor the least ordinary happenstances within what I would later term "zones of encounter" captured my immediate attention. I remembered reading William Foote Whyte's 1943 classic, *Street Corner Society: The Social Structure of an Italian Slum*, and the author's emphasis on understanding "the relations between little guy and little guy, and big shot and big shot . . . ." Through this understanding, Whyte argued, "we know how Cornerville society is organized." He added, "On the basis of that knowledge it becomes possible to explain people's loyalties and the significance of political and racket activities."[4] Beirut is certainly no "Cornerville," and my interlocutors are not gang members, racketeers, or politicians, let alone part of an ethnically and socially marginalized group such as the 1940s Italian-American immigrants in Whyte's pioneering study. While Chick Morelli, Tony Cataldo, and Angelo call one particular neighborhood their own, namely one that is considered by all and sundry a "slum," Rachid, Ramzi, and Hadi, some of the young men with whom

I interacted in Beirut, come from a variety of ethno-religious and social backgrounds and live throughout the Lebanese capital, as well as in its various suburbs.

Yet, Whyte's approach remains methodologically useful for my own fieldwork conducted some sixty years later. In the appendix to his book, Whyte wrote that he "was building up the structure and functioning of the community through intensive examination of some of its parts—in action." In fact, he "was relating the parts together through observing events between groups and . . . members of the larger institutional structures." For him, the chief methodological and theoretical meaning of *Street Corner Society* was "to build a sociology based upon observed interpersonal events."[5] By using ethnography as a critical intervention, I build on this very meaning in *Queer Beirut*.

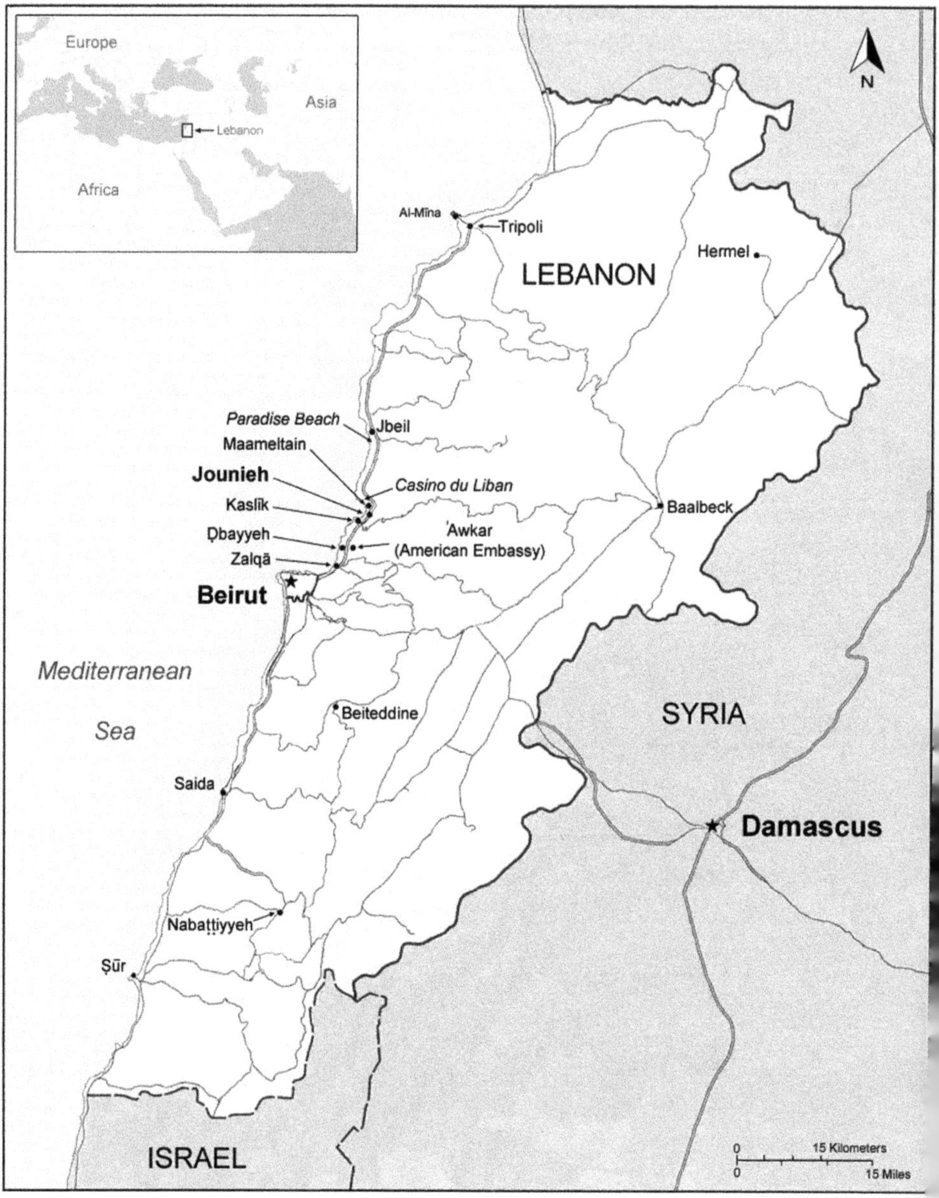

Map of Lebanon

Queer Beirut

Introduction

On the third floor of his slightly dilapidated hotel in Beirut's Ḥamra district, Rachid stands bare-chested on a concrete balcony and looks down on the evening rush hour unfurling along Makdisi Street. He is quite a handsome man in his late twenties. Nonetheless, his red hair and the countless ginger-colored freckles that cover his fine-looking face and brawny body deter a certain number of his contemporaries, who would have otherwise courted him fervidly. Rather on the short side, Rachid is well built without ever having entered a gym. He pays close attention to his outward appearance. His haircut is always meticulous with a hint at the fashion of the moment. Indeed, almost all of his modest earnings are spent on the type of clothes worn in trendy circles in Milan, Paris, or Madrid. Yet, Rachid stands on the hotel's balcony without any kind of ostentation, his eyes fixed on the passersby below as they compete with the countless cars for sovereignty over sidewalk and street.

Rachid is not a tourist, visiting Beirut on a summer holiday. Rather, he had moved temporarily to the capital from his native Tripoli in northern Lebanon to take a job in the advertisement section of one of the main Lebanese private TV stations. In fact, he sort of commutes, albeit not on a daily basis, spending the week in and around the Ḥamra district of Beirut, while "going home," as he would put it, to Tripoli's Al-Mina neighborhood on the weekends.[1] When we met in 2001, Rachid had been working for some two years at a job arranged by his long-time partner, Khalil. His various family connections provided Khalil with lifelong access to power and privilege envied by most men of the Lebanese lower-middle classes, such as Rachid.

Rachid and Khalil had met seven years earlier on Paradise Beach, the southernmost extension of Jbeil's bustling seashore located about thirty-

Paradise Beach, July 28, 2013.

seven kilometers (twenty-three miles) north of Beirut. With a strong Arabic intonation, all and sundry called the sandy stretch *al-baradays*, thus turning the bilabial stop of the English letter *p* into the Arabic-voiced bilabial plosive *b*—as in *bayrūt*, for instance. At the time, Rachid was nineteen and an art student at Ballamand University, a Greek Orthodox institution with a beautiful campus overlooking the southern suburbs of the country's second-largest city, Tripoli. Khalil was twenty-eight, and, for many years, this difference in age made it impossible for Rachid to introduce this mysterious "friend" to his family. His parents and his two younger brothers initially grew to know Khalil through countless stories about the "Christian friend from affluent Rabieh," the upper-class enclave in northeastern Beirut.

But Rachid never revealed his growing romantic relationship in the stories he told his family. He commented to me years later that, even though the subject of his homosexuality was taboo at home, it was not unbeknownst to his parents. He kept saying, "Maʿun khabar . . . bass mā byaḥkū" (They know . . . but they just don't talk [about it]). Instead of talking about his sexual orientation, Rachid's parents advised their eldest son repeatedly to get married. Yet, despite all parental advice, Rachid and Khalil continued their regular rendezvous throughout the second half of the 1990s, meeting almost every Sunday afternoon on Jbeil's Paradise Beach.

An Anthropology of Sexual Difference

This ethnographic vignette sheds an introductory light on the romantic involvement of two Lebanese men and the numerous challenges they encountered within what I call "queer Beirut." The following pages focus on various experiences of queer-identified individuals and explore how men such as Rachid and Khalil navigate the complex microcosm of intimate rendezvous and intricate homosexual relationships in Lebanon. This microcosm is based on a fertile social, emotional, and moral milieu, where the negotiation of dissident sexualities takes place against a heteronormative formulaic backdrop and, at the same time, shapes the human geography of queer identity formation. This complex microcosm also conveys a particular social logic of self-imagining and self-projection, which points to a dynamic interpretation and a potential challenge to a number of normative interpellations.[2] In Lebanon, such interpretations and challenges are enacted spatially and through intricate bodily performances, and they often culminate with a dramatic unfolding on the streets and balconies of Beirut.

Yet, apart from being the story of Rachid and Khalil, this anthropological investigation into sexual difference is also an ethnography of the city within which dissident sexualities live. It traces the genealogy of contemporary constructions of norms and forms of social inclusion and exclusion within the urban fabric of Beirut and, through a focus on its margins, develops a critical socio-cultural paradigm for the study of sexuality in and around the city. Moreover, by examining the formations of Lebanese queer identities in relation to global processes of circulation and translation of gender models and ideas, this book tackles the subject of contested identities and sexual difference through an interdisciplinary approach that positions the importance of gender and sexual identities at the center of an often over-simplified political understanding of the very notion of identity. In Lebanon, that notion has traditionally been defined on the basis of sectarian and religious affiliation. I attempt to complement and expand on such a notion by providing a critical standpoint from which to deepen our understandings of gender rights and citizenship in the structuring of social inequality within the larger context of the Arab world.[3] I explore, therefore, the performative bodily practices of gendering for young Lebanese gay men as they formulate their sense of what it means to "exist" among the numerous physical and mental maps of an urban grid that is perpetually disputed by its various inhabitants.

The present work is heavily influenced by the writings of Pierre Bourdieu and Michel de Certeau on theories of practice or what I call the individual making of meaning within the larger context of everyday life in Beirut.[4] In drawing attention to various manifestations of public culture in Lebanon and the ways in which they take form in daily processes of urban identity formations, I take these manifestations as the framework within which to explore the performative practices of gendering in a highly globalized urban milieu. Based on a broad interdisciplinary approach, my research intends ultimately to open the door for a timely anthropological conversation about gender and queer identities in both Middle East and Urban Studies. It draws on a critical theory of gender and religious identity formations that can disrupt conventional anthropological premises about the contingent role that particular spaces have in facilitating the emergence of various subcultures within the city.

How can an anthropologist write about these spaces, along with the performative bodily practices of gendering, and other modes of queer identity formation? How can one address the local politics of homosexual disavowal and homophobia, especially in conjunction with what I call "queer space" and its contested production in a city such as Beirut? Similar to the analytical subject treated here, one that constitutes a significant part of Lebanon's socio-cultural landscape, the answers to both questions are directly connected to the ways in which one evaluates a perpetually changing global landscape, of which the country is an integral part. It is a fluctuating landscape that needs to be addressed by an intellectual tradition that can be considered neither as one monolithic body, with a coherent thread running through it, nor as a chronological teleology proceeding from a clear-cut beginning to an explicit end.

Rather, to make sense theoretically of queerness in Beirut, one has to draw on different and, at times, competing methodological angles. The knowledge of space, for instance, along with its social and cultural production, constantly oscillates between cohesive description and circumstantial fragmentation. One describes objects within space or unrelated fragments of space while presenting either an anthropological field site or a geographical place. Yet, one rarely reflects on the intricate ways in which space is socially produced and the relations and consequences that a culturally mindful anthropology entertains with the geography of difference within whose realm it operates.

Lebanon's capital Beirut is one of these field sites where the anthropologist is constantly reminded of the historically rich and conflicting nature of the urban landscape, its shifting borderlines, and the entrenched interpretations of a variety of spaces that are persistently contested. As the novelist Rabih Alameddine remarks in *The Hakawati*:

> You take different groups, put them on top of each other, simmer for a thousand years, keep adding more and more strange tribes, simmer for another few thousand years, salt and pepper with religion, and what you get is a delightful mess of a stew that still tastes delectable and exotic, no matter how many times you partake of it.[5]

In trying to illustrate my main point, one that is theoretical as well as ethnographically imbued by storytelling, I shall partake of this "delightful mess" and focus on specific human encounters in different places within the Lebanese capital that come close to the production of queer space. They are often sites in which the socially assumed dichotomy between "public" and "private" cannot be easily applied. Instead, the commonly perceived binary between these two presumably separate spheres gives room to what I understand as being "zones of encounter"—namely, particular urban locations that foster attempts, with various levels of success, to transcend spatio-temporal fixities.[6]

Through various kinds of personal interactions—ranging from the informal conversation on an apparently random street corner to a highly encoded verbal, and at times nonverbal, communication involving suggestive gazes and bodily postures—these fixities, along with their sociocultural correlates, come to be challenged precisely in those locations in and around Beirut that usher in different kinds of individual and collective representations. In dialogue with the French urbanist-philosopher Henri Lefebvre, I argue that these representations, whose queer character I mean to emphasize, are clearly marked by the individual bodies involved in them.[7] They arise out of a dialectic relationship between a controlled and ordered space, on the one hand, and a contested space, actively appropriated, as well as lived in by all sorts of people and their queer performative corporeality, on the other.[8]

Thus, the idea of lived space, with its countless corresponding intersections, becomes most relevant within the interdisciplinary concept of the "moment" purported by Lefebvre, an instant captured by philosophy, literature, and politics that privileges the spatial—physical and mental—over the temporal, yet without discounting the latter.[9] It is this concept that I endeavor to appropriate in part myself. When I write about zones of encounter in the opening chapter of this book, I refer to an epistemological extension of Lefebvre's moment—namely, one within which what I call the "homosexual sphere" in a place like Beirut is best captured in its wide-ranging complexity and its impulse to strive toward possible autonomy.

The encounter itself is an intimate moment of sorts. It is to be located first in time, but equally in space. Such intimacy of the moment points also to the very event of meeting between people who would not necessarily have come together had it not been for this particular time and place. Notwithstanding their discreet character, general encounters in Lebanon are always linked to either one or more publicly accessible places—in many cases, a café/restaurant, but possibly also a movie theater or an Internet café. But more often than not, they are linked to the lesser spatial formality of particular streets or street corners scattered all over the city, and even beyond. For example, life on certain streets and avenues in Beirut unveils a kind of metaphysics of space, a poetic divinity, next to which thousands of people may pass without necessarily seeing anything, and which suddenly becomes sensitively tangible and terribly haunting for those who have a particular social stake in it. This intense sensation is certainly not limited to iconic urban pathways like the Corniche, Ḥamra Street, or Rue Monot. It also includes less exposed roads and alleys located in both affluent and marginalized parts of town.

On some sort of canonical mental map, the individuals I interviewed in Beirut are concerned by these particular intricate differences. They will read the social topography of a neighborhood in the Lebanese capital not merely in terms of a grid of real-life streets. Rather, they will perceive and interpret it as a congregation of sites and cultural references. These sites and references loom large in the imaginations of these local, young queer-identified men with whom I interacted over the years in Lebanon. It is this very reason, having to do with the intricacies of a social topography, that made me choose to capture Beirut's countless congregations of sites and cultural references by literally walking through the entire city, thus indulging in some desperate act of *flânerie*. My choice translated into a challenging enterprise, if not to say one that bears a queering element, which turned the *flâneur* into a sort of queer stroller. The challenge was great, for the social conformities of post-civil-war Lebanon coerce many Lebanese to approach their urban center not via public transportation, let alone on foot, but along the routes of a car driver's paradise, one that is ultimately ill-judged and hauntingly deceptive.

It goes without saying that Beirut is not Los Angeles, so driving the latest American models of sports utility vehicles in the relatively small, and usually car-infested, streets of the Lebanese capital becomes an all-too-obvious exercise in damaging indulgence. Thus, the local politics of prestige and status symbolizations, privileging the unmistaken agenda of the big and brazen, often define a man by his best phallic friend—i.e., the automobile. To willfully walk through the streets and avenues of Beirut, in either a leisurely or a hurried manner, is anything but a commonly shared activity. The trials of coping with the notorious lack of sidewalks is, at best, something that only a "nobody"—i.e., a status-lacking and condemned pedestrian—may be disposed to take up. As an anthropologist, I would argue, however, that by moving against the noxious grain of fumes and honks, it becomes possible for the researcher, and anybody else interested not in mere numbers but rather in the wider urban ramification of a city like Beirut, to experience an invigorating rupture within an otherwise largely limiting scheme of things. It is, therefore, only as a person on foot in a city that almost makes natural locomotion virtually impossible that the observing anthropologist can start to think about distinguishing many of the urban spaces in Lebanon that bear the potential of creating alternative, and perhaps queer, discourses.

Queer, an Analytic Category

The way I define the term "queer," a category I use for analytic purposes, is influenced but not limited by early writings of Judith Butler that posit queer as "a site of collective contestation."[10] In its various redeployments, this potentially rebellious element of the analytic category "queer" can be politically enabling and is etymologically related to the German word *quer*, which, used in common parlance, refers to "transverse, cross, oblique." A *Querkopf* (literally, a queer head), for instance, would be a misfit of sorts, somebody who thinks and translates outside the normative box and against the dominant paradigms. More fittingly, however, a *Querdenker* (queer thinker) is a lateral—if not to say unconventional—thinker whose very habitus is to invest in the countless ramifications of ever-shifting epistemological intersections. But he is also a sort of prisoner of love, whose captivity is ever entangled with the very object of his desire.[11] Similarly, I would like to argue that queerness and its rebellious character, due to their equal analytical and ethnographic relevance, are always also located on the verge not only of captivity, but also of madness. The Arabic term *junūn* marks the border of the obsessive and even ecstatic. It implies passion and the unleashing of strong desire toward an object that solicits fluctuating imaginative horizons and the production of corresponding spaces. The *majnūn* and the *majnūna*, those who are afflicted with *junūn* in their singular masculine and feminine forms, are possessed by their unorthodox love for their respective objects of desire, but come often under attack for it by an array of hostile social forces.

By way of introducing a number of social representations of queerness and their rebellious character bordering on *junūn*, where an apparently controlled and unhampered space is being contested and appropriated by queer-identified individuals who give specific meanings to it, I focus again in the following chapters on the ethnographic example of Rachid and Khalil, who were a romantic couple at the time I met them. At the crucial juncture of the mid-1990s, the microcosm of their intimate relationship paralleled in some ways the macrocosm of a war-torn Beirut trying to forget its violent past. The example also illustrates the dialectic relationship stressed above. The correlation between what is perceived as fixed and what is akin to the individual making of meaning is instrumental in understanding some of the socio-cultural dynamics behind "madness" and "love," as well as the ever-shifting borderlines of a historically compound and disparate place such as Lebanon. In other words, what you are about to read in *Queer Beirut* is also about *junūn bayrūt*.

The Study

Queer Beirut is based on a number of ethnographic journeys I made to Lebanon from 1995 to 2014, including an extended stay from summer 2001 to winter 2003–2004, during which I conducted research for my doctoral dissertation. Since 2004, shorter trips have ranged in length from two weeks to three months. Despite regular Israeli attacks, which culminated in *ḥarb tammūz*, the July 2006 war, and with the exception of my post-2005 fieldwork, my previous ethnographic work reflects some kind of "bubble period," called otherwise *Pax Syriana*. This period followed the fifteen years of the civil war (1975–1990) and preceded the unfurling of internal crises that afflicted Lebanon after the assassination of the former prime minister, Rafik Hariri, on February 14, 2005. It was a period of presumed insouciance—maybe one similar to that of my Algerian childhood—that marked the attitude of many Lebanese at the time, even though the clear-headed observer could have predicted that seemingly eternal sublimation was not possible. The ghosts of the past had to return at some point.

Yet, none of this research, practical and theoretical, would have been possible without exploring closely the importance of bodily performances, especially in such a highly "corporeal" country like Lebanon. In what follows, I thus relate individual and collective bodily performances to larger queer encounters on the national stage. It is a stage located on the border of an assumed public and private sphere. Its spatial boundaries symbolize both the encounter as a "meeting place" as well as "cut-off lines" with other social spheres in and around what Michel de Certeau called the "figure of the City, the masterword of an anonymous law, the substitute for all proper names."[12] I thus want to address different modes of individual performative practices as they interact with the spatial formations of queer gender identities in Beirut. Drawing on de Certeau's writings in *The Practice of Everyday Life*, or "l'invention du quotidien," as he put it in the original French, I locate performance within an everyday life experience and attempt to look at the various ways in which young gay men, as socio-culturally gendered subjects whose identities are performatively "invented" by their bodily expressions, engage in what Judith Butler, in dialogue with Eve Kosofsky Sedgwick in her theory of gender, has called "queer performativity."[13]

However, these "queer" individuals contest and appropriate their alternative life-worlds not only iteratively within the homosexual sphere, but also spatially within the larger urban context of the Lebanese capital. Along these lines, I want to posit two central questions: How can one understand gay individuals who resist self-identification? And, how is a multi-faceted homophobia within the general discourse of such an urban homosexual sphere socio-culturally explicable?

The answer to these questions is partly found in ethnography and the anthropological attempt to capture the complex reality of de Certeau's "figure" (i.e., the city). I thus try to give to my text some of the stylistic range occupied by the various encounters, all of which take place and come to pass within the homosexual sphere in Beirut. For one, I include the most "scientific" genre I could handle, albeit one that is less preoccupied with the felt stringency of empirical "facts" and more by a close consideration of what constitutes *Wissen* and its production within the German notion of *Wissenschaft*. Second, I dare to venture on occasion on an idiosyncratic exploration into the essay form akin to an ethnographic montage, to borrow from Walter Benjamin's eclectic theoretical repertoire. This form, I felt, best suited my intellectual endeavors, where the subject of tragedy is often exhibited in comedic form, even if the tragicomedian in question does not always realize the part he or she is playing. Being as it is, whether my choices are warranted is for the reader alone to decide.

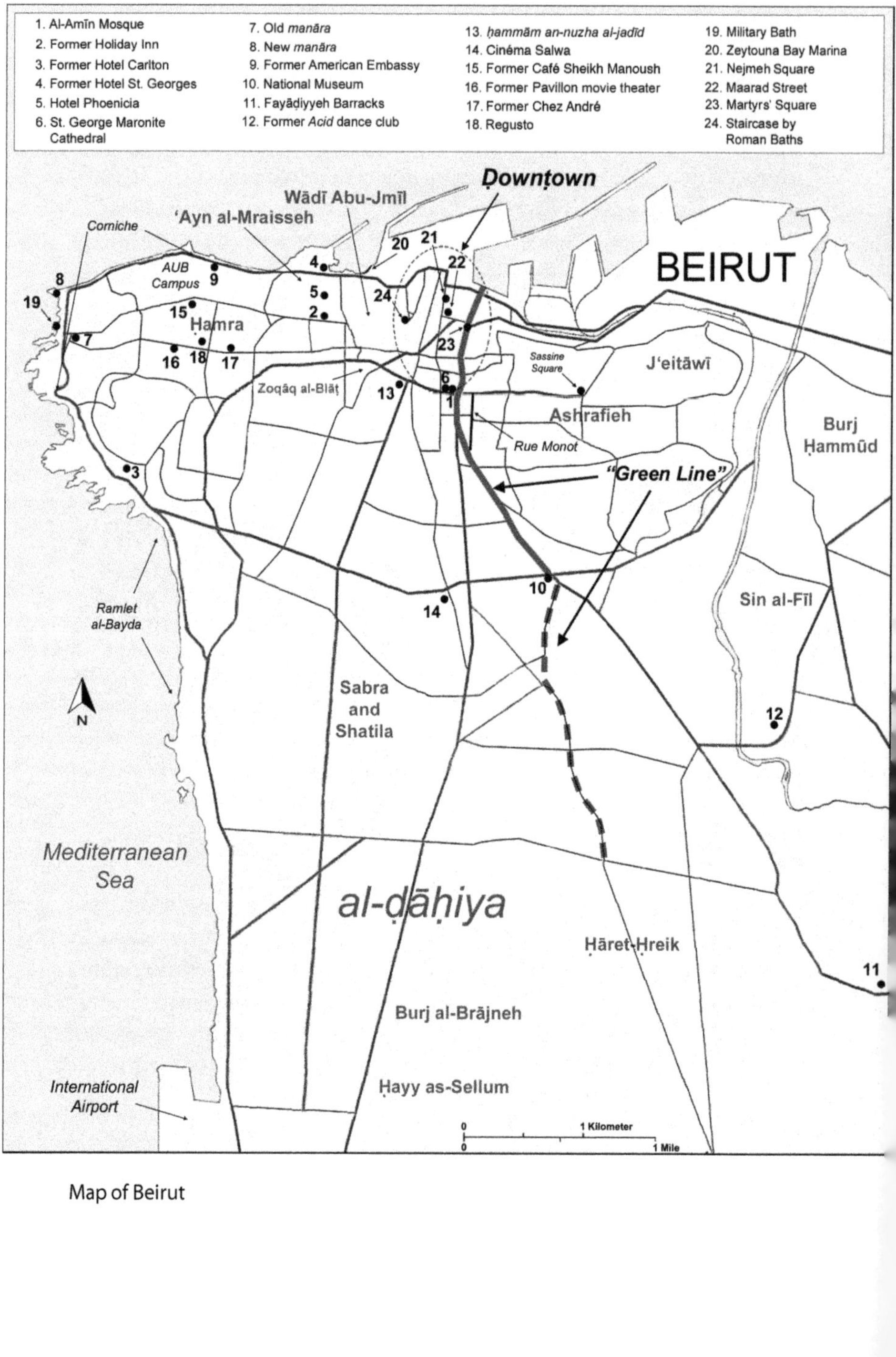
1. Al-Amīn Mosque
2. Former Holiday Inn
3. Former Hotel Carlton
4. Former Hotel St. Georges
5. Hotel Phoenicia
6. St. George Maronite Cathedral
7. Old *manāra*
8. New *manāra*
9. Former American Embassy
10. National Museum
11. Fayāḍiyyeh Barracks
12. Former *Acid* dance club
13. *ḥammām an-nuzha al-jadīd*
14. Cinéma Salwa
15. Former Café Sheikh Manoush
16. Former Pavillon movie theater
17. Former Chez André
18. Regusto
19. Military Bath
20. Zeytouna Bay Marina
21. Nejmeh Square
22. Maarad Street
23. Martyrs' Square
24. Staircase by Roman Baths
Downtown
Wādī Abu-Jmīl
'Ayn al-Mraisseh
Corniche
AUB Campus
BEIRUT
Hamra
Zoqāq al-Blāṭ
Sassine Square
J'eitāwī
Ashrafieh
Rue Monot
Burj Ḥammūd
"Green Line"
Ramlet al-Bayda
Sin al-Fīl
Sabra and Shatila
N
Mediterranean Sea
al-ḍāḥiya
Ḥāret-Ḥreik
Burj al-Brājneh
International Airport
Ḥayy as-Sellum
0 1 Kilometer
0 1 Mile

Map of Beirut

CHAPTER 1

Producing Queer Space in Beirut: Zones of Encounter in Post-Civil-War Lebanon

Rachid and Khalil had met near the town of Jbeil, about one hour north of Beirut, during the summer 1994, a time when the Lebanese rediscovered their country after almost twenty years of civil strife. The 1975–1990 civil war had made it impossible for many to visit parts of the country that were not included within the tightly knit spatial sectarian configuration in which they had found themselves trapped since the mid-1970s. For those like Rachid and Khalil who came of age in the late 1980s and early 1990s, the respective territory situated on the other side of the *khaṭṭ al-tamās* (the line of demarcation—generally referred to as the "Green Line"—that had divided East from West Beirut during the Lebanese civil war) was virtually unknown and to be reckoned with slowly but certainly after the end of the armed hostilities.

During the decade that followed the end of the civil war, the territory of the Other and its various borderlines started to shift, but not without further developing the intricacies of spatial compartmentalization in Lebanon. For many queer-identified men, the beach—or rather, a certain section of the sandy shore—became of pivotal importance. The area in question was located just south of Jbeil, out of which the stretch dubbed "Paradise" made up only one small subdivision. This portion represented parts of the social incongruence that characterized the country at the time. Located outside metropolitan Beirut, the segment of not always clean sand attracted a queer clientele from almost all walks of life.

To be sure, Jbeil's downtown Souq (market) area, adjacent to the picturesque fishing harbor and the modest remains of some Roman ruins just north of the beach, historically had been a magnet for a whole range of leisurely activities enjoyed by citizens from Beirut and elsewhere. These ranged from brief visits to local fish restaurants frequented by countless culinary enthusiasts and arak aficionados to extended strolls through the ruins of those Roman edifices that had been erected on top of Phoenician remains of the ancient Byblos. All of this provided stressed city dwellers with distinctive but affordable small-town favors, otherwise limited to exclusive resorts that started to pop up on other stretches of the coast. As for Paradise Beach, while being public (as is officially the entire seashore), it drew the urban masses mostly from early June to late August. The rest of the year, the beach attracted *majanīn al-baḥr* (sea fanatics), who did not require a minimum of 25°C (77°F) in water temperature. Two of these ardent devotees were Rachid and Khalil, the two lover protagonists from the introduction to this book.

Paradise Beach: A Story about Rachid and Khalil

For Rachid, the reality of being a native of Al-Mina, Tripoli's historic harbor section, as well as an art student at Ballamand University marginalized him momentarily vis-à-vis the dominant Beiruti contingent on Paradise Beach. Not only did he lack significant social ties to the capital, he also had a marked northern accent—all his *a*'s became *o*'s—and this initially made him the target of jokes. The fact that he was gay-identified and from Tripoli added to the instant amusement of his fellow queer sunbathers, some of whom used the word *traboulsi* (Tripolitanian) to connote Rachid's homosexuality. This connotation was based on the stereotypical assumption that the mostly Sunni space of Lebanon's second city was somehow homoerotically marked.

Without discounting the importance of peer pressure, Rachid was able to pick up the Beiruti slang by the extraordinary attentiveness of his ear. In purposefully modifying his intonation and strategically incorporating within his spoken Arabic a couple of English and French words here and there, he quickly became a potentially classy resident of the capital, and this many years before he actually moved into his hotel room on Ḥamra's Makdisi Street. Yet, despite Rachid's seeming metamorphosis, one that continued after he had formally left the North, he remained proud of his origins, frequently highlighting to me the civility he believed prevalent in Tripoli, a quality he contrasted with the self-indulgence of Beirut. As a selectively observant Sunni Muslim, he also prided himself on his fasting during the holy month of Ramadan. But what seemed to provide him with almost equal gratification was that many of his Christian colleagues at the television station thought he was one of them because of what they identified as his worldly demeanor. For example, he peppered his speech with all sorts of French words, which was perceived as a sign of self-gratifying sophistication.

I will never forget how Rachid sang for me, in strongly accented Levantine French, the effusive and catchy tunes of the Egypto-Italian pop icon Dalida. The bleached-blond beauty's career in 1970s France enthralled the entire Mediterranean basin, from Alexandria to Tangier via Tunis and Beirut. Yet, similar to Judy Garland two decades earlier, the idiosyncratic diva, born in Cairo into a lower-class Italian immigrant family, also had a very strong transnational queer following. Like those of Garland, Dalida's fans were so impassioned that their devotion continued even after her suicide at fifty-four in her *grand bourgeois* Paris apartment on May 3, 1987.

Rachid found contentment in his imitations of Dalida and in his acceptance into a world of complex inclusions and ever-so-intricate exclusions. Still, it made him secretly happy to see his coworkers' flabbergasted faces upon finding out about his religious background. Even though Rachid's real name—as well as the pseudonym I am using here—is a distinctively Muslim one, many Christian Lebanese ignored that fact. This socio-historical disregard tended to characterize much of the knowledge about the respectively perceived internal Other, along with the territory presumably associated with this Other. Attuned to this particular aspect of Lebanese identity politics, Rachid loved to perform the Lebanese role of the eternally sophisticated denizen. However, he also felt confident in asserting carefully what he considered his religious identity because it gave him the necessary ammunition in a long-lasting socio-national battle that he was not ready to give up.

Khalil, on the other hand, was the youngest son of an affluent Christian Maronite family. His father had emigrated from Lebanon in the 1950s, temporarily settling in South America. After establishing various business enterprises in the Southern Cone, he returned to his native Lebanon with his Argentinian wife, Graciela, a native of Santiago del Estero. Graciela, whose maiden name was Arid, was a descendant of the early wave of Syrian immigrants who, after World War I, had left the town of Kfar Buhum in the central Syrian province of Ḥamā to seek a better life in South America. Almost half a century later, Graciela, who would rarely talk about her Syrian origins, was the one who returned to the Old World. There she embraced her new home more than a decade before its imagined cultural glory, summarized by the clichéd phrase "the Paris of the Middle East," gave way to the brutality of the civil war. Khalil was in his early teens when the fighting started in 1975. He mostly grew up in the relative safety of the wealthy suburbs of Christian East Beirut. In contrast to Rachid, Khalil never experienced economic hardship. Sheltered by his cronies, he was a pampered inhabitant of a world that assessed him by the social and cultural capital of his family name rather than by his individual character.

And so it was that, according to Rachid, when Khalil turned twenty-five, he drifted into a life of hedonistic pursuit and sexual debauchery. The civil war complicated the coming of age of a gay man like Khalil who, despite—or perhaps because of—his particular affluent background, interacted within a highly restrained social framework. Homophobia in his social environment made it initially difficult for him to engage in any sexual activity, let alone to sustain a homosexual relationship. Contrary to some of his contemporaries I met, who partly experienced the war as a homosocial field of sexual experimentation in which a variety of taboos could be broken without being necessarily reprimanded, Khalil was bound by his social status and the hostility shown to the very idea of homosexuality.

Being rich and sheltered from the world for almost the entirety of the war by overbearing and much older siblings prevented Khalil from mingling with potential gay friends. His extreme bashfulness and his round and heavy physique did not help the equation. By early adulthood, he had become something of an anchorite. Nevertheless, his increasingly guilt-ridden yearning for the male body remained part and parcel of his adolescent life.

All this changed in the early 1990s when the fighting stopped and the Lebanese began to explore and move about the various parts of their former divided country again. Slowly but surely, Khalil began to frequent the numerous bars and clubs that were popping up like mushrooms in East Beirut's then up-and-coming suburb of Kaslīk. In those social venues, he interacted for the first time in his life with his Muslim compatriots, who had been attracted by an unparalleled nightlife unknown at the time in West Beirut. Little by little, Khalil began to venture far into the capital on Saturday nights to look at the boys at the original B018 nightclub. This venue stood in complete contrast to its heteronormative namesake that would open in the late 1990s to great architectural acclaim in the neighborhood of Karantina. A couple of years earlier, however, the old dance club had attracted a large, queer-identified clientele on premises that had a lot of intimate charm but lacked the architectural gravitas of the new club, which would later attract cultural critics from around the world. The new B018, an iron coffin in which patrons would sit at (and dance on) tombstone-shaped tables, was built in 1998 on the site of a former Palestinian refugee camp, razed by Lebanese right-wing militia members in 1976. It was a nod by the architect Bernard Khoury to his taste for the morbid and his cunning assessment of the Lebanese predisposition to amnesia.

But in the mid-1990s, in the old B018, this seemingly provisional club located below the neighborhood of Sin al-Fīl in the little urban vale formed by the ever-polluted—and by now clutched in concrete—Beirut River, Khalil met men he saw dance very intimately with each other, defying all rules of a normative heterosexual behavior he had known until then. In their unconventional interpretation of male homosociality and unorthodox embodiment of masculinity, these men trespassed blatantly the line of what Khalil had considered socially permissible. In reaction to what he identified as overly transgressive, he rejected behavior he deemed as overtly feminine, setting up a clear hierarchical distinction between himself and what he called "those degenerate queens." Yet, his apprehension also included a fair amount of attraction toward parts of a crowd referred to in Lebanese Arabic as either *khassun* (are concerned [with being gay]) or *fāytīn bil-jaw* (part of the [gay] atmosphere) and whom he had immediately recognized as his potential peers.[1]

Over time, Khalil, relatively introverted at first, became conscious of the limitations his heavy physique imposed when it came to mixing with other men. This was especially the case with men committed to a heightened gender-oriented competitiveness that celebrated male beauty along normative lines of masculinity. Moreover, the awareness of his social class made it psychologically difficult for him to bond with some of the men his age, whose local background he considered inferior. Despite these impediments, Khalil eventually managed to connect with several of the gay men he considered his equals. He began going out with them, indulging in all sorts of escapades that the war had prevented him from experiencing. In a way, it was a life that, had it not been for the civil strife sweeping for so long over the country, he might have lived ten years earlier—a post-adolescent rebellion of sorts. But it was only now, in the mid-1990s, that he discovered the putative freedom that followed the end of the violent decade and a half of the Lebanese civil war.

With freedom came excess and with excess came a host of interpersonal experiences that gave Khalil the full taste of Lebanese post-civil-war traumas, general distrust being but one example. He began having sexual encounters with men to whom he grew partly attached. More often, he saw himself in the position of a "hot potato" that was dropped as soon as it developed some kind of painful "stickiness" for the hand that was holding it. At times, he discovered he was a "lemon" to some of the young men he met at the clubs. While feigning affection and genuine interest, they would squeeze him for his potential contacts, and as soon as the preferential treatment, called in Arabic *wāsṭa*, was achieved, they would drop him straight away. These negative experiences only enhanced Khalil's sense of isolation. He began to seek anonymous and semi-anonymous sex, which lacked the most nominal of commitments. It was within this very mood of deceit and false promises, a general atmosphere compensated by the social adrenaline rush of the early postwar period, that the twenty-eight-year-old Khalil strolled on Jbeil's Paradise Beach in the summer of 1994. There, on the first Saturday in June, he saw Rachid, a young man nine years his junior. At that point, Rachid had graduated from secondary school and was a registered art student at Ballamand University south of Tripoli. The oldest of three brothers, he was the first in line for the dreaded national military service.[2] Yet, because of his academic pursuits, he was able to delay the draft for many years.

While still in secondary school in Tripoli's Al-Mina neighborhood, Rachid had overheard some of his classmates having an awestruck, albeit disparaging, conversation about "that beach in Jbeil where faggots meet to have sex." He became intrigued by it, but kept his curiosity to himself for fear of being "outed" by his peers. Whenever he took the bus to Beirut to visit one of his aunts on his mother's side, he longingly looked out the window as soon as the bus passed the town of Jbeil. Once, in twelfth grade, on his way back from Beirut to Tripoli, he saw a group of men barely his senior getting off the bus at the stop that had to be the "stop of Paradise," for the merry bunch had been ecstatic during the entire ride, showing off their eye-catching beachwear to each other. It took Rachid one more year to find the courage to get off the bus one stop over. He enlisted a male cousin, who was twenty-five, to spend the first Saturday in June with him on Tam Tam Beach. This was a strategic move: Tam Tam Beach at the time was part of the same sandy stretch as Paradise Beach, though the latter was confined to the southernmost section of the shoreline. Thus, it was relatively "safe" for Rachid to combine two seemingly distinct worlds. While being firmly anchored on Tam Tam Beach, in the midst of countless groups of wannabe straight alpha-male teenagers and large families with screaming children, he could laze around in close proximity to the queer crowd sunbathing nonchalantly on Paradise Beach.

When his cousin said that he needed to leave early because of a secret rendezvous he had arranged in the town of Batroun with a female classmate, Rachid promised to keep his mouth shut. He willingly obliged, especially given that he was now free to explore more fully the scene that was unfolding to his left. The first thing Rachid did was move his towel and belongings into the highly fluctuating gray zone that lay in the middle between Tam Tam and Paradise. As soon as he entered the water, several young men, who had unmistakably positioned themselves on Paradise Beach, approached him in the most forthcoming way. Reserved as he initially was, Rachid managed to become an integral part of the ensuing conversation, at the end of which he agreed to move his towel next to his new acquaintances.

When I met Rachid, seven years after his introduction to Paradise, he did not remember whether he had seen Khalil on this first Saturday in June 1994. But it surely was during that same summer that they became friends and, shortly thereafter, unruly lovers. In retrospect, it was love at first sight that carried away the teenager. Rachid completely bought into the flirty advances of a young man he looked up to and who seemed to focus his undivided attention on him. During the summer of 1994, they met almost every weekend on Paradise Beach. Their sexual relationship, however, was limited in its early days to Khalil's car, for he could not possibly invite his young partner to his room in his parents' residence in Rabieh. Yet, the twenty-eight-year-old Khalil enjoyed relative autonomy, whereas the situation at hand was much more delicate for Rachid. His parents soon began wondering about his whereabouts on weekends. In response to their questions, Rachid always reacted with a concoction of half-truths and circumlocutory lies. First, he was supposed to meet up at the Rock Restaurant with some random friends from secondary school, for Jbeil's famed venue was known for the best *shish-ṭaouk* sandwiches in all of Lebanon. Second, he was to hang out with a couple of art students from Ballamand University who were originally from Jbeil. It was only toward the end of the summer that Rachid began to mention things about a "nice Christian guy" he had met on the beach.

The additional information that this new "acquaintance" was an advertising agent at a new private TV station and extremely interested in his college art projects was intended to let the air out of an over-inflated parental inquisitiveness. And, indeed, Rachid seemed successful at it—at least at first. Yet, it did not take long before he began noticing a new daily refrain from his father: "We have to start looking for a nice bride for you . . ." Apart from the subtle discomfort Rachid felt whenever his family entertained the subject of marriage, the imagined blissfulness of his semi-secret relationship with Khalil slipped little by little into the uncontrollable realm of sadness and frustration. According to Rachid, by the end of the beach season, Khalil had lost interest in him. Proof of this growing lackadaisical attitude was that the older man became more and more vocal about his erotic investment in other men. He even began pointing out the bodily characteristics that aroused him in some of the many men who frequented Paradise Beach, shattering Rachid's adolescent innocence about first love.

Seven years later, he recalled with pain how he would wake up in the middle of the night, full of yearning and sorrow, leave his dormitory, and walk the high-perched campus of Ballamand University. He would look far down toward the city lights of Tripoli, visible on the horizon, and feel utter grief and soreness in his chest. He would remember this sensation as it was exacerbated by his initial inability to share it with anybody. Yet, over the years, and after the mutual braving of the high and unwieldy waves of romance that left them both with emotional scars, Rachid and Khalil agreed to a working rapport they called in English an "open relationship." As time passed, both of them continued to see each other on a regular basis, an arrangement that also included frequent sexual intimacy. Almost year-round, they met at least once a week on Paradise Beach, regardless of the weather. From April to November, they stretched their sun-tanned bodies out on the sandy beach; the rest of the year, they mostly strolled through Jbeil's narrow alleys. But, as the 1990s progressed, they also made sure to get together in Beirut to check out the up-and-coming social venues that opened there at a breathtaking pace.

When it comes to the declared notion of an "open relationship," I must disclose a tangential role that I unwillingly played in the early days of my fieldwork in Lebanon, but that would haunt me much to its end. Upon meeting Rachid for the first time in summer 2001, I developed a serious emotional attachment to him. At that point, he seemed to reciprocate some of these feelings. Yet, my unfortunate personal episode with Rachid remained clearly what it was despite my difficulty acknowledging this reality. Nothing substantial (apart from my long-lasting heartache) grew out of the affection I had for Rachid, who had initially assured me that his relationship with Khalil was a very loose one at best. Nevertheless, Khalil developed considerable hostility toward me. As is often the case in such emotionally charged and upsetting situations, my role as the occasional—and unwitting—outside lover became the main instrument of reconciliation between Rachid and Khalil. Although their relationship eventually ended, that interlude gave them somehow a chance to work through their differences, even as it created plenty of opportunity for the anthropologist's economy of intimacy to be temporarily disturbed.[3]

Seeking Leisure in Post-Civil-War Beirut: The Emergence of New Queer Space

While the relationship of Rachid and Khalil solidified, its frequent ruptures notwithstanding, war-torn Beirut started to regain some social vitality by attracting a ravenous and leisure-seeking clientele that patronized the increasing number of bars and nightclubs opening in and around the capital by the mid-1990s. It all started in the Christian communities north of East Beirut. Thousands of young Lebanese, regardless of their ethno-religious pedigree, flocked to the chic and trendy clubs that had opened in suburban places such as Zouq or Kaslīk. One of them was the notorious Amor y Libertad, the much-fêted local Latin fantasy of a nightclub where the male belly dancer Mosbah Baalbaki, the self-declared son of a poor Shīʿī family from the Bekaa Valley, made one of his professional debuts. With the help of one of the main luminaries of the booming post-civil-war Lebanese entertainment industry, Michel Elefteriades, Mosbah became over the next decade or so one of the lightning rods of a progressively more visible queer-identified clubbing crowd that reached far beyond any existing or imagined borderlines.

Ever hungry for new and newer locations where one could take pleasure almost unreservedly in the common excitement generated by the end of an ultimately unresolved civil war, many Lebanese sought a short-lived fulfillment in their Saturday night outings. A satisfaction that could never be entirely achieved led to an urge to perpetually explore fresh and—purportedly—superior terrain. Only those who managed to patronize those places considered à la mode at any specific moment were considered hip and trendy.

Thus, the post-civil-war Lebanese display of vanity and indulgence traveled its due course systematically along these socially coercive lines, not only from one club to the next but also from one particular neighborhood to the other. Kaslīk was at the beginning of this trajectory, but, almost a decade later, the fully refurbished downtown district of Beirut was at its temporary end. Until the mid-2000s, the only neighborhood that consistently maintained its reputation as the post-civil-war nightlife district par excellence was the immediate vicinity around Rue Monot (Monot Street), including the SODECO (Société de Développement Commercial) mall with its blockbuster-featuring movie theater. The area retained a spatial perseverance most probably due to its immediate proximity to the former *khaṭṭ al-tamās* (Green Line) but also because other areas, such as the Ḥamra district in West Beirut, were still recovering from the war. On the whole, not all clubs catered to a queer-identified clientele. And those that did also attracted apparently heterosexual patrons, which made it initially impossible to declare such and such place to be specifically a "gay club."

Yet, clubbing oases were scattered all over the city. These included the original B018, as well as the legendary Acid dance club, which would close its doors in 2010 after a decade of seemingly relentless success, and, much later, restaurants/bars such as Wardet Walimeh on Ḥamra's Makdisi Street, followed by T-Marbouta in the Ḥamra Square strip mall and Bardo off Clémenceau Street.[4] Set in motion in the 1990s, this post-civil-war phenomenon of trendy clubs concentrating in the eastern part of the city had drastically changed the map of prewar social patterns in Beirut. With only a few exceptions, the formerly celebrated Ḥamra district was eclipsed by other neighborhoods, its dim postwar character never managing to match a 1960s heyday that many older Lebanese remembered as the country's cultural zenith. All of this would change again after 2006 when the various political appropriations of the downtown district made Ḥamra resurge and almost turned the center of the city into an empty shell.

This initial nostalgia, however, was not limited to those who had grown up during the war. Self-identified gay men like Rachid and Khalil, nearly oblivious to any past map of urban entertainment, took pleasure in socializing in Beirut dance clubs. More importantly, they did not even consider themselves part of the circuit—especially Khalil, who actually abhorred dancing, preferring to stand quietly in the corner in order to check out unfolding scenes. To please his partner, Rachid offered to hang out instead at cafés, a promising proposal at a time when particular outdoor cafés started to attract queer crowds outside—i.e., north—of Beirut. Oddly enough, the biggest magnet for gay men at the time was a Dunkin' Donuts coffee shop next to the highway in Zalqā, roughly 10 kilometers (6.5 miles) north of Beirut. Its strategic location made it the perfect venue for those who frequented Paradise Beach in Jbeil and who, on a weekly basis, stopped there on their way back to Beirut before celebrating Saturday nights in one of the new clubs around town.[5]

The Rise of the "Gay" Coffee Shop: Dunkin' Donuts

The Dunkin' Donuts franchise in Zalqā was located on the first floor of a nondescript office building in a suburban strip mall along the main coastal highway that linked Beirut with the northern city of Tripoli and beyond.

Customers could sit either inside the coffee shop or outside on a small terrace located immediately next to the parking lot, which was the only space between the thoroughfare and the shop. On weekend evenings in the summer, Dunkin' Donuts would be packed with many young men—and a few older ones—all busy showing off their tan lines to each other. Despite the commonality of a heightened homoeroticism looming over the place, a marked hierarchy was just as noticeable, even to the most uninitiated eye.

There was the crucial factor of age. On average, everybody was either in his twenties or early to mid-thirties. A central category that cannot be emphasized enough, along with its correlates class and prestige, age often coincided with the ostensible access to a social and cultural capital. This capital, in line with Pierre Bourdieu's theory, manifested itself in studied performances and the conspicuous display of an otherwise groundless economic capital intended to suggest a normative prestige or a generally recognized "symbolic capital."[6] What Bourdieu called "different forms of capital" include not only material wealth in the form of money and property (economic capital) but also the combination of knowledge, skills, and other cultural acquisitions such as educational qualifications (cultural capital), as well as the mixture of accumulated prestige and honor (symbolic capital). These different forms of capital are instrumental in assessing what I refer to as the *habitus* of the customers at the Zalqā Dunkin' Donuts.[7] Through various bodily performances, this "durably installed generative principle of regulated improvisations [the habitus] . . . produces practices which tend to reproduce the regularities immanent in the objective conditions of the production of their generative principle, while adjusting to the demands inscribed as objective potentialities in the situation, as defined by the cognitive and motivating structures making up the habitus."[8] Thus, for the young gay customers at Dunkin' Donuts, the control over real and—sometimes—imagined cultural capital had to be generated continually through performances that differentiated but also drew together the different hierarchies at hand. Conversely, the deliberate construction of sociability for the purpose of creating a resource (i.e., social and cultural capital) by way of premeditated bodily performances was crucial in order to sustain the larger network of relationships developing in and outside the coffee shop.

While Bourdieu's primary interest was to delineate how social structure asserts itself in individual agency, my attention here is directed toward how queer-identified individuals in Lebanon formulate and negotiate the craft of a bodily performance, the morality of which is established by interacting with an all-too-often hostile world.[9] Moreover, my focus in this book is not on organized activism, but the ethical practice that is at work through the politics of what I like to call a "queer habitus." It is a politics that amounts to the individual challenge directed toward social norms, on the one hand, and the embodiment of alternative identity formations, on the other. However, it is an embodiment that is subject to continual reinventions based on space, time, and circumstance. Accordingly, different customers at Dunkin' Donuts would persist in exhibiting disparate public behaviors in order to distinguish themselves from other people and groups present. For instance, there were the loud and gaudy males in their late teens and early twenties perpetually attempting to capture the undivided attention of some of their seniors sitting on the same café terrace. In response, the latter worked hard at putting on a face of societal magnitude, one meant to enshrine even further the normativity of their perceived social and cultural capital.

This composite context of contrasting courtships revealed itself through calculated bodily performances involving stylish clothes and many chic accessories, including the late-model cell phone positioned meticulously on the table—preferably, next to the keys of an eye-catching car. Thus, the result of this tangled networking became most poignant in the exhibition of the cars parked in the adjacent lot. There, the standard was "the bigger the better," and as important was the place where the automobile was parked. Hence, the significance of the sizeable number of men in their early thirties who would conspicuously place their car keys and their late-model cell phone on the table with an air of utmost self-importance. Based on their elaborate bodily performance, which reached far beyond the theatrical premises of the Zalqā Dunkin' Donuts, these guys knew very well the normative attraction they generated among their peers, even if the BMW in the parking lot was but a borrowed means of attention-grabbing transportation, and the Armani sunglasses but a counterfeited replica.

Khalil was aware of the stunning stage Dunkin' Donuts provided many gay men who, at the end of the civil war, were craving just about any kind of social attention. Like everybody else, he enjoyed simply sitting on the coffee shop's terrace, even with the horrendously polluting and noisy traffic just meters away. Being there enabled him to see a substantial section of the local "gay world" unfolding before him and, at the same time, to be seen and noticed by those with whom he identified most readily. For Rachid, hanging out at Dunkin' Donuts was a way to acquaint himself with the intricate dynamics of Beiruti society. This knowledge seemed to help him after he officially moved to the capital city from his native Tripoli in order to take a job as one of Khalil's assistants in the advertising division of a major private TV station.

In essence, the process that began in the mid- to late 1990s on the premises of the Zalqā Dunkin' Donuts was akin to a post-civil-war "gay café culture" that almost surpassed earlier years when clubbing was one of the major outlets of local male homosociality. Mutually inclusive, however, both socializing practices developed into a general stage on which gay Beiruti sensibilities started to thrive, albeit not without violent repercussions, as discussed later. In the meantime, the biggest revelation for young men like Rachid and Khalil came shortly after the new millennium. It coincided with the complete refurbishment of Beirut's city center, an area that had been bombed and fully devastated during the fifteen years of the Lebanese civil war (1975–1990). A vast unknown terrain and a no-man's-land for anyone who grew up during the long period of sustained violence, it promptly transformed into the platform for a general zone of encounter that, despite many exterior attempts, never managed to totally marginalize the various local queer circles.

Although on weekends the Zalqā Dunkin' Donuts had been a perfect location to see and be seen by one's cronies, the setup was limited in its social capacity and reach. Given the local patrons' everlasting preoccupation with how to make an impression and gain prestige, there was only so much they could look at and talk about while sitting on a narrow terrace squeezed between an uninspiring office building and a jam-packed parking lot on the edge of the busiest highway in Lebanon. After two beach seasons, the business enterprise had come almost full circle, and the overall attention shifted toward alternative venues that would enhance the leisurely excitement and thus maintain the generally cultivated adrenaline rush. For a time, the comparatively small Dunkin' Donuts branch in the heart of East Beirut's Ashrafieh neighborhood became a local queer hub. Irrespective of its prime urban location on Sassine Square, where customers could readily observe whatever was happening on the turnabout while being sure of being seen by all sorts of passersby, the importance of this coffee shop remained minor due to the heavy sectarian character of the neighborhood that generally excluded many potential Muslim patrons. Similar dynamics applied to other social venues in the vicinity that, at regular intervals, would open and close on and around Sassine Square. One of these venues was Columbus Café inside Ashrafieh's ABC shopping mall, which opened its doors in 2004. While the café attracted gay men who identified as "bears" (and their respective "chasers"), it did not last more than a few years before closing in 2011.

Ḍownṭown: The City's New-Fashioned Center

For at least five years after the turn of the millennium, Beirut's new-fashioned center became, for many gay men in and around the city, an alternative large zone of widespread encounters. The social diversity of the many ethno-religious groups reached far beyond any previous possibilities, all superficial uniformity notwithstanding. Somehow or other, what would readily be referred to by most denizens, regardless of the language, with its particular intonation, as *ḍownṭown* transformed into the very setting where all kinds of controlled and unhampered spaces melded in the most unpredictable and, sometimes, uncanny ways. For people like Rachid and Khalil, the numerous chic and stylish cafés in the new city center turned into prime destinations not only on weekends, but also after work during the week.

Before I further elaborate ethnographically on how the production of queer space and the formation of individual and collective identities affected each other within the spatially small but socially significant context of Beirut's city center, let me turn first to a historical and political overview. This is intended to provide an understanding of the dynamics behind the symbolism of what has come to be called by many urban dwellers, using an idiosyncratic plosive intonation, *ḍownṭown*, as well as of the collective relations unfolding there. As we will see, these relations managed time and again to transcend spatio-temporal fixities as well as their socio-cultural correlates, ranging from the intricate practices of gazing to studied bodily postures and performances.

Since its official opening in the summer of 2001, the remodeled section of downtown Beirut functioned, with a few exceptions, as a broad, albeit far from inclusive, zone of encounter where people of diverse backgrounds converged. This continued even in later years, despite the constant tension evident in Lebanese politics. Remembered as a sectarian "salad bowl" that integrated spatially many different socio-religious groups in prewar times and that exhibited a markedly popular character, the area encompassing what has been called the *Central Business District* surrounding Martyrs' Square—or the *Burj*, as it was commonly referred to by older locals—was considered one of the few public places in prewar Lebanon with a decidedly mixed ethno-religious pedigree. Thus, early on after the beginning of the civil war in spring 1975, the area between the commercially oriented Martyrs' Square and the civic edifices built during the 1920–1943 French Mandate period around Nejmeh ("Star") Square became the principal target of attacks launched by a variety of armed militias. These militias, along with their respective sectarian identity politics, did anything they could to defy the spatial symbol of a "common ground." The result was that, for most of the civil war period, the Burj was a no-man's-land, an area in which civic and commercial buildings had been almost entirely destroyed at the beginning of the hostilities and, consequently, had promptly fallen into ruins.[10] In the late 1980s, some of the more peripheral structures were turned into makeshift shelters for the disenfranchised populations fleeing the pervasive fighting flaring up recurrently in the southern part of the country.

In the two years following the official agreement signed in 1989 by Lebanese parliamentarians in the northern Saudi Arabian town of Taef, armed combat effectively ceased in Lebanon and fifteen years of a deceptive *Pax Syriana* began.[11] During that time, the former Central Business District, next to both Nejmeh and Martyrs' Squares, began to undergo a slow but certain refurbishment, initiated by the big business cronies flocking around the then prime minister, Rafik Hariri. Holding most of the stock, the high-flying businessman-turned-politician had founded a "joint-stock construction company" in May 1994 called Solidère (Société libanaise pour le développement et la reconstruction de Beyrouth, or the Lebanese Company for the Development and Reconstruction of Beirut).[12] The company, in charge of planning and redeveloping Beirut's city center, proposed to bring in a decidedly amnesiac and "future-oriented" era of prosperity. One sign of this looming and increasingly pervasive amnesia was that some people even started to refer to the entire area around the Burj by the suggestive entrepreneurial acronym Solidère.

The manifest symbolism of the Burj—whose popular and multisectarian prewar reputation had, in almost a sardonic way, caused its demise as soon as the skirmishing started in the mid-1970s—was once again brought into play twenty years later. This time, the symbol was transformed into a glitzy stage of affirmed ultimate urban living. The chic boutiques and expensive restaurants were intended to attract a financially potent clientele—ideally, wealthy Arab tourists from the Gulf. Historical amnesia and projected intentions notwithstanding, Solidère's planning did not go well with all parts of the local population, whose collective relations transcended in many ways the spatio-temporal fixities imposed on them. The overwhelming majority of Beirutis could barely relate to, let alone afford, the riches on display in their capital's renovated downtown district. By summer 2001, after more than twenty years of total spatial concealment, Beirut's geographic and historic center had become once again an alien space to most citizens of the capital. The district's new-fashioned physical and, by extension, social fabric could not provide a more poignant contrast to the generally dilapidated surrounding neighborhoods, if not the war-torn country as a whole.

While collective relations transcend spatio-temporal fixities, and oftentimes their socio-cultural correlates, they have been subject to constant change in Lebanon. Over and over, collective relations in Beirut have been symbolically displaced by way of a steady compromise meant to sustain the avatars of social normativity, be they in the form either of an imposed and physically concrete space or of an enforced moral conduct. Yet, as I show throughout this book, these relations can also be dissimulated altogether, that is to say, withstood by various people whose respective representations are marked punctually by detailed bodily performances. In both cases, social relations call for the emergence of zones of encounter located beyond a readily ascertained public-private opposition. Thus, displacement and dissimulation are but two examples of how a particular place like the downtown district of Beirut becomes a platform on which all sorts of identities can stake out the territory that allows them to be seen, and possibly even heard, by society at large. It is a platform that can lend an avowedly transgressive character to a queer individual whose contestation and appropriation of space always happens in conjunction with his or her studied bodily performance.

The 2001 summer season marked the official "opening" of an a priori alien space that, apart from being flatly called *Solidère* by some, soon enough was referred to, regardless of whether one spoke Arabic, English, or French, as *ḍownṭown*. What distinguished the vernacular intonation of this word was one striking oral release coupled with an oral stop that highlighted a voiced alveolar plosive at the beginning of each syllable. All of this resulted in an uncanny rapprochement between the English letters *d* and *t*. Linguistically, the phenomenon one heard was a voiced alveolar release (the initial *ḍ* or ض in Arabic) along with a voiceless alveolar stop (the final ṭ or ط), producing a sound that could be deemed eccentric by many native English speakers. As outlandish as this pronunciation may seem, the actual physical space designated by the word *ḍownṭown* began to acquire in due course a similarly eccentric aura. From the neighborhood of Gemmeyzeh in the east halfway to ʿAyn al-Mraisseh in the west, the restored French Mandate buildings along the arteries of Maarad, Allenby, and Foch Streets—all of which adjoin Martyrs' and Nejmeh Squares—started to feature high-class eateries and stylish stores. To see and be seen there was equated with having reached the goal of utmost social distinction and prestige in post-civil-war Lebanon.

It was reminiscent of the Situationist Guy Debord's book *La société du spectacle* in which he argues that for "societies dominated by modern conditions of production, life is presented as an immense accumulation of *spectacles*. Everything that was directly lived has receded into a representation."[13] *Ḍownṭown* provided the platform for such spectacles to unfold. Yet, despite these spatio-temporal fixities asserted by a dominant space strikingly controlled by the rich and famous, where the suggested social synchrony may have appeared difficult to confront, spatial counter-appropriations had been equally present from the very beginning. For instance, in the wake of the February 14, 2005, assassination of the former prime minister Rafik Hariri, these counter-appropriations of certain downtown streets and intersections were epitomized politically by a major spatial rivalry. Physically speaking, this spatially inscribed and foremost political enmity opposed Martyrs' and Riād al-Ṣolḥ Squares, or, to be more precise, the followers of the Western-backed government of Fouad Siniora and later of Hariri's son Saad, on the one hand, and the supporters of Ḥizballah (Party of God) and its allies, on the other.[14]

Just as important in this spatio-political equation were those men who made spatial appropriations and counter-appropriations in downtown Beirut possible in the first place. Thus, one can hardly forget the many Syrian laborers who were customarily positioned at the bottom of social hierarchies in Lebanon. Coming in throngs over the border in the 1990s in order to find jobs, working-class Syrians were instrumental in re-erecting the swanky façades of those buildings in the Central Business District of Beirut. By 2001, the new ostentatious style of the district, despite its original French Mandate architecture, had acquired an almost Disney-like quality. Yet, as soon as the new emerging pedestrian walkways, flanked by those sandstone buildings constructed to provide expensive store and office space to the bold and beautiful, came to be used, the men directly behind the change vanished completely, as much as did most of the war rubble that the great reconstruction was meant to replace.[15]

At the turn of the millennium, what was physically destroyed by a civil war remained visible in many parts of the country. In the center of the capital, however, where reconstruction was paramount, destruction gave way to a new space of coerced joy and happiness that made social and political resistance difficult to perform. This difficulty notwithstanding, dissent manifested itself, even if half-heartedly at the beginning. It came in the form of spatial counter-appropriations through the very presence in the downtown area of local individuals, young men who, for the most part, despite lacking the otherwise necessary financial capital, persisted

Maarad Street, with Nejmeh Square and the *sāʿa* in the background, July 29, 2010.

in integrating the "new" city center into their mental as well as physical spheres of action. To be sure, this integration can be interpreted in, at least, two different ways. I will discuss the first one here before tackling the second one later within the wider context of transgression and its various limitations in Lebanon.

Whereas the rich and self-identified Lebanese glamour classes sat at the tables of fancy cafés and restaurants, where the exposed setting made the well-rehearsed ritual of seeing and being seen a thing of unquestionable eminence, those young males, unable to afford either expensive *arguīleh-s* (water pipes) or extravagantly prepared cappuccinos, made their presence *ḍownṭown* equally felt. Such a state of being physically present manifested itself, for example, through the elaborate practice of steadily parading around the *sāʿa* ([Big] Clock), which faces the Parliament building on Nejmeh Square, or by leisurely promenading on a pedestrian catwalk like Maarad Street, the new city center's main artery. The meticulously studied exchange of daring looks and gazes was often turned into an art form by young men checking out both the wider scene and each other while wearing the trendiest outfits. Even though fashion and the access to it have always played an important role in Lebanon, the brand names worn by most men did not necessarily reflect material standing. If anything, the coveted labels pointed to a prevalent practice of conspicuous consumption of global commodities. Being dressed up in certain clothes was understood as giving temporal access to a physical and mental space of social importance otherwise unattainable by the compulsive wearers of Armani jeans and Gucci sunglasses (oftentimes fakes).

Albeit highly contradictory, these kinds of demonstrative spatial contestations and counter-appropriations, where an imagined and widely sanctioned capitalist consumption compensates for the lack of actual social status, are certainly no random happenstance. However, the practice of transcending spatio-temporal fixities in Beirut's new downtown, an urban setting in which space and class have been coinciding in a mundane way since it was made fully accessible to the public in 2001, has been an exceedingly incongruous matter. To be sure, the routine of defying and outdoing controlled space in Beirut has always been closely linked to meticulously demarcated locations that draw a fine conceptual line between what is generally considered daring, on the one hand, and socially (un)acceptable, on the other. Expressed differently, the socially marginal—albeit geographically central—space of a parading ground like Maarad Street, where young men from materially deprived suburbs congregate among members of different social groups, remains different from the umbrellaed bistro tables occupied by those who can afford the costly service. As far as these separate, even if overlapping, spaces are concerned, both attract in their own ways different clienteles that are respectively shaped by disparate socioeconomic backgrounds, as well as by a contrasting social standing that plays itself out unequivocally on the pedestrian walkways of the city's center.

Despite being sometimes poles apart from one another, the various groups of individuals appropriating these different spaces engage in a range of interactions that go well beyond the mere bodily exchange of looks and gazes. As will be shown through the ethnographic example of Georgette below, these interactions can point to the limits of social transgression. Apart from often being finite, any postures of defiance also highlight the immense attraction the overarching sociopolitical discourse of the local bourgeoisie has managed, over the decades, to exercise over the rest of Lebanese society.

A good example for some of the consequences of bourgeois enticement in post-civil-war Lebanon would be the instructive relationship of Rachid and Khalil. The two found in some of the new downtown cafés and restaurants the perfect place in which to hang out any day of the week. I remember well the excitement with which Rachid welcomed the opening of Caspar and Gambini's, the high-end coffee shop at the top of Maarad Street. The venue was next to what was supposed to become the Garden of Forgiveness, or *jenaynat al-samāḥ* in Lebanese Arabic, adjacent to the Maronite Cathedral of St. George—itself rebuilt in a neo-Italianate style after it was partly demolished during the war. However, the unintended bitter symbolism of a café eclipsing a failed project intended to fight rampant amnesia and commemorate the civil war by extending pardon to the foes could not have escaped even the most oblivious of bystanders. But maybe it did, for everybody I knew at the time talked about Caspar and Gambini's as *the* place to order one's overpriced cappuccino.

Despite the elevated prices, the café remained a self-declared social venue of prime importance until it closed some years later. The management introduced Caspar and Gambini's as being part of a world-class Italian coffee chain, although in reality, it was not a franchise, but the local project of an influential, and evidently quite cunning, Lebanese businessman. Yet, few cared about authenticity; rather, being part of the particular scenes in and immediately outside of Caspar and Gambini's was what most mattered to the majority of the café's patrons. The social pressure to participate in this normative extravaganza was so great that people like Rachid, who were bound by the realities of a small income, felt it necessary to return time and again to the restaurant's posh premises.

While many Beirutis may well have felt tempted by this collective show of vanities, few could even consider sitting at a table at Caspar and Gambini's as a remote possibility. Rachid might have had only a modest income, but he embodied social and symbolic capital, including the "looks" and the required clothes. Moreover, he had an affluent boyfriend. For others, to indulge directly in the pleasures of the bourgeoisie was a much more difficult undertaking. However, the financial obstacles involved in the appropriation of downtown Beirut did not prevent those with limited contents in their wallets from the contestation of what they called *ḍownṭown*. Even if, for a majority of local denizens, ordering at a venue like Caspar and Gambini's was out of the question, asserting a physical presence in a highly contested part of the city remained of crucial importance.

Contesting Space with an Empty Wallet, but with an Attitude: A Story About Georgette

During the time of my ethnographic fieldwork in Lebanon, I came across countless young gay men whose socio-material backgrounds prevented them from partaking actively in a lifestyle for which they nonetheless yearned. I followed one of these young men for quite a while and he captured my attention with his unequivocal ability to turn the newly refurbished downtown district into his unchallenged domain. I met Georgette in late summer 2002 through my friend Ramzi, who had previously filled me in on some of the stories regarding "one of those heavily built *tantāt*[16] who don't give a shit"—mostly in response to negative comments targeting either their size or their heavy makeup. Georgette was a true *adīra*, a key term used in the grammatical feminine form by queer-identified men in and around Beirut to refer to a strong person who inspires others. About nineteen years old at the time we met, Georgette embodied without any doubt a larger-than-life ideal of a queer city dweller. Beneath the layers of foundation and mascara, his baby face revealed his very kind disposition. As benign as his personality may have been, it would transform into a fury at the slightest sign of perceived outside hostility.

Georgette's Christian name was, of course, Georges, but he almost always introduced himself as Georgette to anybody he considered either *khassun* (family) or otherwise "safe" because they appeared to be *fāytīn bil-jaw* (part of the [gay] atmosphere). On two occasions, I saw him insist vehemently that he be called Georges. Both times, his doggedness translated into an act of defiance aimed at anyone whose potential antagonism he sensed.[17] A lower-class Christian Maronite, Georgette lived with his mother and three older siblings in an unassuming apartment building in East Beirut's deprived Jʿeitāwī neighborhood. He never spoke much about his father, so rumors started to circulate about his untimely demise during the civil war. Others alleged he had left the family—and possibly the country—for a better life elsewhere. Although I was never able to find out the truth about the absence of a father in Georgette's life, I knew that he entertained a very thorny rapport with his mother. It was a relationship that replicated itself with both his older sisters as well as his younger brother, who openly treated Georgette like the black sheep of the family.

After dropping out of secondary school, Georgette found it increasingly difficult to land a permanent job. Yet, he could sew, a skill he developed over the years by watching his seamstress mother, and this helped

Classic "service" out of service, May 29, 2011.

him gain temporary employment in the backroom of several cheap garment stores in the Armenian quarter of Burj Ḥammūd. Unfortunately, whatever formal work he got, losing it shortly after receiving the first paycheck turned into a painful routine for Georgette. As a result, he began staying at home during the day. There, in the confinement of his mother's living room, he would take out all kinds of fabrics and transform them into the most daring clothes, which he would wear for parading at night, preferably in and around the new downtown. As opposed to the other young gay men who, wearing stretch pants and tight body tops, considered their clothes the pinnacle of smart styles and chic trends, Georgette enveloped his voluptuous body with all sorts of lofty accoutrements, all of which would attract the attention of virtually everybody he passed on the street. Instead of spending the one thousand Lebanese liras (L.L.)[18]—a sum that would double a few years later—for a shared taxi, otherwise referred to as *service*, Georgette preferred in most cases to walk all the way from Jʿeitāwi to *ḍownṭown*, crossing through Ashrafieh and parts of Gemmeyzeh. If he managed to catch a ride or a *micro*, one of the common minivans that only charged five hundred L.L. per trip in the early 2000s, he would get out as soon as he reached Martyrs' Square and walk straight toward the Virgin Megastore before doing his customary rounds on the centrally located Nejmeh Square.

When I first met him, Georgette was in the company of his then-best friend, whom he referred to as Monica. On some level, Monica, whose actual full name was Mohammad Harb, could not have been more different from his all-too-conspicuous mascara-wearing buddy. However, despite obvious distinctions, the two of them undeniably shared many similarities. The main difference was size. While Georgette was a bulky queen with an evidently marked personality who, on the face of it, could put down the most aggressive thug, Monica was his opposite. Petite and extremely skinny, he could not have measured more than 160 cm (approximately 5 feet, 2 inches) in height. Contrary to his assertive and outgoing friend, Monica exhibited one of the most reserved demeanors I had encountered during my time in Lebanon. With a few exceptions—sometimes he exclaimed over things he found funny and that would seem to come out of nowhere—he generally did not talk much in a group setting and always left the conversation to Georgette, who would repeatedly look warmheartedly at his smaller partner. Most noticeably, Monica was a compulsive gum chewer of the local brand of Chiclets; his nervously masticating mouth would suddenly stop whenever awe struck him after hearing something he found noteworthy or seeing somebody he fancied.

Georgette and Monica were born in the early 1980s and shared a relatively deprived upbringing in the wake of the Lebanese civil war. While Georgette was a Christian Maronite from East Beirut's underprivileged Jʿeitāwī neighborhood, Monica grew up in Ḥayy as-Sellum, a mostly Shīʿī locality that is part of the southern suburbs of Beirut and located next to one of the landing strips of the international airport. Like thousands of other Shīʿī families from the country's south, his parents, whose respective kin had been local peasants for generations, left their ancestral village near the town of Nabaṭṭiyyeh during the Israeli military invasion in the summer of 1982. They sought refuge in what would shortly thereafter become Beirut's southern "misery belt," called *al-ḍāḥiya*, the southern suburb of the capital.[19] Pregnant with her youngest son at the time, Monica's mother decided to move in with her sister, whose husband owned a tiny apartment in the neighborhood of Ḥāret-Ḥreik. Slowly but surely, the Harb family moved from one small dwelling to another before settling in a two-bedroom apartment in Ḥayy as-Sellum in the early 1990s.

After the official end of the Israeli invasion, countless armed skirmishes continued in the southern Lebanese border region and extended well beyond into the post-civil-war period. Given this perpetual insecurity, Monica's parents never seized the opportunity to return and live permanently in their village. However, together with their five children, the Harbs remained registered as residents of the Nabaṭṭiyyeh district. Thus, the entire family became part of a growing number of formerly rural peasants who, over a period of twenty years, had not only become unmistakable city dwellers but who also contested and actively appropriated the various urban spaces in and around the Lebanese capital. While the mother did not have a formal job, she worked occasionally for a political organization close to the Shīʿī Amal Movement that provided social services to some of the inhabitants of the *ḍāḥiya*.

Monica's father, on the other hand, counted himself among one of the many *service*—or shared—taxi drivers. He steered his dilapidated but ever-running old Mercedes Benz along pretty much all the major roads in West Beirut, including the highly lucrative route from and to the airport. Monica had a brother and a sister still in school, and two older siblings who excelled in whatever occupation they could find. His sister Khulūd, who was engaged to an auto mechanic from the Ouzāʿī section of the *ḍāḥiya*, worked part-time in a children's clothing store located in one of the smaller shopping malls that had opened up in the late 1990s. His brother Ali moonlighted from time to time as a chauffeur for the Marriott Hotel in Choueifāt. Nobody in the family had ever had a steady job, but, with the help of all family members, the Harbs managed somehow to brave the country's harsh economic reality.

Ali had suffered from polio in his early childhood, so it was Monica, the second male in line, who was drafted by the Lebanese army as soon as he turned eighteen. When I first met him on that late summer evening in downtown Beirut, he had just come back to the capital from a week-long army duty at a roadway checkpoint between the southern coastal towns of Saida and Ṣūr. Watching him in a bright T-shirt that prominently featured the Calvin Klein brand name and looking at his meticulously done nails and eyebrows, I had a very hard time imagining this skinny and slightly bashful youngster carrying a machine gun at some random checkpoint in south Lebanon. However, when I asked him half-jokingly about this odd scenario, he proudly showed me a Polaroid picture that proved the unimaginable to be reality.

When, on a different occasion, I asked Monica questions about his experiences in the army, he turned teasingly to Georgette, his inseparable companion at the time, and exclaimed: "This one, she almost became a female officer!" Similar to the widespread usage of feminine first names among some young gay men who, depending on the context, considered themselves to be part of a larger queer-identified "family," the grammatical feminine in Arabic would be used whenever it seemed to fit the particular situation. Given that in Arabic the shift from one grammatical gender to the other not only affects the structure of names and nouns but also that of adjectives and verbs, the total grammatical feminization of the language by young gay men would oftentimes become a highly stylized verbal performance carrying all sorts of implications for intonation and bodily posture. Thus, affected oral inflections, coupled with dramatic gestures, habitually complemented a behavior intended to distinguish its protagonists from their otherwise heteronormative—and often hostile—environment.[20]

Apart from this linguistic particularity, Monica's exclamation about his friend Georgette opened the door to a whole set of complicated and painful issues that I was not in the least aware of—let alone prepared for—when I initially interacted with the two of them. The materialization of those issues only happened much later. That evening, Georgette's reaction was one of unusual marked silence. A shadow engulfed his face instantaneously, and it did not take long before I realized that something was wrong. At the time, I naively thought that Georgette was being a drama queen for no reason, displeased by a silly comment he thought made fun of him. However, it was only weeks later that I found out through my friend Ramzi about the traumatic memory that Monica's statement had triggered in Georgette who, on that very evening, abruptly stuffed his big rimless sunglasses in his yellow handbag and left the rest of us baffled, but not before having uttered a disgruntled, "Ḥa shūfkun ba'deen!" (See you later!) Lacking sensitivity toward his friend, Monica exclaimed, "Ya allah shū ṣān'a!" (My God, what a fake woman you are! [Can't you understand a joke?])

Under regular circumstances, Georgette could understand a joke. However, he had almost been drafted by the Lebanese army the previous year. As the older of two sons in his family, he was technically required to perform what was then the compulsory one-year military service. Since he had dropped out of secondary school, there were no officially valid grounds on which he could have obtained a postponement for the mandatory draft once he turned eighteen. Nevertheless, he got an unmitigated exemption, and it is the ordeal that led up to this exemption that was behind his distressed departure following Monica's unfortunate remarks. Georgette did not personify, by any account, the masculine model of a soldier that would have fit the ideal of any modern army. He was also far from anything resembling a *jaggal* or an *'abaḍāyy* that would have put him

"The Life of a Gigolo Is Hard," July 1, 2011.

on the same level as some of the gay men on Paradise Beach who celebrated what they considered the advantages of being a "gigolo" or a "big man" in a crowd of self-important queens.

Rather, Georgette embodied two major disadvantages, both of which immediately disqualified him for any military entrance exam. For one, he was considered overweight, which was why he sometimes suffered from respiratory problems, despite his young age. Second, his personal demeanor exhibited a high degree of what others perceived as effeminacy. This had made him a prime target for homophobic slurs ever since puberty.

Moreover, the way he typically dressed and the bodily performances—including the explicit use of eyeliner, eye shadow, and bright nail polish—that he was keen to put on for his usually disapproving social surroundings aggravated, more often than not, many situations in which he found himself. Paradoxically, the more Georgette received contemptuous and judgmental responses to what he represented, the more he accentuated the eccentricities that, in turn, became the standard motivation for many around him to engage in nearly constant antagonism. While, at the beginning, he contented himself with having his eyebrows regularly plucked, as time passed, he started to accentuate his eyebrows with eyeliner. Later, I would meet him downtown on weekend evenings and he would be in full makeup with—if need be—some fake leopard fur dangling around his shoulders. Not that all reactions incited by Georgette could be interpreted as exclusively disgraceful and discreditable, some were even appreciative to some extent. Nonetheless, a good number of individual responses continued to be an intricate combination of silent condemnations, on the one hand, and the most unsympathetic of looks, on the other.

Part of the reason behind Georgette's own resentment was undoubtedly his experience at the Fayāḍiyyeh barracks a year earlier—the very story that prompted his response to Monica's unfortunate statement. Located on the main road to Damascus near the Ministry of Defense in the foothills of Mount Lebanon, these barracks represent the headquarters of the Lebanese army, and, in many cases, are also where young recruits registered and, in some instances, spent the first three months of their military service. In this emphatically martial place perched high above Beirut in the country's Metn region, Georgette had an appointment, like any other potential new soldier, with an army physician who was to assess his fitness for the national service. While Georgette told me the story, I could not help but notice how trepidation and anger gradually transformed his otherwise gentle facial features. He recalled how frightened he had been to take the public bus up the mountain slopes to make sure he would be on time for his scheduled medical appointment at the Fayāḍiyyeh barracks.

Of course, he wore neither mascara nor his customary sweet perfume on that particular fateful day in late January 2001. His exceedingly feminine behavior, however, could not be hidden, even though, at that specific moment, he had meant to appear as the man everybody in his family wanted him to be since he was a young boy. Standing in line for three hours outside the barracks medical ward turned into a nightmare, for Georgette dreaded the many oblique comments he expected from the other young men waiting with him. Some of them made explicit fun of him, but never by addressing him specifically, let alone looking directly into his eyes. The juvenile giggles, signs of hostility, increasingly got to him. Yet, at the time, he was incapable of saying anything to his sheepish aggressors. In fact, he felt paralyzed. More than a year later, he remembered with painful disdain this woeful episode preceding the medical examination. Little did he know then that the confrontation with the physician would actually be an experience far worse, emotionally as well as physically.

By the time it was his turn to be examined by the military doctor in residence, Georgette had already waited in line for hours, enduring one disdainful glance, if not to say one antagonistic comment, after another. When he was ushered into the medical ward by a male nurse, Georgette began to feel a sense of relief, hoping that, with the health check, his ordeal would come to an end. The nurse, a man in his late thirties, asked him to sit on a white plastic chair in a decrepit antechamber. After about ten minutes, the nurse returned and directed him to the doctor's office. Georgette could not but notice the derisive and slightly mocking expression on the nurse's face.

In the consulting room sat a man, probably in his early forties, who was wearing a long white doctor's shirt. He never looked into his patient's eyes or introduced himself, although Georgette suspected his name to be Dr. Marwan Khoury due to the sign posted next to the door. But it may as well have been an entirely different person who examined him on that unlucky day in January. "Enta lūṭī, ma heyk?!" (You are a faggot, right?!), said the presumed doctor in an amused tone that married cynicism with contempt. He pretended to formulate a question, even though his expletive pitch suggested a fait accompli. Georgette recalled how this unexpected statement baffled him completely. For some reason, he had never imagined that the examining doctor would tackle the subject of his homosexuality by invoking the pejorative term, *lūṭī* (son of Lot), generally used to describe gay men in Lebanon. As a professional medical doctor, he would have used instead the neologism *mithlī*, as in *mithlīyya* (sameness, i.e., homosexuality), a word the doctor had certainly come across before. However, the reference to the biblical Lot, the unfortunate prophet of Sodom and Gomorrah, flummoxed Georgette and made him wonder what to expect from this intimidating overture.

Before Georgette could even say anything, the doctor ordered him to take off his clothes and lie down on his stomach on a consulting table in the corner behind a dirty baby blue plastic curtain. At that point, Georgette noticed that the male nurse was also present in the room, making some undecipherable signs to the doctor, who started grinning in a mischievous way. Georgette felt mortified, taking off layer after layer of his clothes and then lying on his stomach on that table in front of two men in positions of undisputable power, who were evidently making fun of him. He wanted to leave immediately. The worst thing was that he did not know what was supposed to happen. The doctor put on a pair of plastic gloves prior to ordering Georgette to turn his head toward the wall. Then, he felt his buttocks being touched by the doctor, who blatantly started to finger Georgette's rectum. After about five seconds that seemed an eternity, the doctor commanded his male nurse: "Aʿṭīnī al-bayḍa!" (Give me the egg!) At that moment, Georgette turned his head and saw the nurse hand his superior a large gray egg, which was then placed between his buttocks, on top of his anal orifice.

"Does the egg fit?" asked the nurse, acting as if this was all part of some major entertainment. "Pretty much," said the doctor, whose voice, by now, had taken on a tone of unrestrained glee. Then, as far as Georgette remembered, everything went very fast. The egg the doctor had squeezed between his buttocks broke. The physical sensation was deeply unpleasant, especially given the slimy substance that started to cover the lower parts of his body, and the stench from the egg was unbearable. The doctor and nurse knew that the egg was rotten. The doctor shrieked, called Georgette a *shādh* (pervert in Arabic), while the nurse blamed the breaking of the egg on him. Terrified, Georgette cleaned himself up as best as he could with a dirty towel that had been wrapped around the upper part of the table. While the nurse insulted him, the doctor told Georgette that the Lebanese army did not need a bunch of *ṭabājna*[21] like him and that, moreover, he was excluded from the military service.

Georgette left the barracks of Fayāḍiyyeh in a state of long-lasting trauma. He found out later through a couple of friends that the revolting experience was not at all out of the ordinary. According to what he was told, the sanctioned rationale behind the "egg treatment" was to determine whether or not the potential recruit had the habit of being anally penetrated. If the egg "fit" into the anal orifice, then the person in question was a homosexual and, therefore, likely to become the subject of further humiliation, including the possibility of official persecution. On the face of it, Georgette could consider himself "lucky," said some of his friends, for he was sent home immediately after the "medical checkup," and no further official mistreatment followed.

There are at least two other aspects that should be discussed in relation to the "egg treatment" employed by some army physicians in Lebanon to determine male homosexuality. First, the widespread perception—albeit one that defies actual practices—of homosexuality as being limited to those men who are anally penetrated by other men is crucial in order to understand the pervasive obsession with the shape and size of the rectum. It is an obsession that partly holds because the "penetrators" are not necessarily identified as homosexuals themselves, unless they are penetrated as well. According to this logic, if the anal orifice appears to be bigger than that deemed to be "normal," the person in question must be a homosexual and, therefore, a possible target for harassment. The centrality of harassment is why I prefer to talk about a "(mis)treatment" rather than a "test," for the term "egg test" would only convey one aspect of the painful and humiliating procedure. With respect to Georgette, however, the officially shared notion of the socio-medical consequences of anal penetration did not apply whatsoever, for the patient in question was an eighteen-year-old whose sexual experiences had yet to become a part of his young life.

This leads me to my second point: it is safe to say that it is "external appearance" more than anything else that determined the perception shared by both physician and nurse at the Fayāḍiyyeh barracks. As far as these medical practitioners were concerned, Georgette's effeminate behavior, along with the associations they made from it—and not the size of his anus—motivated their decision to identify him as *lūṭī*. Never mind the disparaging definition of homosexuality shared by the doctor and his assistant, on the one hand, and the problematic equation made among male homosexuality, effeminacy, and perversion, on the other. The amount of random humiliation targeting young men like Georgette remains considerable. In retrospect, the fact that the egg broke and that, in addition, it was rotten is unlikely to have been a coincidence. The occurrence rather points to a contemptuous intent meant to blame and bring further shame on the victim.

Georgette was and felt dirty in more than one sense. On the bus down the foothills and back to Jʿeitāwī, he avoided all eye contact with the other passengers sitting next to him. Although his eyes were filled with tears, it was only after he reached his mother's apartment, where he stood under the flowing waters of the shower, that he burst out crying, feeling a deep sense of disgust not only toward everybody who had visibly harmed him, but also toward himself. He looked down at his voluptuous body and closed his eyes in sickened revulsion. Why had God made him both gay and fat? Thankfully, Georgette's self-revulsion did not last, and soon after the Fayāḍiyyeh incident, he regained the resiliency that so prominently distinguished his character.

As a result of his experience, Georgette was exempt from being drafted by the Lebanese army. More than a year after his exemption, he meekly showed me his *daftar al-jaysh* (army pad), a small white leaflet that included, next to his name and the information about his sectarian affiliation, the entry: "UNFIT FOR MILITARY SERVICE DUE TO AN *INCURABLE ILLNESS*," or, as the original Arabic would have it, "marad ghayr qābel lil-shifā'." Given the lack of any clear laws regarding homosexuality, the intention by the state to regulate it never failed to be a source of concern to many Lebanese officials.[22] This formal lack notwithstanding, nothing can really prevent the state from discriminating against individuals it identifies as being "in opposition to nature." After all, Georgette's military exemption could have been based on the actual physical health problems he had due to his relative obesity. However, there was no mention of it in the official medical report he received in the mail a couple of weeks following his checkup.

Moreover, despite its small size and inconspicuous design, the *daftar al-jaysh* was more than just a way for the state to record all male citizens according to their confessional affiliation. To be recognized right away as Christian Greek Orthodox or Druze is one thing, along with the problematic implications that became evident during the civil war. To be identified as having "an incurable illness" is quite another. This qualitative difference became a significant issue whenever one left or entered the country and could also be of fundamental importance when employers required the *daftar al-jaysh*. Many business owners knew about the potential connection between a military exemption and homosexuality, and few did not share the homophobic outlook manifest in the notorious entry on the *daftar*. This might have also been one of the reasons why Georgette never truly managed to land a proper job: his lack of formal education; his physical and behavioral presence, which daunted many; and the tarnishing note in his army pad, all resulted in an explosive combination of ill-fated characteristics that made him, as well as others in a similar situation, into some regrettable sort of social pariahs.

Despite all his mishaps, Georgette seemed by and large to approach life with buoyancy. For sure, his sense of optimism did not prevent him from going through frequent depressions. In general, however, his good-natured personality prevailed and he was unfailingly generous with his friends and acquaintances. It is in this same vein that Georgette continued to assert his presence even in those places where he was regarded negatively by people whose judgmental gawps he tried to ignore, even if always with difficulty. In an almost ironic way, the experience he went through at the Fayāḍiyyeh barracks made him stronger—akin to his qualities as an unquestionable *adīra* (strong queen)—at least as far as his outside demeanor was concerned. I am not entirely sure, but I believe it was during the following summer that he began to apply full makeup before setting out on his regular weekend outings that usually led him to the streets, squares, and alleys of Beirut's refurbished downtown district.

CHAPTER 2

Producing Prestige in and around Beirut: The Indiscreet Charm of the Bourgeoisie and the Assertion of a Queer Presence

By the time the first summer season of Beirut's new city center ended in late August 2001, one could have argued that the entire area had been completely usurped by the local bourgeoisie. The wealthy tourists from the Gulf only started to arrive in massive throngs about a year later, partly because the attacks on the United States on September 11, 2001, had made it more difficult for them to vacation in Western countries. The actual picture was more complicated, however. While plenty of local bejeweled bleach blondes conspicuously shared café tables with their gold watch-wearing male counterparts, there were also much more unassuming men and women, mostly young, who made their presence downtown equally felt. Even though the majority of them could not have afforded the district's high prices, they still actively appropriated what they called *ḍownṭown* in all sorts of ingenious ways.

Yet, despite the apparent heterogeneity in Beirut's city center, the social backgrounds of the young gay men with whom I interacted were an assortment of individual experiences that remained, for the most part, couched within a general uniformity in terms of behavior, clothing, and, especially, overall aspiration. Take Rachid, for example. A lower-middle-class native of Tripoli, he could buy himself only a limited number of drinks at a café like Caspar and Gambini's. Yet, what began to unfold in downtown Beirut that summer was a bourgeois fantasy in which Rachid willingly participated by donning a range of fancy outfits purchased with the modest income he earned at the private TV station. Sitting at a café table on Maarad Street, he thus pretended to be an integral part of a world based on material wealth that he could only dream of. In contrast to this conspicuous consumption, which managed to sell itself as economic affluence, the respective contexts from which Georgette, Monica, and their friends emanated were less auspicious. In most cases, their particular backgrounds and perceived social behaviors prevented them from tapping directly into the riches that surrounded them, notably in a well-heeled spatial setting such as *ḍownṭown*. None of them could allow themselves to spend money that was mostly needed elsewhere in their financially constrained lives.

Georgette and Monica still went at least once or twice a week to the area around ʿAzarieh Road, Nejmeh Square, and Allenby Street, sometimes stopping at a more reasonably priced coffee shop like Dunkin' Donuts or Cinnzeo. They always wore their best clothes and paraded so as to see a maximum number of people and, possibly, to be seen by even more. In other words, the spatial contestation of a place such as downtown Beirut was and, throughout the early 2000s, continued to be a multifaceted matter, including an indiscreet and self-imposing bourgeois charm coupled with the marginal but significant assertion of a queer presence. The ostensible paradox that was found in the complicated relationship between latent—and at times sublimated—practices of a tacit resistance as embodied by Georgette and Monica, on the one hand, and the dominant normative bourgeois discourse, on the other, had to do with a shared conspicuous consumption and the intricate politics of prestige that the appropriation of a socially valued space, such as *ḍownṭown*, entailed.[1] For me, it quickly became important to assess the very presence of the lower classes in a place originally intended for the rich and affluent. Yet, of equal significance was the apparently widespread compulsion to pretend to be part of the local establishment, even if one's wallet reflected a different reality altogether.

Conspicuous Consumption and the Intricate Politics of Prestige

After fifteen years of civil war and more than ten years of a concerted effort at selective reconstruction, the area that people started to call *ḍownṭown* in 2001 slowly but certainly transformed into a huge three-dimensional canvas. Many fantasies were projected on to this canvas, inspired by all the new and chic things that had captured the obsessive attention of post-civil-war Lebanon. Common among them was the pervasive and dreamy vision of becoming part of a perfect world, materially and socio-politically. Thus, at the turn of the millennium, the vigorously articulated fascination in Lebanon with all things new and upscale resulted in a performative and imaginary blurring of almost all observable differences in exposed urban locations, such as downtown Beirut, where the need to look and act in a bourgeois fashion, even if one was far from actually embodying affluence, surpassed all other preoccupations.

Accordingly, the practice of keeping up appearances, *maẓāhir* in Arabic, was very much de rigueur among many of the urban youth I interviewed. The dictum of *maẓāhir* turned into a general pursuit of perceived happiness that increasingly included all strata of Lebanese society—its highly disparate makeup notwithstanding. The local conspicuous consumption of global commodities came into play here, a practice that ranged from wearing clothes featuring particular labels and brands to sitting in cafés and restaurants that conferred the feeling of what was understood to be "cosmopolitanism."[2] Yet, the element that gave a young man access to *ḍownṭown* was not limited to the otherwise necessary ownership of a precious bank account. For the bodily performance of somebody like Rachid to be socially persuasive for his surroundings, a wardrobe displaying seeming stylishness was essential, but it needed to be prominently highlighted by a personal attitude and overall behavior that made men like Rachid convincing candidates in their highly competitive surroundings. Thus, within the convolution of this bonfire of vanities, the obsession with trends and looks—all of which fit common social expectations—was never limited to the visible surface of clothes and hairstyles. It always included a studied performance in attitude, along with particular bodily postures that suggested the resilience of the respective character.

This fixation on the mundane leads me to an additional interpretation, namely one that is removed from the controlled space of a fancy café or restaurant. This interpretation further helps elucidate the many ways in which Beirut's new city center was integrated into the mental, as well as physical, space of those young gay men who—despite their various performative attempts—generally failed to partake fully in the sky-rocketing consumption politics prevalent in the decade and a half following the end of the civil war. In this vein, I would like to advance a couple of thoughts by expanding on the intricate production of prestige in post-civil-war Lebanon.

The wide area around Nejmeh Square, which extends all the way to Martyrs' Square to the east and the offices of the Lebanese government located within the large and renovated Grand Sérail to the west, is a central neighborhood where all promising leisure activities of the early 2000s were carried out by the wealthy classes in and around cafés and restaurants. However, there remained a multiplicity of alternate and less controlled spaces where official function was not terribly clear to the uninitiated eye, but that nevertheless got appropriated by those individuals who, due to limited financial resources, found no formal place on and around Maarad Street to declare their own. In the shadow of the late Ottoman edifice of the Grand Sérail, perched on the hill overlooking the old quarter of Wādī Abu-Jmīl, there remained indeed many niches that, to a certain degree, were subject to almost anybody's contestation. It is this contestation to which I turn now, after a brief historical introduction to the area that would become *ḍownṭown*.

The streets converging onto Beirut's Nejmeh Square form, as the Arabic name indicates, a star shape, even though two churches—one Greek Orthodox and the other Greek Catholic—have spoiled the intended symmetry since the beginning of the 1920s. The original urban plan, which included a series of civic buildings, was elaborated under the French Mandate in the 1920s and 1930s and intended to strike a chord with the Lebanese and improve their loyalty vis-à-vis their post-Ottoman authorities. After independence from France in 1943, the square became an imaginary symbol that spatially reinforced the coveted, but utterly deceptive, self-image of the "Paris of the Middle East."[3] Yet, far from being a physical replica of the Champs Élysées's Place de l'Étoile, the Lebanese version is a national center stage *en miniature* where Napoleon Bonaparte's colossal Arc de Triomphe is replaced by an ordinary clock tower, *al-sāʿa*. "The clock" faces the comparatively undersized Parliament building, an edifice from the Mandate period that, since the 1930s, has been the unglamorous stage of the country's ever-diverging sectarian power politics.

In modern Lebanon, the command of political power has been concentrated customarily in the hands of those patriarchs who time and again move about in an emblematic fashion through the house of national representation (*majlis al-nuwwāb*, or Assembly of Deputies) with the main purpose of giving voice to their respective clan allegiances. Generation after generation, exactly the same male names keep popping up. On the face of it, this performative routine seems to have translated over time into an unalterable political status quo. While many have tried to dispute it, only a few politicians have actually been able to defy this state of affairs in some consequential way. For decades, fixed sectarian quotas, coupled with the political monopoly of a relatively small number of affluent families, have dominated the national scene. In principle, no single crisis—politically, economically, or even militarily motivated, as in the case of the civil war—has put an end to a system that is distinctly sectarian and nepotistic. Ironically, even those who could have altered it to a significant extent decided to continue their political operations within the broader logic of this often loathed—albeit unconditionally espoused—official arrangement.

As sectarian and clan-based as this system may be, political influence and economic wealth in Lebanon have often boiled down to membership within a single yet multi-sectarian social class, where affiliation with one or another notable family is the worldly *conditio sine qua non* for access to—and appropriation of—resources. Thus, it is class, more than any other social category, that holds the key to these resources, which can be socio-economic just as spatial in nature. As for those many contenders whose pedigree falls short of this limiting social requirement, the lack of unequivocal political command turns out to manifest itself especially on the level of spatial contestation. However, in referring to spatial contestation as openly practiced by some Lebanese in Beirut's refurbished downtown, I do not have in mind primarily the explicit historical challenge clearly identifiable in the various political camps set up in the wake of the 2006 Israeli war by Ḥizballah and its allies in defiance of the then-American-backed government.[4] Certainly, this spatially inscribed stalemate was of great importance regarding the overall political situation in the country in 2005. Yet, what is far more interesting is how the daily difficulties of earning and maintaining one's "right to the city [center]" (to paraphrase Henri Lefebvre) are surmounted by the everyday man who embodies anything but the prototype of a "son of a family." Since these difficulties had been even larger for most young gay men, it becomes imperative to look out for those exact locations within the urban fabric that have managed, despite all odds, to be appropriated by those decidedly vulnerable protagonists.

Below the eastern façade of Beirut's Grand Sérail extends a great staircase that crosses partly over the excavated ruins of the Roman baths. Not that there is much left from these baths, which must have been a lively meeting place in antiquity. A couple of marble pedestals and a number of old red bricks are part of a mid-sized public garden that has been landscaped on a rather steep slope. To borrow a notion from Timothy Mitchell's pivotal 1991 book *Colonising Egypt*, the garden is "enframed" on all sides by either banks or government buildings.[5] While the ruins of the Roman baths are confined to the southeastern corner of the garden, there are little paths up and down throughout, as well as about half a dozen benches. To sit on one of these benches for too long can be a liability for anybody perceived as unsuitable by the security guard on duty. In the northern section of the garden is a little stage reserved for piano recitals or other sorts of musical performances intended to cater to an ex-

The staircase at the Roman baths, July 3, 2010.

clusive audience on warm summer evenings. The great staircase, on the other hand, is located more or less in the center of the garden and spans it from east to west. Coming from the west—that is to say from the hill on which the Grand Sérail rests—and walking down the set of a hundred steps or so, one reaches Bank Street, the notorious access road that, incongruously, after the beginning of the civil war in 1975 remained almost entirely intact. Everything else in downtown and in its immediate vicinity was either randomly shot or completely destroyed by deliberate shelling, but not the daunting Fascist-era buildings from the 1930s and 1940s on Rue des Banques, as it is called in French. The reason for such paradoxical immunity must be traced back first and foremost to the money laundering activities carried out in those buildings by the wide mixture of banking institutions, all of which were of vital importance to all the fighting parties.

Seventy years after their construction, the area offices on Bank Street formed a physical boundary that separated the Grand Sérail from the rest of the city center. These offices provided a place of liminality and "inbetween-ness" for those people who sought to appropriate a space that was less exposed to the general public but that, nevertheless, remained close enough to it to give the concerned individuals a sense of being part of the overall commotion unfolding just two blocks away. Following the summer of 2001, this combination of proximity and relative distance from the center stage—one that amounts to a physical as well as a mental isthmus—took on the potential to overcome binaries of either/or. It is the performance of an ostensibly subordinate discourse that called my attention to the staircase of the Grand Sérail. While the dominant ideology was represented by nearby Maarad Street, the ideal arrangement for young gay men in Beirut who were not able to afford the high prices at the cafés and restaurants on and off the city center's main artery but who were still keen on partaking in the general atmosphere of *ḍownṭown* was precisely to keep some—but not much—distance. In so doing, they were able to formulate their own, even if short-lived, discourse, one distant from but still in relation to their immediate surroundings.

Resting on the railing or sitting on the steps of the large staircase that connects *ḍownṭown*'s lower part around Bank Street and Nejmeh Square with the Grand Sérail located uphill, many young males congregated there regularly on Saturday nights. Generally, they were joined by a few of those mature men who, for various reasons, were eager to enjoy the young men's company. In that homo-eroticized crowd were always some of the local security guards, who tended to treat their young subjects of control, and sometimes desire, with a paradoxical mixture of arousing attraction and executive harassment. Several of the adolescent men were each other's friends or, at least, acquaintances. They checked out the wider scene from within the relative safety of their respective circles. In fact, it was rare, but not unheard of, to find a young man standing or sitting alone on one of the steps to the Grand Sérail. Even from the vantage point of these otherwise socially marginalized youngsters, such a solitary person was generally considered an oddball and rarely engaged in a conversation.

Flirting on and Beyond the Steps: A Story of Elio, *Ḍownṭown*, the Beach, and the Internet

I started to go to these weekly gatherings on the great staircase near the Roman baths after a young acquaintance of mine, Elio, told me he would meet me there one warm Saturday evening in spring 2003. I had seen Elio for the first time on Paradise Beach the previous spring, but it took us almost six months to become friends and start meeting on a regular basis. I suppose he did not know what to make of me, which may have limited his interest in getting to know me. Given that he did not live in Beirut but

Snāck al-sakhra, August 2003.

on the southern outskirts of Jbeil, he spent at least three days a week during the hot season among the *tantāt* who, coming from all corners of the country, flocked throughout the entire summer to *al-baradays* (Paradise Beach). By 2002—and even more so in following years—what had been Paradise Beach, roughly a third of the sandy area, began to be reduced by the development of "private beaches" with names like "Voile Bleue," "Bay 183," and "Eddeh Sands." These new developments, which required an entrance fee of up to US$30, first took over Tam Tam Beach before pushing Paradise toward the southernmost edge of the stretch—ironically, next to a military base of Lebanese navy SEALs, whose recruits were regularly the topic of conversation among the beachgoers next door. When I returned to the area ten years later, the site was almost completely transformed, occupied by expensive private beach bungalows the Lebanese like to call *chalets*—or *shalehāt*, to use the Arabized plural. By that point, the navy barracks had relocated, and it was only possible to reach the remaining stretch of Paradise by walking along the entire beach, past three private resorts all known for their loud music.

In the early 2000s, however, concerns were of a different nature. Very important to the entire Paradise population at the time was the legendary Labiba. She held sway over her devoted queer following a short distance from the navy base on her *snāck al-sakhra* (Snack of the Rock), located on one of the very rocks that would later be moved to make space for the luxurious *shalehāt*. Seemingly undeterred by what was going on, Labiba—the female equivalent of what I imagined a fifty-year-old ancient Phoenician sea captain, marked by wind and weather, would look like—spent three out of four seasons in her cooking shack on Paradise Beach. From there, she catered to the basic culinary wishes of her queer clientele (including the signature dish of *man'ūshat jibneh-jambon*—Lebanese pizza with cheese and ham). She and her partner Georgette (not my young friend mentioned earlier) often charged rather excessive prices, which led Elio to say, "Labība, 'asʿārha mithl 'asʿār ḍownṭown!" (Labiba's prices are like prices *ḍownṭown*!)

By the time I got to know him, Elio had just failed his *baccalauréat* exams and was preparing to repeat his last year of secondary school. As I understood Elio's personal state of affairs, his educational failure was not a major problem for him because his priorities were elsewhere. One of the beach regulars, he was one of the few elected "princesses," who were distinguishing themselves from the larger sea of pleasure-seeking queens. Elio very much enjoyed being courted by the right people.

He had three sisters, two of whom were older, and one little brother who was about ten at the time we met. His mother was a Maronite native from Jbeil, and his father, although from the same religious group, came from the Shūf. As a young married couple, his parents initially settled in a village situated below the Barouk mountain chain. They fled that area with their children during the War of the Mountains in which Druze and Maronites fought each other following the withdrawal of the Israeli army in the early mid-1980s. An infant in 1984, Elio claimed to remember how his family would hide from the Druze militiamen in the basement of their former house, a memory that might have been imbued by countless stories he heard recounted during his childhood. According to what Elio told me, it was very difficult for his peasant father to leave the mountainous Shūf region of his ancestors in order to settle permanently on the Lebanese coast in Fidār, about one kilometer south of Jbeil. But as the civil war found no end, the old man reconciled himself with the idea that he would never return to the village of his birth as well as with the painful thought that his children would grow up without any substantial ties—physical or emotional—to the Shūf.

Fit and slender without being scrawny, Elio was quite the social butterfly. I liked being in his affable presence. The unparalleled joviality of his face was highlighted by orthodontic braces that made his smile all too endearing. He loved to interact with all sorts of people, but he also indulged in biting gossip sessions that, for some of his contemporaries, marked him as a tittle-tattle princess to be avoided. He also excelled in cozying up to Western European gay men who lived in Lebanon and spent most of their weekends sunbathing on Paradise Beach. Older blond men from Germany were especially prized acquaintance material: to be seen mixing with them enhanced one's prestige among the young local gay crowd. It also, however, made somebody like Elio the subject of resentful bad-mouthing. His independent and free spirit always amazed me. Despite many obstacles—including age, class, and the moral values of some of his critics—he unquestionably lived his sexuality to the fullest, even if not always fighting off jealous accusations that he was a *sharmūṭ* (male prostitute), which surely he was not. His family was aware of his homosexuality, although the subject was taboo and had never been discussed explicitly. The notable exception was his third sister, barely one year his junior, who periodically teased him about his possible escapades on the "queer" beach half a kilometer north of their house.

I met Elio's family on two occasions. The first was a late fall Sunday in 2002 when he invited me to come over from Beirut and spend the day with him at his family's house in Jbeil. The house was one of the modest old stone dwellings that have become a rarity in Lebanon. It was nothing like the late Ottoman square residences that feature the iconic three arches on their façades and that, based on an invented tradition intended to spur nationalism, were celebrated everywhere as the quintessential "Lebanese house." Rather, it was a farmer's house, built to store agricultural goods and harbor hard-working residents. Elio told me proudly that his family did not need air conditioning during the otherwise excruciating coastal high temperatures of the summer because the walls of their rustic house were at least three-quarters of a meter thick and, therefore, the best remedy against the summer temperatures of up to 40°C (104°F), coupled with unbearable 90 percent humidity.

The interior of the modest house was impeccably arranged, and, true to local hospitality, I was offered excellent food and shown around a private garden of trees and brushes full of seasonal fruits and vegetables. I was also introduced to everybody in the family, all of whom were puzzled in some expected measure by my identity as a non-Lebanese Arab man with a dark complexion, who was teaching at the American University of Beirut and who spoke Arabic with a Lebanese accent. Never mind my Muslim name and the fact that I had French and German connections. All of it made me an oddity—albeit a dark one—Elio wanted absolutely to introduce to his family as one of his acquaintances. One of my main interlocutors was his older sister, a nurse who commuted regularly to Beirut where she worked at the military hospital next to the Franciscan monastery in the Badaro neighborhood. Even though we were mostly communicating in Arabic, she loved speaking French with me, and she told me that she had been short-listed for an immigrant visa by the Canadian embassy because the Province of Québec was actively recruiting professionals who qualified as half francophone.

Elio's second sister was rather reserved. The day of my visit was approximately one month before she was to marry a young man from Nahr Ibrahim, and everything in her life at that point was determined by her fast-approaching wedding date. She planned to move to the village of her future husband and was wondering about life away from Jbeil and her family. Elio's third and slightly younger sister, who could have been his twin in more ways than one, shared her brother's quick wittedness, and it was no wonder that it was she, more than anybody else, who teased him about what she knew was his homosexuality. Her relentless energy impressed me quite a bit. At school, she was in the same grade as Elio. But in contrast to his flakiness, she excelled in all subjects. On top of that, she spent her summers working at the nearby SANITA paper towel factory for a meager income, which she planned to save for what she described as her "professional future."

The second time I met Elio's family was at his sister's wedding. He had also invited a gay German engineer, who lived in Rabieh but agreed to pick me up at the busy Dora roundabout on the northeastern outskirts of Beirut, so that we could go to the wedding together. Jürgen was a forty-two-year-old employee of the German technology company Bosch and had been living in Lebanon for about two years. He spoke no Arabic, nor French for that matter, but got around quite well with his heavily accented English, which singled him out right away as the Swabian he was. I had seen him on Paradise Beach, always surrounded by an ever-changing group of at least three young men in their early twenties. He initially mistook me for Lebanese, but given that my age was almost ten years over the limit of his erotic typology, I did not count for him in any meaningful way. The fact that I was actually from his country of origin provoked perplexity at first, but that bewilderment quickly faded into indifference.

At the wedding, Jürgen was the only foreigner noticeable as such, for I blended in fairly well with the other local guests, mostly due to a common language and my Arab identity, which could not have been put into question easily by anybody present. For the celebratory occasion, the patio at the entrance of the old stone house had been transformed into some kind of large outdoor *maḍāfa*, or formal reception area, lined with several rows of white plastic chairs on which a majority of the guests sat, including the bride's mother. I barely recognized her that night because she looked so different. She had experienced a total makeover at the hairdresser earlier that day, but she continued to carry her rather plump body proudly, with a rural dignity that could not be missed. Everyone was wearing his or her best clothing for the occasion—except Elio's father, who stood at the entrance of the patio, greeting the guests with a big smile and dressed as if he had just come back from working in one of his orchards. Like everybody else, Elio was visibly elated, but he was also anxious to see the party end on a good note. Earlier, he and his father had installed a chain of multicolored lights, which were blinking nonstop over the heads of the guests and into the darkness of the Lebanese night. Unable to afford to hire a band, the two men had borrowed a stereo system with three huge speakers, which blasted recordings of previously taped *zajjal* performances, traditional musical poetry slams intended to sing the praises of the newlyweds and anyone else of importance.

The Jbeil wedding was far removed from the world of affect and mimicry into which many of Beirut's *nouveaux*—and *vieux*—*riches* had settled. The indiscreet charm of the Lebanese bourgeoisie was far from the stone house. As much as I could tell, it was an entirely Christian affair. Yet, for even the most initiated eye, the religious affiliation of those present might as well have been a different one altogether. I never saw the groom, for Jürgen decided that he wanted to leave before midnight, citing his professional commitments for the following day and avoiding the more likely possibility that the wedding procedures had made him feel a bit marginalized. Although I wanted to stay, I opted for Jürgen's ride because I dreaded the idea of catching a taxi in the middle of the night while standing at some random highway stop. We thus left the wedding ceremony, but not without paying our respects first to the bride. She was wearing a graceful pinkish dress made of silk and covered with beads, which looked truly great on her. Everybody complimented her on her dress and she responded with a facial expression that conveyed her high spirits. I knew quite well that the evening was still young and that the rounds of arak, accompanied with all sorts of delicious nibbles and appetizers, were far from coming to an end.

It was only two weeks later that I saw Elio again. He did not own a cell phone at the time, which made long-distance communication quite difficult. Also, he had been out of the house the day I called his family's landline to express my thanks for their exceptional hospitality. There was something that preoccupied me. I wanted to know the reasons why Ralph, one of Elio's best friends, had been absent from the wedding. I also knew Ralph from Paradise Beach. I had expected him to be at the wedding because he was the only other gay guy on the beach in his late teens who was from Jbeil proper and not from Beirut or any other part of the country. Even though they were friends, the tension present in the room whenever I spent time with them together was tangible and, at times, as stinging as the moon jellyfish that invaded the Lebanese coastline every August. Despite their recursive mistrust, each considered the other to be a good friend with whom to share intimate secrets. Mutual jealousy occasionally rendered these secrets public, and this with disastrous consequences.

In contrast to Elio, Ralph was not as outgoing, let alone gregarious. He celebrated his gayness with much less luridness, even though he did not hide his erotic penchant for mature Western men. Elio was a short and slender young man with a relatively auburn skin tone, who looked athletic without engaging in any significant physical exercise. Ralph was his opposite. At the beach, one could not but notice the considerable amount of baby fat enveloping his body. Despite the flesh spilling over his green swim trunks, his relative chubbiness in no way made him plump. Rather, it made him even more endearing to those of us who recognized in him the distinctive characteristics of a very enjoyable person. More importantly to others, his deep blue eyes were often the subject of envious conversations on the beach. In addition, he was very blond, a physical reality that won over countless admirers who fantasized about a possible Teutonic heritage on his part. However, this possibility remained an imagined legacy that nobody could substantiate. I knew he had siblings, but they never materialized in our conversations, let alone in an actual physical way. From what I was told, his father lived in Dubai, and it seemed as if his parents did not have much of a marriage, especially given the short paternal visits that were limited to one per year.

Ralph's queerness, on the other hand, must have been—at least in part—a sensitive issue in his family because he disappeared unexpectedly one day in the winter of 2002, apparently sent to the Arab Gulf and to a father who purportedly had plans to transform a son who was perceived by some as lacking strong male qualities. After a mere two months though, Ralph was back in Jbeil, not as a "real man," but rather vigorously cursing Dubai as if it was synonymous with utter misery. It turned out that during one of his visits to Lebanon, Ralph's father had noticed a pointed effeminate demeanor on the part of his son, which he blamed on his wife's negligence in raising him appropriately. A heated argument ensued and the mother decided that if her husband was unhappy with the way she raised his children, he should try to do a better job and take Ralph with him to Dubai. The subject of effeminacy and latent homosexuality was completely eclipsed by a gradually overarching family discourse that focused exclusively on all the possible educational advantages Ralph was to have in the United Arab Emirates, advantages that supposedly did not exist in Lebanon.

I never learned what exactly happened to Ralph in Dubai, but his stay lasted barely eight weeks before he became once again an integral part of the young *tantāt* scene in and around Beirut. While Elio went to a public secondary school in Jbeil, Ralph attended a semi-private *lycée* run under the auspices of the Maronite Patriarchate in Bkerke. Apart from being a superior student, Ralph received a much better formal education, and so his prospects of getting into university were also better. This qualitative difference was crucial in understanding parts of the rivalry that characterized much of the relationship between the two friends. Yet, it was not the dissimilarities in social and cultural capital that had led to a temporary cold war between Ralph and Elio. Rather, it was a jealousy of a different kind, one that just happened to coincide with the marriage of Elio's sister.

With the spread of Internet cafés in Lebanon around the turn of the millennium, chatting with people at home and around the world became commonplace. This would change slightly with the increased use of personal computers in people's homes five to ten years later when platforms such as Manjam spurred the erotic imaginations of countless gay users. This was followed by the proliferation of smart phone applications—like Grindr, Scruff, and Hornet—that inserted a clear element of class into the convoluted equation of conspicuous consumption and access so important to the production of prestige in Lebanon.[6] By 2010, most people had access to a computer and could, therefore, easily open an account on Manjam. To have a profile on Grindr, however, meant that one was the proud owner of a smart phone. This required significant economic capital, given that the iconic iPhone, for instance, went for roughly US$800 at local phone stores. Yet, in the early 2000s, what many practitioners would later consider "conventional chatting" on the smart phone application Whatsapp actually started on such generic social media platforms as AOL and, later, Facebook. Also, while romantic motives were often behind the various chatting practices, the number of pornographic gay sites visited by many surfers astounded me whenever I visited one of the semi-public dark caves of virtual excitement that constituted the Internet cafés at the turn of the millennium.

To give a concrete idea of how some of these chatting practices were conducted, let me zoom in on a particular example intended to highlight not only the very form of communication between two interlocutors I call "douwara69" and "t2borni," but also the language, often explicitly sexual; based on a mix of Arabic and English, via French phonetics; and used to channel identity, desire, and fantasy.

douwara69@hotmail.com says: (7:54:45 a.m.) hi
douwara69@hotmail.com says: (7:54:53 a.m.) ana jean 22 beyrut sin el fill [I'm John 22 Beirut Sin al-Fīl]
t2borni@hotmail.com says: (7:54:53 a.m.) hi
douwara69@hotmail.com says: (7:54:55 a.m.) u
t2borni@hotmail.com says: (7:55:09 a.m.) marwan 24 bil ashrafieh [Marwan in Ashrafieh]
douwara69@hotmail.com says: (7:55:45 a.m.) 3endak ma7al? sekine wa7dak? [You have a place? You live alone?]
t2borni@hotmail.com says: (7:55:56 a.m.) la. enta? shu? [No. You? What?]
douwara69@hotmail.com says: (7:56:08 a.m.) ana hala2 wa7de bass mich deymann [I'm alone now, but not always]
t2borni@hotmail.com says: (7:56:46 a.m.) ma3ak siyara? [Do you have a car?]
douwara69@hotmail.com says: (7:57:31 a.m.) la. [no.]
douwara69@hotmail.com says: (7:57:40 a.m.) looking for?
t2borni@hotmail.com says: (7:57:57 a.m.) sex ma3a 7ada bottom. enta? [Sex with a bottom guy. You?]
douwara69@hotmail.com says: (7:58:04 a.m.) kamena [Same]
douwara69@hotmail.com says: (8:01:51 a.m.) badak nilta2a? [Do you want to meet?]
t2borni@hotmail.com says: (8:02:16 a.m.) halla ma fiye. 3ashiyeh? [Now, I can't. At night?]
douwara69@hotmail.com says: (8:02:25 a.m.) ok
t2borni@hotmail.com says: (8:02:51 a.m.) bas ma 3ende matra7 [But I don't have a place.]
douwara69@hotmail.com says: (8:02:59 a.m.) chou bit7ib bill SEX w2adeh toulo ayrakk? [What do you like in terms of sex? What's your cock size?]

t2borni@hotmail.com says: (8:03:11 a.m.) 19. enta? [19 cm/7.5″. You?]
douwara69@hotmail.com says: (8:03:28 a.m.) 16 cm cut chwey t5ine. U? [16 cm/6.5″ cut and quite thick. You?]
t2borni@hotmail.com says: (8:03:57 a.m.) enta bottom, ma heyk? [You're a bottom, right?]
douwara69@hotmail.com says: (8:04:31 a.m.) yes.
douwara69@hotmail.com says: (8:05:49 a.m.) ana yimkine ykoune 3inde matra7 3achiye. btije aw dabirlak chi top tene nrou7 la3andooo? [I might have a place tonight. Will you come or should I get a second top for us to travel to?]
t2borni@hotmail.com says: (8:07:55 a.m.) mithl ma badak [As you wish]
douwara69@hotmail.com says: (8:10:03 a.m.) chou bit7ib bill sexx wi wen bit7ib tjibo [What do you like in terms of sex? Where do you like to cum?]
t2borni@hotmail.com says: (8:10:13 a.m.) beddi iyak bas! :p [I just want you! :p]
douwara69@hotmail.com says: (8:10:38 a.m.) wen bit7ib tjibo? [Where do you wanna cum?]
t2borni@hotmail.com says: (8:11:45 a.m.) 7asab, wen ma kan. [It depends. Wherever.]
douwara69@hotmail.com says: (8:12:24 a.m.) aha ok. bitnik ma3 condom aw bala [Aha OK. You fuck with a condom or without?]
t2borni@hotmail.com says: (8:12:51 a.m.) kaman, 7asab. shu bt7ib enta? [Again, it depends. What do you like?]
douwara69@hotmail.com says: (8:14:03 a.m.) 7ayala no problem [Whatever. No problem]
douwara69@hotmail.com says: (8:14:09 a.m.) ayrak t5ine? [You have a thick cock?]
t2borni@hotmail.com says: (8:14:56 a.m.) yes
douwara69@hotmail.com says: (8:15:50 a.m.) good fi chi soura la 2iloo? [Good. You've got a pic of it?]
t2borni@hotmail.com says: (8:16:14 a.m.) la, ma 3endi, sorry. [No, I don't. Sorry.]
douwara69@hotmail.com says: (8:16:30 a.m.) ok
douwara69@hotmail.com says: (8:16:54 a.m.) bit7ib lchab hairy aw no? [You like the guy to be hairy or not?]
t2borni@hotmail.com says: (8:17:50 a.m.) b7ib izza kan hairy ktir. enta hairy? [I like it if he's very hairy. Are you hairy?]
douwara69@hotmail.com says: (8:19:39 a.m.) eh [Yep!]

t2borni@hotmail.com says: (8:19:56 a.m.) good!
douwara69@hotmail.com says: (8:20:49 a.m.) bikib ma3ak ktir? [Do you cum a lot?]
t2borni@hotmail.com says: (8:21:31 a.m.) 7asab. izza mhayej ktir, eh. Enta? [Depends. If very horny, then yes. You?]
douwara69@hotmail.com says: (8:22:05 a.m.) eh
douwara69@hotmail.com says: (8:23:12 a.m.) 2inta bitmous? [You suck?]
t2borni@hotmail.com says: (8:23:38 a.m.) akeed! [Of course!]
douwara69@hotmail.com says: (8:23:58 a.m.) aha wen bit7ib jib ayreee [Aha. Where do you want me to cum?]
t2borni@hotmail.com says: (8:24:30 a.m.) wen biddak tjibo enta? [Where do *you* wanna cum?]
douwara69@hotmail.com says: (8:24:50 a.m.) bitimak [In your mouth.]
t2borni@hotmail.com says: (8:26:03 a.m.) yimkin, bas ma ba3ref izza beddi tjibo bitimi [Maybe, but I don't know if I want you to cum in my mouth.]
douwara69@hotmail.com says: (8:27:08 a.m.) wen ma badak bjibooo [I'll cum wherever you want me to.]
t2borni@hotmail.com says: (8:27:21 a.m.) ok
douwara69@hotmail.com says: (8:28:11 a.m.) bitawil ta yije ayrakk? [You take a long time to cum?]
t2borni@hotmail.com says: (8:29:19 a.m.) fi yije aktar min marra [I can cum more than once.]
douwara69@hotmail.com says: (8:32:19 a.m.) bitnik bi 2ouwe aw houdou2? [You fuck hard or mild?]
t2borni@hotmail.com says: (8:33:46 a.m.) bi houdou2 WA bi ouwwe, 7assab . . . [Mild AND hard, it depends.]
douwara69@hotmail.com says: (8:35:22 a.m.) ok
douwara69@hotmail.com says: (8:37:32 a.m.) 2iza 3indak sou2al tis2alo s2all [If you have a question to ask me, go ahead.]
t2borni@hotmail.com says: (8:38:43 a.m.) fiyye shufak al yom? 7a tkoun la 7alak? [Can I see you today? Will you be alone?]
douwara69@hotmail.com says: (8:38:56 a.m.) eh, yimkine [Yep, possibly.]

Apart from the sexualized tone and content of the virtual conversation, in which both protagonists check out each other's physical qualities and preferred sexual acts, what becomes clear right at the beginning in the above chat is the problem of finding a place to have sex. Both "douwara69" and "t2borni"[7] do not live alone and depend on the temporary absence of their housemates (generally family members) in order to invite visitors. Due to the difficulties of finding a *maḥal* or *maṭraḥ* (place), the possibility of a physical encounter, even if in a *siyāra* (car), is usually aborted from the outset. Thus, the chat platform becomes a site of projections and dreams that, for the most part, are impossible to realize.

What is of equal importance is the linguistic form within which these projections and dreams take shape. This form carries a particular logic and structure, but its consistency is not always guaranteed within the rushed act of chatting. While Lebanese Arabic is used to communicate, the language is written in Latin letters and includes a whole set of numbers used to convey particular letters in the original Arabic. For example, when douwara69 asks t2borni, "3endak ma7al? sekine wa7dak?" [You have a place? You live alone?], the number *3* stands for the Arabic letter ع (generally transcribed as *ʿa[yn]*), while the number *7* stands for the Arabic letter ح (generally transcribed as *ḥ*). Also, douwara69 inquires about whether his chatting partner's penis is *t5ine* (thick), using the number *5* to represent the Arabic letter خ (generally transcribed as *kh*). The number *2* recurs throughout the chat and stands for a glottal stop and the Arabic letter أ (generally transcribed with an '—i.e., hamza), as in *houdou2* (mild or quiet) or t2borni, even if the *2* in the screen name actually stands for the Arabic letter ق (generally transcribed as *q*), which is silent in Lebanese Arabic. Moreover, what is striking is that douwara69 is most likely "French-educated," based on the various *e*'s he puts at the end of his words and the French letter combination *ou* that stands for the Arabic or English sound *u*. In contrast to t2borni, who writes *shu* for *what*, douwara69 writes *chou*, according to French language conventions. If many expressions remain in English, such as "looking for," "OK," "sorry," and "hairy," they form part of a globalized lingua franca in which local practices of chatting co-opt a widely circulating terminology. However, this terminology is met with homegrown grammatical and semantic standards where idiosyncratic intonations (such as the rolling of the *rr* in "sorry") form only the tip of a complex sociolinguistic iceberg.

With the advent and continuous development of modern technology around social media, local practices of chatting in Lebanon grew, adopting particular conventions that were increasingly perfected as far as their formulaic structure was concerned. Invariably, this structure highlighted recurrent themes, including all kinds of sexual fantasies and the dilemma of place. But it also included the longing for other places, and the hope to "meet" Mr. Perfect in some faraway fantasyland.

To return to the story of Elio, it happened that he was one of the early chatting practitioners in Lebanon. In fact, in 2002, he "met" a young American man, barely seventeen, from Orange County, whose family was originally from the largely Druze village of ʿAyn ʿOnūb, located in the foothills flanking the southern outskirts of Beirut. For about two months, according to Elio, a great love story unfolded across a sea, an ocean, and an entire continent—only the two lovers had never set eyes on each other. Yet, for weeks on end, Elio could not talk about anybody else, and he even stopped being the sexually charged social butterfly he usually was. He gave the impression of being focused only on the upcoming day when "Sal" (Sleiman was his proper name) would visit Lebanon. Needless to say, almost everybody around Elio was unnerved by his constant stories about how he and Sal would get married, live in Hollywood, and share the life of a glamorous couple to whom nobody would ever fail to give due attention. Ralph especially grew increasingly angry with his friend, although there was a substantial portion of unconcealed jealousy that accompanied his extreme annoyance. More than just exasperation, however, caused the rift between the two friends. Ralph had asked to see pictures of Sal, as well as some of the correspondence between the two lovers. Somehow he managed to convince Elio to give him his e-mail password. Shortly thereafter Ralph, pretending to be Elio, sent a long message to Sal, detailing how he had met somebody else, a man in his thirties whom he considered to be close to his heart, "closer than anybody else, ever!"

It did not take Elio long to find out what had happened, and he reacted with a fearsome fury, doing everything he could to discredit Ralph within the small group that they both interacted with on and off Paradise Beach. The dispute happened in late fall 2002, and Elio made it clear to me, shortly after his sister's wedding, that he was in no hurry to be friends with Ralph again. Each stopped frequenting places at times when he suspected the other might be present, avoiding at all cost the possibility of sharing space, let alone spending time, with each other.

Luckily, not everything was lost, mostly because Elio had managed to explain to his transatlantic lover what had happened and convince him of an unadulterated devotion he promised to substantiate in person as soon as Sal came to Lebanon. For quite some time, the plan had been for Sal to spend parts of spring 2003 in Beirut, an arrangement backed by his parents who very much wanted their son to be in touch with his Lebanese roots. An additional incentive was the possibility of Sal registering for a freshman year at the American University of Beirut, an academic environment that, by the parents' accounts, would not constitute a major culture shock for their son.

During all these weeks, when strategies of moving from Southern California to the Levant were being carefully devised, Elio spent hours on end in Jbeil Internet cafés, chatting his time away with Sal. Occasionally, they also talked to each other on the phone, using an extraordinary mixture of Lebanese Arabic and American English. During this time, people like Ralph were totally out of Elio's frame of interest, and I often wondered, had it not been winter, whether he would have had the guts to boycott Paradise Beach. When spring came, Sal moved to Beirut, staying with one of his uncles, who owned a big house in Choueifāt, part of the capital's southern suburbs, not very far from the family's ancestral village. At that point, I ceased to follow all that unfolded between Elio and his American "boyfriend," whom I met for the first time in Jbeil on one of these warm days in early March when a jump into the Mediterranean is irresistible. Sal was quite pleasant, baby-faced and a bit on the shy side. In other words, he was not at all what I expected a SoCal boy to be. His braces lent a little lisp to his otherwise forthcoming, though soft-spoken speech. One could not help but notice the obviously amusing fact that both lovers wore retainers, a happenstance that made them even more amiable and charming.

Shortly thereafter, however, what had seemed to be the love of a lifetime faded away swiftly, but not without leaving a bitter aftertaste for both protagonists. There was a short initial phase during which Elio had all kinds of bad things to say about Sal. But even that disappeared without much ado, and by the time I met up with Elio on the large staircase below the Grand Sérail in downtown Beirut, he was his old self again, socializing actively with almost any adult male who let himself be captivated by Elio's enchanting wit. To my initial surprise, a few steps down stood Ralph, who was visibly in good spirits, to say the least, and chatting with a number of other fellows who had gathered next to the ancient Roman baths. For all I could see, the two friends had finally resumed their friendship, even though tension continued to be a part of their relationship.

Hierarchies, Differences, and the Performance of Wealth

The large staircase above Bank Street may have been a comparatively significant zone of encounter for a young queer-identified crowd from a variety of backgrounds. These young men congregated there on a regular basis on Saturday evenings before some in the group would hit clubs scattered around the city. However, the area two blocks away from the centrally located Nejmeh Square did not attract every young gay man in Lebanon. Denizens like Georgette, for example, never set foot on the staircase, although his friend Monica fit the ideal type espoused by this group of adolescent men who looked down on bodily flamboyance such as that exhibited by Georgette. In a similar vein, men in their late twenties and thirties—notably those, like Rachid and Khalil, who enjoyed a professional career and could afford to patronize an expensive café such as Caspar and Gambini's—made sure not to mix with a considerably younger—and, therefore, easier to dismiss—set of people. To be associated with them could have been interpreted as debasement by somebody perpetually preoccupied with maintaining social prestige. Vis-à-vis a larger public with significant homophobic tendencies, it was "safer" for men like Rachid and Khalil, who were comparatively mature and had the money to spend, to sit in a café on Maarad Street than to stand on a staircase with people who would have clearly marked them, along with their entourage, as potentially marginal.

Of course, this is not to say that age limitation was subject to a necessary reinforcement by the mix of people who contested the liminal space of the staircase. Occasionally, I saw a few men, in their forties or fifties, appropriating a social space that at first may have seemed to exclude them. This appropriation ranged from a marginal participation, limited to a cautious exchange of gazes, to regular rendezvous set up between older men and the younger subjects of their undivided attention. This transgenerational attraction managed to hold its ground in a multiplicity of ways, including the various policing activities undertaken zealously by some middle-aged security guards who actively participated in a spatial economy of desire that caused the range of scenes enacted on the staircase to be all the more disputed and multifaceted.

Whenever I met with Elio and his pals, apart from the particular configuration at hand on any given weekend evening, everybody present on the spot would catch up on the latest gossip and show off his most recent outfit: a pair of authentic, or sometimes fake, designer pants or a tight tank top. These clothes were among an extensive list of accoutrements with explicit, trendy qualities that set the tone for the highly performative interactions taking place on the staircase. Indeed, hanging out at the Roman baths on Saturday nights soon became a weekly ritual for one specific category of young gay men in Beirut. These young men momentarily immersed themselves in a homo-social world of dabbling flirtation, where everyone *khasso* (concerned) or *fāyit bil-jaw* (part of the [gay] atmosphere) could feel safe from outside social criticism and, at the same time, hip and stylish in a place that was considered à la mode by everybody. Most importantly, this sense of safety came without the financial cost of sitting in one of the expensive cafés located behind the monumental office buildings along Bank Street.

Despite this alternative world that was recurrently created on the steps to the Grand Sérail on Saturday evenings as a realm of "in-between-ness" and made into a zone of unconventional encounter by young gay men, I want to point to the paradoxical discontent these young men and their actions embodied for some onlookers. On the one hand, to hang out on the steps leading to the refurbished (and slightly altered) late Ottoman-style seat of government proved that socioeconomic depravity could be an outward impediment. It was an obstacle that prevented those who constituted the unfolding social encounter from completely conquering a world where being a full-fledged member of the bourgeois establishment was a difficult—if not impossible—task. On the other hand, for these young gay men, as well as for a large number of Lebanese, regardless of their gender, sexuality, or age, this projected world, with its quintessentially materialistic and image-driven outlook, continued to be perceived as representing their societal aspiration par excellence.

To sit "properly," as did Rachid or Khalil, outside a café or restaurant on either Maarad Street or Nejmeh Square would have rightly constituted the complete achievement of such an aspiration, one that was clearly shared by Elio, Ralph, and their mutual acquaintances. However, to gather in a place that might be perceived as marginal by all local accounts did not necessarily do away with one's active contestation of "prime space"—that is to say, virtually any part of coveted *ḍownṭown*, regardless of whether its spatial location was deemed central or peripheral. The ostensibly inconsequential location of the staircase still constituted an integral part of the fashionable city center according to which all sorts of local identities were being formulated on a perpetual basis. Consequently, something else must have constituted the paradox inherent in a state of affairs where young Beiruti homosexual men, in preparing for their long-awaited weekend outing, flocked to a location imbued with a significance that was anything but accidental.

The significance of space and its appropriation notwithstanding, the assertion of a queer presence on the staircase below the Grand Sérail cannot be separated from the conspicuous consumption in which many young gay men engaged, despite their limited access to economic capital. The dominant lifestyle of the local bourgeoisie attracted many segments of society, even if the former would repeatedly emphasize the "deviant" character of the latter. Though queer-identified men such as Elio, Georgette, or even Rachid were de facto incapable of indulging in the opulent lifestyle that was limited to a few, the general desire nevertheless remained widespread among many to become a part of it, albeit an ultimately rejected part.

Historically, this type of striving for what was imagined as "civility" and access was also found in élite discourses of morality and "deviance," going all the way back to the late nineteenth century. As Jens Hanssen observes in *Fin de Siècle Beirut: The Making of an Ottoman Provincial Capital*, the attempt of the late Ottoman bourgeoisie at "a geographical alignment of evolving class and gender notions . . ." led to the labeling of social activities "as deviant precisely because they occurred in central places that were envisaged to represent more enlightened urban images for Beirut." Consequently, he writes, "elite notions of civility generated gender and class tensions that were fought over urban space."[8]

About a century later, the outwardly ceaseless and pervasive effort of avoiding the stigma of the lower classes in an exposed location, such as *ḍownṭown*, was based on a widely perceived indignity that, as a matter of fact, revealed the country's persistent social inequity at the turn of the new millennium. In the end, such an effort involved the elimination of observable difference. The fear of being associated with poverty, and thus the stigma of the social gatecrasher, fueled this attempt to do away with an otherwise visible reality. Moreover, it was an embodied teleology that included—but was evidently not limited to—young gay men and that amounted to a "performance of wealth" in Lebanon. Again, like the overt display of tangible wealth, such a performance was certainly not limited to Lebanese gay boys who checked each other out on the comparatively small—yet significant—number of explicit cruising grounds Beirut had to offer. Nor was it restricted to an avowedly superficial and socially marginal group, one that was solely preoccupied with exterior looks. Aside from unsympathetic interpretations of what was "actually going on" at the Roman baths, we are far from dealing with a group of people that was operating in some sort of socio-cultural vacuum. Rather, these young gay men were part of a wider Mediterranean society, one that locally counted among its primary obsessions the infatuation with everything believed to be at the height of fashion. These obsessions often ran the gamut from the most basic piece of clothing to a foremost local sense of bodily magnificence.

In post-civil-war Lebanon, the performance of wealth became emblematic within the relatively small social context of young gay men, even if it was obviously far from being limited to it. The active appropriation of spaces in and around Beirut by people like Elio and his friends tended to be coupled, by and large, with studied bodily performances that fit, on the one hand, a larger model of material reality concealment and, on the other, a highly coveted social aspiration with an ambition that remained continually difficult to achieve. In sum, a considerable number of these young gay men continued to exemplify the way in which several of the fundamental aspects that characterized the scuffles of ordinary life in the early 2000s in Lebanon came together, including the contrived living of a life removed from an economically and socio-politically dire reality.

More importantly, some of the struggles determining the daily existence of numerous young gay men in and around Beirut had to do with difference and the local difficulties of its social acceptance. Once more, the splendid exterior appearance on display in an exposed setting like *ḍownṭown* in no way reflected the actual socioeconomic standing of the person in question. On the contrary, the deteriorating economic situation, one that gathered speed in the late 1990s and came to a devastating end in the new millennium, led to the embattlement of the traditional middle class. The historical importance in Lebanon of this class was replaced by an uneven binary positing a gradually disenfranchised majority against a numerically small, albeit exceedingly potent, class of tremendously wealthy businesspeople, whose imagined way of life captured large parts of society. Many of these economic barons excelled—and, in some cases, continued to do so during the postwar years—at national politics.

While the local bourgeoisie managed to set the tone regarding many social practices, it also succeeded in doing so without notable opposition by a majority whose weight in national politics had been gradually eclipsed and substituted by an ostensibly upward-looking social mimicry. More than anything else, the disenfranchised majority did its best to imitate some of the most notorious bodily and attitudinal fashions brought up and sustained by the various performances introduced by the local élites. A counter to this argument is the contention that, on a broader historical scale, socio-political opposition in Lebanon had always been systematically cultivated and channeled through a range of parties and associations. In the wake of the civil war, some of these political groups had emerged from the sectarian fabric of previously marginalized sections of the population and, consequently, challenged the role of the privileged classes.[9]

Although my own analysis here is not focused on any sectarian group in particular, be it Shīʿī Muslims or any of the other seventeen officially recognized sects in the country, it remains important to elucidate the relationship an identity—informed by politics, religion, and gender—entertains with one based on the broader acceptance of perpetual social and cultural change. My work is thus informed by an understanding of identity that goes beyond the mere inclusion of the strictly socio-political components of this pivotal concept. In an attempt to gauge the many seeming contradictions of contemporary Lebanon, where a multi-layered modernity is fueled by conspicuous consumption and the performance of wealth, I have intended in this chapter to reach for an understanding of local identities that is informed by a composite confrontation with the dynamic effects of a perpetual social and cultural transformation. My theoretical focus is informed by the ethnographic reality at hand, especially when it comes to how I approach the categories of gender and sexuality and the ways in which both inform the formation of a particular identity, which I deem as queer. First, my interlocutors do not belong to one single sectarian group. Individually, religion may on occasion play a considerable role, but it rarely does so during the various personal interactions within the range of spaces I have earlier described as "zones of encounter"—namely, spaces where mostly young men from different horizons interact on the very basis of a common erotic desire. Second, in a strongly hierarchical society like that in Lebanon, social categories such as age and class need to be factored in as well. Most of those individuals with whom I interacted only benefited from a limited social and cultural capital, a limitation that, on the one hand, can be explained by their relatively young age.

On the other hand, however, even though some possessed sufficient funds to partake in a world of material wealth, most of my interlocutors had to be content with the prospect of "performing" it, and sometimes "queering" it, but in general without actively "participating" in it. Third, their dissident sexuality, albeit not always visible to everybody, put them outside the realm of social acceptability—including the lack of access to particular resources, as we will see in subsequent chapters—and repeatedly on the receiving end of homophobic affronts that manifested in both subtly covert as well as blatantly unconcealed ways.

I certainly do not discount the overriding significance of organized social and political movements in the formation of identities that are consequently mobilized by political parties like Ḥizballah or, for instance, by the human rights activism of particular groups discussed later. What both political parties and activist groups have in common, and this despite all differences, is a concerted attempt to bring change to a status quo deemed as lacking righteousness for their respective clientele.

Moreover, while I acknowledge the importance of social and political action in contemporary Lebanon, my interest in *Queer Beirut* remains more focused on the apparent, although often ephemeral, fringes of daily social performativities, and less on the tangibility of exceedingly structured socio-political associations that have formed the primary center of attention in many social studies of the country. This focus has allowed me to access a broader view as far as the complex social realities in Lebanon are concerned. By assessing individual and collective performances that some may allege to be inconsequential due to their lack of a common political denominator, my view may certainly be a broad and perhaps even a scattered one. Nonetheless, it provides me with a perspective where the extensive focus on the complex formation of gender identity manages to capture the local pulse of time, including its potential for generating queer practices, in a way any exclusive discussion of political factors would arguably miss.

CHAPTER 3

Walking through the Concrete Jungle: The Queer Urban Stroller Traveling amid de Certeau, Benjamin, and Bourdieu

If one thinks about post-civil-war Beirut, many of the immediate associations that emerge are connected to the dismal realities of the concrete jungle that the city became during the last two decades of the twentieth century. Almost completely covered with ordinary roads, somewhat plain boulevards, and unexceptional buildings, the Lebanese capital has been increasingly perceived by many of its inhabitants as an impervious and unreceptive environment that renders daily life a rather fractious enterprise. The devastating legacy of the 1975–1990 civil war brought about a frenzy of construction. This was fueled by a proliferation of building permits signed by corrupt officials all too willing to partake in a sprawling economic and political system sustained by the fallacies of widespread endemic preferential treatment, the archetypical *wasṭa*. However, topography and population growth have also factored into making Beirut the congested city it has become since the beginning of the 1990s.

About 4.5 million (2014) people live in Lebanon, half of them in Beirut and its suburbs. It is a small country of roughly 10,400 square kilometers (4,015 square miles) with a coastline on the Mediterranean Sea to the west, Galilee to the south, and the Anti-Lebanon mountain chain, which forms the official border with Syria, to the east. The country's geographically central regions are dominated by what has been referred to over the ages as Mount Lebanon, a string of adjacent rugged mountain peaks with foothills that, in many places, are near the coast. Such is the case with the immediate topography surrounding the country's capital. Although Beirut is mainly located on a relatively flat triangular peninsula with a northern flank that gives form to the adjoining St. George Bay, its eastern edge meets the slopes of the mountainous areas that are part of the country's Metn region.[1]

From Fishing Village to Capital

Until the mid-twentieth century, Beirut grew mostly around what is still today considered to be its geographical center.[2] Despite the city's relative importance in ancient times, due to the local site of the Roman law school, Beyritus, as it was called then, soon vanished into historical oblivion, thus paving the way for neighboring cities like Tripoli and Saida to become major regional centers throughout the Middle Ages and into modern times. As the famed Lebanese historian Samir Kassir argued, it was the decision to build a railroad between Damascus and Beirut in the 1860s that transformed Beirut's trajectory from a fishing village to a major modern urban player.[3] Moreover, during the civil war of 1860, significant numbers of Christians from the mountains and from Damascus sought refuge in a then mid-sized town that soon became the unofficial capital of the newly proclaimed *mutaṣarrifīyya* (province) of Mount Lebanon. This special district would remain a nominal part of the Ottoman Empire, while functioning de facto as some sort of protectorate under the auspices of the great European powers at the time, Britain and France.[4] Many of the refugees stayed and were joined by other—mostly rural—populations attracted by the burgeoning commerce around the rapidly growing local port, which soon enough became the most important one in the Levant, catering to what Jens Hanssen calls "a nation of provincials." In *Fin de Siècle Beirut*, Hanssen notes that, in becoming a capital, "Beirut extended its political power far beyond the confines of geographical, confessional [i.e., sectarian], or familiar ties with Mount Lebanon. . . . The creation of the Province [the *mutaṣarrifīyya*] consolidated Beirut's economic position through the political functions performed by a late Ottoman provincial capital."[5]

My purpose in *Queer Beirut* is not to deliver an exhaustive chronological account of important past events, for it would be a sheer impossibility to provide a boiled-down version of such brilliant introductions into Beirut's intricate history as those provided by Hanssen and the late Samir Kassir.[6] What interests me more, especially in this chapter, are the broad patterns along which the city grew during the decades of the twentieth century before it covered the entire space available for its expansion.

In his classic pre-civil-war socio-cultural study of urbanization, *From Village to Suburb: Order and Change in Greater Beirut* (1975), the late anthropologist Fuad Khuri examined the political function of sect and divided local history into three phases: ancient, peasant, and suburban.[7] Khuri mostly focused on the southern "suburbs" of Chiyāḥ and Ghobeiri.

An enormous number of rural migrants had settled in these primarily lower-class areas. This influx, as he argued, disrupted the physical and social arrangement of old neighborhoods. Khuri saw "suburban" settlement patterns in 1960s Lebanon as social in nature. Functioning along the lines of family, class, and sect, these patterns affected occupational structures and political alliances. More importantly, they pointed to a shift from kin to sect politics. In other words, sects fused and enabled the formation of sectarian identities unheard of within the village setting.

Despite regular visits to Chiyāḥ over the years, I did not initially focus on that "suburb," its national importance notwithstanding. In the 1960s and early 1970s, it was, to a large extent, Christian but acquired a Shīʿī identity during and in the aftermath of the war. One is reminded in reading Khuri's theses about sectarianism and class today that it was in the immediate vicinity of Chiyāḥ, in the Maronite "suburb" of ʿAyn Al-Rummāneh, that the Lebanese civil war started around the time his book was published. Although my interests are based on the complexities of class, the emphasis on sect is important, but not central, to my analysis. Apart from my concern with gender and sexuality, my limited treatment of sectarianism also has to do with the very spaces in which I conducted the initial stages of my fieldwork. Less concerned with Beiruti "suburbs" or with the image of a "house of many mansions" that Lebanon as a whole was supposed to convey, according to the late historian Kamal Salibi, I was more interested in urban neighborhoods that were relatively mixed in terms of their social and confessional pedigree.[8] For that matter, let me shift my attention to the Ḥamra district, an area important to the modern history of Beirut—if not to the country as a whole—that cannot be highlighted enough.

A major turn in the local urban development was the post-World War II building frenzy in the northwestern part of the peninsula, along a former dirt road. The road was called *ḥamra* (red) because of the auburn color of the mud covering it. In the mid-1860s, American Protestant missionaries appropriated a large amount of land west of Beirut's city center to found what they initially called the Syrian Protestant College, the forerunner of the American University of Beirut (AUB). Over the years, entire quarters to the west and south of the new campus emerged, creating a major focal point, political and cultural, for the entire country, if not the region at large. In the late 1950s, but especially during the politically significant decade of the 1960s, what had become the Ḥamra district rapidly transformed into the epicenter of Arab thinking at the time, mostly due to the considerable influx of Palestinian refugees following the *naqba* (the 1948

Palestinian "catastrophe") and to the sad but simple fact that Lebanon had become one of the few places in the wider region of the Arab world where a certain freedom of expression was not totally impossible. Writing fifty-five years later, shortly before his brutal assassination, the eminent Lebanese historian Samir Kassir contended, however, that, since then:

> [L]e Liban a entamé un singulier voyage à reculons. À peine sorti d'une guerre qui, en plus d'avoir déchiré sa société, a privé le monde arabe de l'un de ses laboratoires de modernité, le Liban a perdu en quinze ans d'après-guerre la plupart des atouts qui l'avaient longtemps distingués. À commencer par la liberté d'expression et l'inventivité médiatique. . . . Sans parler d'une tradition républicaine qui, si incomplète qu'elle ait été, avait pu survivre à la guerre qui l'avait grièvement blessée.[9]
> (Lebanon has started a peculiar journey backwards. No sooner had the country left a war behind, which, while having torn apart its society, deprived the Arab world of one of its *laboratories of modernity*, than Lebanon lost in fifteen years of post-civil-war most of the assets that had distinguished it for a long time. Starting with the freedom of expression and media inventiveness. . . . Without talking about a republican tradition that, no matter how incomplete it was, had been able to survive a war that had seriously injured it. [My translation, emphasis mine.])

Despite this "journey backwards," which, according to Kassir, has been haunting Lebanon ever since the beginning of the country's civil war, the initial influx of people during the middle of the twentieth century led also to an influx of money, followed by an extensive building sprawl in the 1950s and 1960s. The Ḥamra district, as well as most other neighborhoods in Beirut, became dotted with new high-rises, which successively dwarfed the few remaining late-Ottoman houses that had, until then, put an identifiable mark on many boroughs of the capital. Even though this kind of urban development was quite advanced by the time the civil war began in 1975, it was only during and after the fifteen years of uninterrupted fighting that Beirut experienced its concrete coup de grâce. The physical destruction of buildings did not prevent the city's inhabitants from replacing whatever had become rubble with new structures that seldom reflected any sensitivity as far as urban planning or design was concerned. Moreover, an unusually high number of parking lots spread across the urban landscape, making one wonder about the link between human suffering and the potential consequences it had on the environment. In other words, the presence of a parking lot in Beirut marked an absence of something that had been destroyed, but it also indicated a presence of a different nature. It was a presence that pointed to the damages people inflicted on themselves and their surroundings, motivated by a sense of rage at what they believed other people had done to them.

Also, during most of the second half of the twentieth century, Beirut had been anything but a green city. Today, public places, regardless of whether they feature trees or not, remain a rarity. So it is no mystery as to why many—if not all—Beirutis regard the sea as a welcome respite from their otherwise all too concrete quotidian. The Corniche, the celebrated seashore promenade that circumscribes the entire western part of the city, therefore became a prime destination for anybody who wanted to *shamm al-hawwa*—or "smell the air," as "having a stroll" is pointedly called in Lebanese Arabic. Yet, anything that is located within the perimeter of the Corniche's pedestrian sidewalk is subject to the exhaustive reality of countless internal combustion engines. Over the years, the population has suffered from an excruciating traffic problem. Indeed, cars were to be seen everywhere, slowly but surely making their way through the tightly knit web of asphalt roads and alleys. They were even parked on the few sidewalks that initially were intended for pedestrians, who, marginalized in numbers and overall social prestige, were required to be highly inventive when braving the urban pavement.

Therefore, since the end of the civil war, getting around Beirut, which is spatially small compared to other cities in the region such as Damascus, Cairo, or even Istanbul, had become a driving affair. For sure, there was a clear-cut hierarchy attached to urban mobility. To own and drive a car placed one at the top of a pyramid, a spot that was constantly subject to a fierce contestation, and where factors like size and brand were of major importance. To prioritize prestige in such a fashion often compensated for the frequent inconvenience of spending too much time moving one's vehicle along congested city roads and alleys. Furthermore, the driver was not always the actual owner. The mere fact of sitting behind the steering wheel of a new model Mercedes or BMW was important because it bestowed upon the operator—mostly, but not exclusively, male—an instant elevation in status. This was especially the case in exposed places where one could be seen by fashionable people. Such a gendered performance went hand in glove with the unruly ramifications of life in and around Beirut in the postwar years.

Hierarchies in Urban Mobility: The Service and the Micro

For a variety of reasons having to do with limited public transportation in general and an increasingly grim economic situation in particular, many Beirutis move about the city by using cars they call, irrespective of the language used, *service* (pronounced *sarvīs* in Arabic). A service is a shared taxi that operates along a more or less predefined route. Customers can hop on and off, providing their destination is concomitant with the initial route devised by the "chauffeur" of the service. Despite continuously changing dynamics in the new millennium and for a long time since the end of the 1975–1990 civil war, most of the services were Mercedes Benz automobiles, typically 1980s models. Many of these vehicles were rumored to have been stolen from the streets of Western Europe at a time when "Lebanese gangs" were notorious in cities like Berlin or Vienna. The many Mercedes service cars came in all conditions, often including half-broken engines that produced excruciating sounds and unbearable exhaust smells. Yet, because it offers relative speed and affordability—LL (Lebanese liras) 2,000 per ride (less than US$1.40), an amount that was initially LL 1,000—this mode of transportation, although not limited to the Mercedes brand anymore, still has no major competition to speak of in terms of public transportation.

Starting in the mid-1990s, the various offices that made up the still-divided municipality of Beirut introduced a number of fixed bus lines that connected faraway parts of the capital with each other. Called *micro*, these long motor vehicles complemented an already existing fleet of privately run minivans, which were the cheapest mode of transportation the city had known since the end of the civil war. It became possible for the first time in more than twenty years to travel other than by car from the Ḥamra district in West Beirut to the locality of al-Fanār or even to the town of Antelias, both well beyond the city limits of East Beirut. Not many individuals rode the entire length of the various bus routes because using and transferring from one service to the next was actually much faster. But the mere fact of their existence was almost revolutionary at a time when the city was still clearly separated into east and west. Although the buses were slow, the cost of transportation remained its biggest attraction. Regardless of the final destination, a rider paid as little as LL 1,000 (approximately US¢70), and, at the turn of the millennium, the amount was half that, namely LL 500 (approximately US¢34).

Since I did not own a car, the only way to get around Beirut and beyond relatively quickly (providing there was not much traffic) was by either service or micro, unless I happened to catch a ride with somebody who had a private car at his or her disposal. Whenever I chose to take a service, however, I was startled by the mixture of people who would share a taxi. With the exception of the elites, almost everybody—all ages and, as far as I could tell, genders—flagged down services. Riding the micro-bus, however, was a different experience altogether. I rode the micro on many occasions, especially when I was not in a hurry. The slow pacing of the bus, which would come to an abrupt standstill anytime and anyplace a customer wanted to get on or off, allowed me to take in the urban landscape fully along with its moving panoply of human realities.

But despite the pleasure of an unhurried ride through a city constantly on the move, the micro, more than any other mode of transportation in Lebanon, carried a social stigma. Those who could—or had to—put up with it were either outsiders like myself or one of the many city dwellers for whom LL 1,000 was a significant sum. The stigma was such that many riders of the micro-bus lacked any substantial social status. It was almost as if a noxious spell had been cast on micro-bus riders, leading to rejection by society as a whole. I was often met with complete incomprehension by people who could not understand why I—an instructor at the American University—would enjoy sharing the bus with Syrian workers, sub-Saharan or African janitors, and Sri Lankan maids. For many Lebanese from the established bourgeois classes, as well as those eager to mimic them by regularly indulging in the most barefaced of racist discourses, the micro was synonymous with material, and thus social, marginality, if not to say human inferiority—a condition to be avoided at all cost.[10]

The Art of Walking: The *Flâneur*, the "Participant Objectifier," and the Queer Stroller

Walking through Beirut is not a simple endeavor for a variety of reasons, ranging from many physical obstacles to numerous barriers that, more often than not, tend to be of a mental nature. It is comparatively difficult for a pedestrian to move at a moderate pace from one Beiruti neighborhood to the next. The lack of actual sidewalks complicates the matter. Many lie broken and await repair; others are used as parking spots ingeniously set aside by the resident rooster for one or several of the ubiquitous cars that dominate most sections of the city. All this poses a veritable challenge to anybody who braves the streets on foot, for one must constantly circumvent all sorts of vehicles, regardless of whether they are parked or moving along roads that, by default, have also become a pedestrian space, all inherent dangers notwithstanding.

The social stigma attached to riding the micro is concomitant with the many prejudices projected onto walking denizens. With the exception of the Corniche, there is no significant stretch of land within the city limits of the Lebanese capital that most Beirutis would consider suitable for walking. Apart from the occasional power-walking bourgeoises, even in a place such as the Corniche, the point is to be *present* on the seashore promenade, not necessarily to be walking on it. The same thing applies to those leisurely bicyclists who started appearing in the mid-2000s as a sign of indulging in fashionable activity. Yet, to this day, the most frequent occurrence is a group driving to a particular spot on the Corniche, getting out of the car, and then appropriating a strategic spot from where they can see and be seen. To walk for reasons other than recreational or economic necessity is an entirely different matter, however. Why would anybody want to do that, especially given the many impediments involved in taking to the streets on foot? Moreover, is it not better to take a service, providing traffic allows it, that will drive a person anywhere and in a timely manner? Therefore, if one still opts for the pedestrian approach, it can only point to foolishness or to a lack of material means and thus adequate social standing. For many puzzled and rather disapproving people, any kind of pedestrian activity suggests a questionable pedigree and therefore cause to distance oneself.

And yet, whenever I am in Beirut, I make a point to spend most of my days walking, strolling across the city and wandering aimlessly through narrow streets in sections to which no regular service would ever take me. And as the urban sociologist William B. Helmreich notes, "You need to walk *slowly* through an area to capture its essence, to appreciate the buildings, to observe how the people function in space, and to talk with them" (emphasis mine).[11] If riding the micro was some sort of societal sin, then walking everywhere was one of the "queerest" practices one could possibly indulge in. But, depending on the season, I still persist in roaming slowly around the capital at different times of the day and, occasionally, at night because this is the only way that I have been able to put together a mental map of an urban environment I continue to actively appropriate. True to the ideals of a *Querkopf* (queer head), I have found that walking has helped me to highlight those zones of human encounters for which I have searched. Access to the very spaces that manage to transcend the latent—and, at times, manifest—rigidities of spatio-temporal fixities seems possible only through some acquired art of pedestrian mobility.

Active appropriation, however, never precluded extended moments of introspection. During such moments, the practice of walking became almost some sort of therapeutic exercise. Walking enabled reflections bitterly needed within the context of ethnographic fieldwork that often pushes the boundaries of the socially sufferable. Thinking and intent on translating outside the normative box and against the dominant paradigms, the ethnographer often aspires to be a *Querdenker* (queer thinker), whose lateral and unconventional assessment is to invest in the countless ramifications of ever-shifting epistemological intersections only understandable through intimate involvement. I fondly remember getting a daily breath of air in the wintertime as I walked eastward on the Corniche toward the snow-covered mountaintop of the majestic Sannine, looming behind a city that carried a seasonal crisp atmosphere I tried to take in as much as I could. On occasion, I had to be careful not to get soaked by one of the forceful waves that sweep effortlessly over the seashore railing, as if asserting a natural power to which the comparatively small size of a single human being could never face up.

In those moments, full of momentous melancholia and a sense of irrefutable alterity, I wanted only to hold my old-fashioned Discman and listen to Miles Davis's *Kind of Blue* or other jazz tunes I felt expressed my incongruous feelings of momentary alienation and elation. The same applied to Astor Piazzolla's inimitable *Adiós Nonino*: its smooth movements and abrupt pauses mirrored my frequently tortuous emotions. As soon as I hit the "play" button, the expected disjuncture between the music and my physical surroundings metamorphosed into seamless coexistence. And so I spent countless winter hours listening to the sounds of syncopated rhythms and improvisation while I negotiated the various roles that I, as an anthropologist, was supposed to play on an urban stage that at times cost me too much mental energy and bodily vigor. Only a few lonely souls haunted—as I did—the Corniche in the early hours of a wintry day. More attuned with local habits, groups of people would appropriate a spot far away from the potential danger of a seasonally raging Mediterranean.

The summer, however, provided a completely different picture. The baking heat of the day gave way to a momentary respite starting in the late afternoon. The break in the heat brought Beirutis out to congregate in large numbers on the Corniche. Many city dwellers walked from the neighborhood of ʿAyn al-Mraisseh toward the *manāra* (lighthouse) at a time of day when the most glorious of sunsets was to be observed behind the western tip of the neighborhood of Rās Beirut. Albeit omnipresent, the sea is much less capricious between the months of May and

Commotion on the Corniche, May 29, 2011.

October, gently rocking the numerous fishing boats dotting the horizon. These walks of mine were certainly not limited to urban spaces such as the clearly exposed Corniche. They also included parts of the city where physical openness was replaced by the tight network of streets and avenues from where the sea could only be presumed to be nearby. As some kind of ethnographic *flânerie*, this pursuit permitted me to explore urban sites of general interest to me, such as neighborhoods with a socio-cultural configuration that varied in part from one street to the next. But I also looked for zones of queer encounter. At times, they were to be found in unequivocal social venues, like a café or a restaurant. Sometimes, however, these zones were much less tangible in their spatial arrangement. Particular stretches of roads or street corners would, for example, transform into explicit male cruising grounds at any given night hour, and this despite the fact that these same areas projected a totally different identity during the day.

So is this *flânerie* or but a transfiguration into voyeurism that the anthropologist indulges in? As Michel de Certeau remarked in his chapter, "Walking in the City":

> The ordinary practitioners of the city live "down below," below the thresholds at which visibility begins. They walk—an elementary form of this experience of the city; they are walkers, *Wandersmänner*, whose bodies follow the thicks and thins of an urban "text" they write without being able to read it.[12]

The anthropologist might not be able to read this "text" either, save s/he pays close attention to the countless lost footsteps that de Certeau's "wanderers" on the ground—and s/he is necessarily one of them!—leave behind. These "pedestrian speech acts," as de Certeau calls them, turn the experience of walking into a space of enunciation where "making it work" can easily turn into "making it walk," unless the impersonal pronoun becomes personal and "making *him* walk" quickly amounts to pulling his leg or taking him for a ride.[13] The latter is out of the question for the queer urban stroller. He intends to make sense of what constitutes zones of encounter, where individuals meet who would not interact if it were not for places that are part of a larger urban fabric full of obstacles but also possibilities and countless associations. Because of this intent, he engages in perceptive and attuned observation that carries gravitas but also the subtlety of *flânerie*.

As the young Walter Benjamin grew smitten by Paris and what he understood to be French culture, a central figure emerged from the German thinker's eclectic work. It was not that of a queer urban stroller—although, given his propensity for *querdenken* (queer thinking), it may as well have been. Rather, the figure in question was what he perceived the quintessential—i.e., male—Parisian to be: the *flâneur*.[14] This idle but always well-dressed stroller is continuously adrift in the metropolis, his passive senses exquisitely tuned. His greatest luxury remains one of having no specific purpose. He walks for the sake of walking. As an indulgent and solitary figure, he loves to contemplate the panoply of street life as an ambler whose own reflection is mirrored in the alleys and thoroughfares. With the seemingly impartial gall of an infant, or sometimes of a predator on the move, the *flâneur* gazes at passing strangers—one of whom, due to a reflection in a random mirror, may be himself. Such alterity becomes manifest in fleeting one-on-one encounters, but also in a fractured form that may be reflected in some unexpected shop window. Yet, there is probably no more impersonal, and for that matter, no more concentrated, distillation of an intimacy originally "made in *fin-de-siècle Mitteleuropa*" than that of the Benjaminian figure of the Parisian *flâneur*. This three-dimensional figure unremittingly strolls, loafs, or idles through the streets and avenues of metropolitan Western Europe, observing and critically reflecting within an intricate "dialectics of seeing."[15]

Beirut is no Paris—or Berlin for that matter. Yet, possible human intangibility and gender hierarchy notwithstanding, I do not find it utterly improper to use the altogether male figure of an early twentieth-century suit-wearing Berliner, most likely carrying some kind of mahogany walking stick, on the boulevards of Paris, to convey my own methodological approach. On the contrary, in order to make some sense of the vicissitudes that rage in the Lebanese capital, I find that such an idiosyncratic and decidedly queer figure comes in quite handy. What some would see as unforgivable aimlessness is, after all, one of the city dwellers' most critical *arts de vivre*. Then again, the anthropologist who is walking through Beirut's urban maze—and this on an everyday basis for several years—cannot be reduced to some allegedly elitist theoretical icon, regardless of its practical significance. After all, most anthropological fieldwork encompasses individual struggles with a daily life that, by definition, lacks conventional glamour and is decidedly un-academic in outlook. Therefore, in the best Aragonian tradition of a peasant walking through Paris, whose rather detached and fresh glance allows us to appreciate anew the seemingly most ordinary urban locales, being part of the larger picture, even if continuously out of place, becomes somewhat of an asset for the anthropologist, irrespective of whether he is a *libre penseur* (free thinker) or a *Querdenker*.[16] Consequently, rather than the becoming—even if undoubtedly confining—figure of the male *flâneur*, I favor in my own work to talk about the rather ordinary but multi-gendered walker, stroller—or perhaps even the combination of an easy roamer and a simple drifter, akin to de Certeau's *marcheur* or, maybe, to a Lefebvrian "rhythmanalyst" of sorts, who walks through space and time, as well as through everyday life.[17] Therefore, I concentrate on such a person's abilities to master the arts of impressions, circumnavigating the city as whim dictates and giving himself or herself over to the spectacle of the moment (or the encounter!), without the manifest limitations of any particular agenda.

But such a contemporary version of the Benjaminian *flâneur* is certainly not without moral consciousness, even if he gladly sees himself as the occasional *dragueur* (flirt). In an endeavor to capture a necessary social awareness, I focus such an idle drifter-cum-researcher's various attempts at making sense of reality around a concept that Pierre Bourdieu called "participant objectification" within the larger context of his research during the Algerian War (1954–1962).[18] Such objectification, Bourdieu explained, is a moral stance of sorts that, at best, forms an integral part of the social scientist's overall ethical responsibility. Along these ethical lines, I assert that of equal moral importance is the activation of all senses on the part of the anthropologist. It helps him or her to comprehend the complexity of the various spaces and neighborhoods in such a heavily segregated city like Beirut. Such sensibility is of crucial human and methodological assistance when it comes to evaluating the ways in which all kinds of subjects manage to succeed in coping with the general hardship of daily life in Lebanon.

In an additional effort to illustrate my personal interpretation and adaptation of Pierre Bourdieu's participant objectification, as well as what I mean by the activation of the senses on the part of the contemporary *flâneur*'s alter ego—i.e., the anthropologist—I return to one ethnographic episode that illustrates my theoretical point. The example below depicts a range of elements I would deem as "queer" in the historical life and topography of one of Beirut's historically most vibrant neighborhoods, the Ḥamra district in the western part of the Lebanese capital. First let me say, however, that the activation of the anthropologist's senses should never discount the importance of humor and irony, coupled if need be with a bit of voyeurism.

The Ḥamra district of Beirut, the "Big Red" as it were, is a prime example of a busy neighborhood. It is a modern part of the Lebanese capital that each day goes through different stages of presumed collective perceptions and individual discoveries. During the day, store after store, snack stand after snack stand, and a myriad of cars, compete for the passerby's attention. At night, however, it is an entirely different set of human configurations and competitions that manifest themselves between the neighborhoods of ʿAyn al-Mraisseh in the east and Manāra in the west. Regardless of whether it is daylight or the relatively secretive wee hours, one has to ask whether and, if so, how a large part of this human stream, which on an everyday basis transports innumerable waves of personal dreams on the city's streets, is influenced by its very urban environment. If such an influence actually exists, how may an ostensibly mutual impact between city and people possibly modify the entire current of thoughts of a particular neighborhood, an entire city, or perhaps—on the unobtrusive face of it—the whole world?

Writing on the rapid urbanization in the late 1960s of the area around the Ḥamra district, Samir Khalaf and Per Kongstad noted, "Rās Beirut's side-walk cafés and snack bars have in fact become notorious for sheltering the so-called coffee-house intellectuals with varying political

View from the American University of Beirut "beach" to ʿAyn al-Mraisseh, July 3, 2013.

shades and ideological leanings."[19] Both authors surveyed a dying world of seeming insouciance, one soon to become entangled in the numerous bloody struggles that epitomized the fifteen years of Lebanon's civil war. They borrowed Carleton Coon's much debated concept of a "mosaic," a term intended to convey the emblematic image of a socio-political and ethno-religious coexistence in the Middle East that was ideologically popular among early twentieth-century social scientists and based on a highly specified ethno-sectarian division of labor.[20] Despite its originally patronizing connotations, Coon's image of the mosaic and its theoretical rendering helped Khalaf and Kongstad in their sociological study. Using data collected in the late 1960s, both authors characterized the distinct urban communities in the Ḥamra district, arguing that these groups lived together for a host of reasons, many of which were of a practical nature. In other words, the various communities in the Ḥamra district "needed" each other for the basic requirements—political and economic—of daily living in this highly urbanized part of Lebanon.

Interestingly, according to Khalaf and Kongstad, Ḥamra's pre-war moment was marked by an unrestrained vitality when it came to larger forms of entertainment and the ways in which these forms managed to permeate ordinary life in the district. Compared to the decade and a half that followed the 1989 Taef Agreement, which ended the war, what was initially represented—physically as well as ideally—by Ḥamra's *khaṭṭ al-raīsī* (main artery) and its environs in the 1960s and early 1970s in terms of entertainment venues was scattered all over the city thirty years later. At the same time, the celebrated sphere of commonly perceived cosmopolitanism in the pre-civil-war Ḥamra district lost its international cachet and became decidedly Lebanese. While the favorably remembered old cosmopolitan character of the neighborhood was based in part on ready consumption, it also included a genuine artistic character that was influenced by diverse inside and outside factors. However, the new globalization that started in the early 1990s had been markedly reduced to all kinds of patterns of geared-up consumption.

Local conspicuous consumption notwithstanding, the increasingly declining economic situation that had been haunting the country in the new millennium was quickly exacerbated on the ground after the end of the first decade by a civil war that brought multiple waves of refugees fleeing Syria. For many Beiruti neighborhoods, that conflict, which had started in spring 2011, had as its immediate consequence the influx of countless Syrian families, from the very wealthy to the bitterly poor, with the latter roaming the streets and alleys of the Ḥamra district. This contrasted with the immediate Lebanese post-civil-war period, during which the remaining practices of blind expenditure, for which Ḥamra had been famous, conquered neighborhoods that historically had never been known as urbane and sophisticated—namely, the refurbished downtown section, Rue Monot, and other socially strategic sites spread around many different neighborhoods of Beirut.

Despite the fact that almost everything hip and trendy had left Ḥamra, before returning to it about ten years later, the specter of a certain past remained omnipresent within the iconic district. In the bustling streets around the main artery, a multiplicity of bars and so-called amusement centers, including brothels and other "super night clubs," like Candle Bar and Rock Inn, were barely noticeable in daytime, but came to the fore soon after sunset. Although these establishments had long catered to a wide range of heterosexual patrons, historically, there have always been a number of social venues clearly drawing on gay customers of all ages.[21] However, these queer-identified spaces have never been fixed places that remained stable in terms of their locations, names, or design. On the contrary, these bars, cafés, and clubs have emerged on a queer topography for various reasons at some point or another in the history of this pivotal neighborhood. Some have vanished and been forgotten; others, while ceasing to exist, still continue to be remembered by those individuals who, for reasons of their own, associate them with memorable times.

During the 1975–1990 Lebanese civil war, the most popular hangout for gay men in the area was to be found at the eastern end of Ḥamra Street—namely, within the modernist architectural premises of the so-called Horseshoe Building. The street-level café bearing the same name disappeared long ago, and a fast food restaurant opened in its stead in 2003, followed by an international coffee franchise shortly thereafter. The new owners may have initially resuscitated the old alias, but they made the Horseshoe Café into an entirely new place, not only in design but also in terms of an entirely different—i.e., family-oriented—clientele. In fact, the civil war, and especially its immediate aftermath, brought about an active spatial contestation and various practices of (counter-)appropriation on the queer mental map in and around Beirut. Now vanished and almost completely forgotten nightclubs, like the indelible King's on the Corniche, harbored composite crowds of gay men of various ages in the days when the city was in physical shambles. These crowds congregated at an interesting moment in time when all sorts of social combinations were possible. This was before the forced order of the post-civil-war establishment of the late 1990s and after put a premature end to an entire range of contested and appropriated freedoms that had been mushrooming—not always quietly—on the margins.

Up until the early 2000s, two run-down movie theaters in the Ḥamra district, the Edison on Bliss Street and the Khayyam in an apartment building off Sidani Street, hosted occasional sexual encounters among men framed against either European soft pornography shot in the 1970s (often staged in German and featuring either Greek or Turkish subtitles) or East Asian Kung-Fu films, where spoken language mattered less than seemingly liberating—albeit sometimes aborted—cries of violent anger and forceful release. However, the main cinema that, for a long time, was the prime hub for ready man-to-man sexual interactions in the Ḥamra district closed its doors in 2000. The Pavillon, located in the basement of the Hotel Pavillon on Ibrahim ʿAbd al-ʿĀl Street, is said to have attracted huge crowds of men during the civil war, many of whom took an active part in militia fighting. According to a number of stories I have been told, the power generators of the Pavillon movie theater worked in splendid isolation from the terrors of the outside world when West Beirut was under shelling and deprived of electricity. The cinema became the main guarantor in matters of sexual gratification for its faithful patrons, including members of competing militias.

Not having been there at the time of the Lebanese civil war, I cannot vouch for the total accuracy of these stories. Nevertheless, these years of overheard commentary, along with later personal visits to the theater preceding its closure, made me realize the insinuated sharp dichotomy between an apparently licentious inside and a regulated spiteful outside. For the potential aficionado, knowing about places like the Pavillon meant also knowing about their socially illegitimate character. Thus, by becoming a form of release (or delusion, for that matter) to be indulged in furtively inside the movie theater, the strictly sexual encounter was often being recollected in shame on the streets outside. Especially in the 1990s, when the relative stability of state order and the ensuing willful moral sanitation had not yet completely swept the many locales of marginal gay *jouissance*, I talked to many men who regularly patronized movie theaters like the Pavillon or the Edison. Most of them were over thirty, and very few actually lived in the Ḥamra district. In fact, these men lived all over the metropolitan area, including almost all the neighborhoods of East and West Beirut, but also other regions in Lebanon. The ethno-religious background of this regular clientele was equally diverse and consisted of Armenians and Druze, as well as Syrian laborers and everything in between.

The Ḥamra district was in no way the only neighborhood in Beirut with dilapidated movie theaters that were patronized by men urgently needing ready homoerotic or sexual release. On a queer mental map of the city, there were many such venues, notably Cinéma Salwa in Tarīq al-Jdīdeh and Cinéma Beyrouth on the Barbīr end of West Beirut's Corniche al-Mazraa, which by 2010 was turned into a small cheap shopping mall and in 2012 destroyed by sectarian riots, as well as the infamous Cinéma Canard located in front of one of Burj Ḥammūd's police stations. It was rumored that many officers were either "guardians" of some of the theater's customers or patrons themselves.

The clientele that in the 1990s went to movie theaters in the Ḥamra district and in other neighborhoods of the Lebanese capital distinguished itself considerably from the category of young interlocutors I would interact with only a few years later in places so varied as outside cafés, nightclubs, or Paradise Beach. The men at the movie theaters, most in their thirties or forties, would rarely have used the English word *gay* to identify themselves. In many instances, even the most local notion of homosexuality was outside their frame of mind. Some of them were married and

Cinéma Salwa in Tarīq al-Jdīdeh, July 22, 2010.

had children. But, as one of my interlocutors put it to me, he "needed the occasional release"—never mind the fact that, in this particular instance, "occasional" had readily become, as far as I could tell, a matter of staunch bi-weekly observance.

The regularization of the occasion can easily become the substance of homosexual desire, perhaps even of potential voyeurism. Selective recollection—along with the issues of daydream, fantasy, and delusion—cannot be eclipsed completely by the complex existence of an otherwise rampant socially sanctioned politics of homophobia in Lebanon. Even if they might be part of such homophobia in other contexts, the middle-aged men who regularly patronized one or the other movie theater in the Ḥamra district, in their discreet attempt to achieve sexual gratification, tried to escape temporarily society's notorious disapproval by creating—albeit for just an hour or two—an overall enclosed space of possibilities that had the capacity to run against any outside social prescription. Through its spatially projected dimension, the local contestation of values (as inconsequential as it may ultimately be), together with the various lived realities and collective performances that were—and continue to be—put into daily practice in Lebanon, all have a continuous impact on the panoply of individual dynamics—notwithstanding any kind of spatial confinement—and on social interactions in the country at large. Methodologically, these dynamics and interactions, I would argue, can only be made sense of by adopting, on the one hand, Pierre Bourdieu's morally inspired "participant objectification." On the other hand, what I have introduced as the walking anthropologist's activation of the senses is of equal importance, and it is an homage of sorts to the fieldworker's *Doppelgänger* of yesteryear, the Benjaminian *flâneur*.

Views from Ashrafieh: Walking through the City with Ramzi

With a few exceptions, my daily excursions on foot were undertaken alone, probably in response to social and professional exigencies that put me almost constantly in the presence of people. Moreover, informed by a particular character and biography, my previous experiences had often shown that solitary travels also facilitate access to places and people's lives that would be more difficult to gain when traveling with company. Yet, I end this chapter on a note of walking and companionship.

Starting in the summer 2002, I frequently met up with my friend Ramzi in *sha'bī* (popular) Beiruti neighborhoods like Barbīr or Burj Ḥammūd in order to spend hours strolling around the urban grid with no fixed direction in mind. The two of us would often meet at Sassine Square, for it was close to where Ramzi lived, and walk down the "little mountain" eastward before crossing the polluted and almost completely dried-up Beirut "River." From there, we would reach Armenia Street bustling with cars and shoppers browsing the cheap clothing, furniture, and home appliance shops that crowded the entire area of "Ḥammūd's Tower." Ramzi loved parading on these busy streets, which were full of people carrying plastic bags containing their many purchases. He knew that his willfully studied bodily performance would attract a lot of curious looks, which, apart from a couple of antagonistic instances, he enjoyed quite a bit. In a neighborhood like Burj Ḥammūd, the two of us would sometimes enter a store where he knew one of the employees from past visits during which he had bought the occasional dress he would finish himself for one of his many drag performances around town.

I met Ramzi in July 2002 through a mutual friend who called him the "drag queen from Sassine" and "a very gentle and incisive young man" I absolutely needed to talk to. I still vividly remember that summer day when I saw Ramzi for the first time. We had e-mailed and then talked on the phone before setting up a time to meet. Of all places, we decided to meet at the Starbucks on Sassine Square, the only one at the time that did not feature the coffee shop's name in Arabic letters. As it turned out, Ramzi could not have cared less about that Starbucks. Given that he lived nearby, he merely thought it would be a good idea to meet at such an exposed location. It did not take me long to figure out that the "sons of families" (i.e., the male offspring of the local bourgeoisie), who prominently displayed their gold crosses on their hairy chests while sipping their lattés, were not necessarily his type.

Because of the excruciating July heat and the fact that I was a bit worried about being late for my meeting with Ramzi, I took a service from Ḥamra to the SODECO roundabout. As I walked past Zaatar W Zeit (Thyme and [Olive] Oil), the local branch of a popular fast-food chain that served all kinds of Levantine dishes in a calculatedly hip and trendy environment, I managed to catch a micro uphill to Ashrafieh's Sassine Square. Even though I was on time, I saw a tall and slender man waiting. In his late twenties, Ramzi wore dark shorts and a white t-shirt. A bandana was wrapped around his head and topped by a baseball cap in an obvious attempt to hide a receding hairline. His face was unusually pale, I thought at the time, and his remaining hair, despite either being covered or shaven, must have certainly been black.

In that moment, I was not completely sure if the man I was looking at was actually Ramzi. Apart from a group of well-dressed society ladies, who must have just come back from the hairdresser, and a couple of suit-wearing male office workers in matching blue dress shirts, there was virtually nobody else at Starbucks. Therefore, the man who was sitting alone and nervously reading the French daily newspaper *Libération* had to be Ramzi. As soon as he saw me, he got up and, in a strikingly polite tone, inquired about whether I was indeed the person he was waiting for. He said, "*ʿamiltillak* missed call" (I left you a missed call [on your cell phone]), wanting to make sure that I knew that he had been serious about meeting me.[22] In return, I asked him whether he wanted to order a coffee, but he declined and offered instead to take a walk around the area.

At that time, Ashrafieh was no terra incognita for me. Even though I lived and worked in the western Ḥamra district, I regularly went to East Beirut's centrally located "Christian" neighborhood to meet friends and acquaintances, go to an exhibit or two in one of the local galleries, or catch a movie at Centre Sofil. I particularly enjoyed walking though the streets of Ashrafieh because the neighborhood was pretty much the only one within Beirut's actual city limits that was topographically ele-

View from Ashrafieh westward, August 6, 2010.

vated and occasionally provided—as indicated by its very name—lovely views toward both the sea and the peaks of Mount Lebanon.[23] However, the local construction frenzy had eliminated some of the ever-receding number of outlooks and turned the entire area into a haven of steel and concrete. At first sight, the Ashrafieh in the early days of the twenty-first century had little in common with the neighborhood described in Elias Khoury's *Al-jabal al-saghīr* ([*The*] *Little Mountain*).[24] The book was written at the beginning of the Lebanese civil war at a time when Khoury, due to his leftist political convictions, was denied access to the neighborhood in which he had grown up. Some thirty years later when I read his book, I could not help but start mapping his memories onto the various places I frequented on and around this jam-packed hill of bustling urban life.

On the afternoon I met Ramzi, the two of us left Sassine Square and went downhill toward the northwest in the direction of the city's Mār Mitr section, where we stopped at Spinney's Supermarket to get a bottle of Tannourine water to help us withstand the heat on our little journey *ḍownṭown*. We continued walking all the way past Rue Sursock, where the legendary Lady Cochrane resided along with other members of the Christian Lebanese upper class.[25] Then, we stepped down the long and picturesque Gemmeyzeh staircase, which sometimes served as an open-air exhibition space, before turning left and continuing until we reached Martyrs' Square and, behind it, *ḍownṭown* with its newly refurbished buildings along Maarad and Allenby Streets.

It quickly became clear that Ramzi and I had many things in common. In fact, within minutes I realized that our meeting would be followed by numerous other encounters. Only a year my junior, he shared many of my diverse cultural and social interests, all of which were influenced by his sharp intellect and his fluency in five languages. Apart from sharing my passion for queer strolling, he opened many conceptual doors to the intricate world of queer life in Lebanon. Moreover, Ramzi instructed me in contemporary French literature, as well as in international film history and theory. Although he had never been there, he told me everything I needed to know about filmmaker John Waters's Baltimore. He opened my eyes to countless details in Pedro Almodóvar's early films, half of which I had admittedly not even heard of at the time. And whatever I know about Rainer Werner Fassbinder's work beyond a superficial reading is due to the many private lectures I enjoyed from somebody who, over the years, had grown to become a close, albeit highly complicated, friend.

This ethnographic vignette about Ramzi is illustrative of some crucial aspects of the practice of walking in the city as formulated by Michel de Certeau. Regardless of whether consumed by *flânerie* or voyeurism, the anthropologist and his companion become "ordinary practitioners of the city" who "live 'down below,'" where visibility and assertion are a daily struggle. While I end this chapter as both men walk to experience the city, I take note of their aspiration to follow the thick and thin of an urban "text" that they want to be able to read. And, by looking closely at the footsteps left behind, some of which are lost while others are recovered, I begin the next chapter with this *will to read*, one that is informed by queer performances and the politics of place in Beirut.

CHAPTER 4

Queer Performances and the Politics of Place: The Art of Drag and the Routine of Sectarianism

Born and raised in East Beirut, Ramzi spent the end of the 1975–1990 civil war in France in order to finish high school away from the deadly skirmishes that had begun to engulf the eastern part of the capital. When he returned to Lebanon, he realized that it would be very hard for him to find his particular niche in a society where deep-seated trauma often prompted violence against people who were either unwilling or unable to fit narrow social molds. Especially as a young adult whose newly asserted homosexuality expressed itself outside a socially prescribed frame—namely, one that took the shape of a physical and mental trap that was as limited in scope as it was limiting to the concerned individual—Ramzi had to face a very large number of complicated undertakings that would quickly become part of his daily life.

The Embattled Lebanese Middle Classes: A Story of Ramzi

Although part of the embattled social strata of the Lebanese middle classes, Ramzi had still had the chance to begin high school at one of the best schools the divided city had to offer in its eastern sector. Academically, he very much excelled there, albeit at the cost of occasional marginalization induced by the homophobic attitude exhibited by some of his *grands bourgeois* classmates. After his return from France, he was thrust by his parents into studies in economics at Beirut's Jesuit Université Saint-Joseph. However, it did not take him long to abandon that course of study. Instead, Ramzi enrolled in audiovisual studies at the Académie Libanaise pour les Beaux-Arts (ALBA), the local arts school, from where he graduated with excellent grades.

Yet, despite his various successes in school, he had a hard time finding work as a visual artist. He had always written for a variety of student newspapers, so he decided to register as a journalism student at the Lebanese University. But even after receiving his second academic degree, he remained unemployed, unable to land a permanent job either at some local magazine or in the country's television industry. Moreover, his obstinate and forthright character sometimes made it difficult for him to compromise, especially with whims that were informed by an arbitrary injustice that all too often characterized the general atmosphere in countless Lebanese offices. Ramzi's unwillingness to cozy up to enemies—a game that was almost a necessity in order to achieve anything—may have been part of the reason why nobody wanted to hire him. More importantly, he simply did not possess the indispensable means that turned access to resources in Lebanon into an exceedingly skilled game involving *wāsṭa*, the high art of preferential treatment.

Far from being from one of the few affluent—and, therefore, influential—families in Lebanon, Ramzi was the son of a retired civil servant, who was one of the few remaining members of a Lebanese middle class that, until the civil war, had not only held progressive political convictions but was also significantly comfortable in economic terms. Although all this changed drastically with the economic decline in the wake of the war, Ramzi's father continued to hold strong beliefs regarding state institutions, and he did everything possible to ensure that his two children enjoyed an excellent education, one intended to enable both to conquer their respective worlds without ever having to fall back on the nepotism that was becoming rampant in his country.

Things did not altogether work out that way: for the longest time, Ramzi's older sister was the only one who managed to get a relatively stable job in Lebanon's post-civil-war free market economy. As for her younger brother, he continued to write at irregular intervals for various media outlets, running the gamut of remarkably colorful Lebanese magazines and newspapers. For some time, Ramzi's written contributions included short articles for the business page of a local trade journal as well as feature-length pieces on the history of drag, put together for a local glitzy and glossy society magazine, the notorious Lebanese French-language gossip monthly *Mondanité*.

During his years at ALBA, Ramzi had met the publication's editor at a soirée in Beirut. These events were organized by one of her wealthy Christian companions and intended to generate a "cosmopolitan atmosphere" designed to make those present forget that they were actually in an Arab country. The editor, an aesthetically "surgeried" middle-aged fake blonde and the niece of one of the doyens of the Maronite establishment, did everything she could to never utter a single word in Arabic. The *Mondanité* editor and her peers inhabited a bubble of total denial and make-believe in which Lebanon was "different," that is to say, conceptually—but also spatially—removed from what they felt to be the alienating region of the Arab—i.e., Muslim—world. Paris and—if need be—New York were their frames of reference. In contrast, Damascus, just a two-and-a-half-hour drive east, was hell to them. Given who Ramzi was, I never fully understood the relationship between him and the *Mondanité* editor. Even if they were part of the same sectarian group, their respective class backgrounds were different. For sure, his sharp and captivating intellect must have charmed her, but I also suspect an intermittent desire on the part of the middle-aged fake blonde to interact with somebody who was decidedly young and "queer" and who provided her with the opportunity to play on occasion the public role of a matronizing and open-handed "fag hag."

Ramzi's undeniable strength, however, was his ability to move seamlessly from one socio-cultural context to the next without any sense of superiority or inferiority whatsoever. I very much admired him for that, especially given the often-hindering circumstance of a highly stratified context in which movement was made extremely difficult by a solidified set of social rules and structures where prejudice was rampant. Ramzi clearly understood the rarified air of Lebanese high society and the ways in which members of that class projected paradoxical images onto themselves and each other, often oblivious of the social reality at hand. I very much respected Ramzi for his ability to combine theory and practice, so as to scrutinize critically the various Lebanese social strata, on the one hand, but nonetheless to engage actively with them, on the other. Most likely, the broad-mindedness of his family background helped him to transcend all sorts of social boundaries. Importantly, however, it was his queer identity that made it difficult—if not virtually impossible—for him to be confined in a particular box, an imposed limitation that would have satisfied the urge for categorization heralded by many of his contemporaries. All of this reflected unmistakably the combined reasons for why Ramzi was the perfect person for me to walk around the diverse neighborhoods of Beirut. Always genuinely curious and interested, he would point out to me every different street scene that, as far as he was concerned, characterized the Lebanese capital's intricate social fabric at the transitional time we met.

Although I had already heard from common friends about Ramzi's career as a local drag queen, it was only during one of our extended walks through Beirut in the summer of 2002, and in the following years, that Ramzi told me about his experiences. Forever fascinated by the cultural phenomena of camp and drag, he related how, early on, he read French historical and sociological accounts on these subjects. Later, he befriended Dominique Fernandez during one of the *académicien*'s travels through the Levant, and he told me how Fernandez's novels, and their highly critical approach to the formation of queer identities, had made a great—if not to say lasting—impact on him.[1] Further, Ramzi immersed himself in gender-bending films from Western Europe and North America. In addition to John Waters's Divine and Pedro Almodóvar's Antonio Banderas and early Carmen Maura, the adolescent Ramzi of the late 1980s and early 1990s added a range of stars from the music industry to his list of idols. Notable among them were Madonna, who would remain one of his favorites, and Boy George, whose performing styles, including the extravagant clothes and the heavy makeup, Ramzi soon started to imitate in the privacy of his Beirut family home.

Queering the Saint: Between Barbāra and Drag

Not long after he returned from the two years in France, during which his eclectic interests as well as his sexuality were subject to a lot of probing questions, Ramzi became acquainted with a circle of young Lebanese drag queens who, after the end of the civil war, started performing in and around the capital. Western pop influences notwithstanding, male-to-female cross-dressing in Beirut historically had been part of a wide spectrum of performances that every so often received partial social acceptance. Most noticeable were the ritual celebrations of St. Barbara (*barbāra* in Arabic), one of the many north Lebanese patron saints. Unfortunately, nobody I asked in Lebanon was able to tell me anything specific about the genealogy of this avowedly proto-Christian rite.[2] What I can say, however, is that one of its later, profane incarnations revolved around young men in drag, who, irrespective of their sectarian background, meet yearly in early December for a large-scale lavish social event in one of the many entertainment venues located below the prominent Casino du Liban in the notorious local pleasure haven of Maameltain, north of Jounieh. Having prepared themselves for months, some of these young men compete for the best outfits and—sometimes—for the best drag performances. These performances are very much reminiscent of Mikhail Bakhtin's analysis of the topsy-turvy atmosphere of the carnival in relation to Rabelais's writings, or, comparable to the Uptown balls in the iconic 1980s movie, *Paris is Burning*.[3]

It was during one of these rambunctious *barbāra* celebrations in the mid-1990s that Ramzi met Khaled, a Palestinian man his age who had grown up in the Burj al-Brājneh refugee camp on the southern outskirts of Beirut. Without much romantic involvement, the two soon became best friends and, shortly thereafter, started to perform together as drag queens at an increasing number of private events, ranging from the occasional bachelorette party to all sorts of social bashes at a variety of local nightclubs. Without the legal privileges of a Lebanese citizen, Khaled had virtually no prospect of landing a stable job, either inside or outside the camp in which he had grown up. Since childhood, his dream had been to become a hairdresser and own a salon where he could express his artistic talents freely. His schooling had been limited to the official United Nations Relief and Works Agency (UNRWA)[4] school in the refugee camp, and he never earned a diploma. His family support network was limited and very much affected by his homosexuality, which was met with a great deal of hostility wherever he went.

Further, the more successful Ramzi and Khaled became with their drag performances, the more they became visible to a wider public, and, therefore, also prone to homophobic slurs and attacks. Although Ramzi was much better placed within the knotty fabric of Lebanese society, he was not spared the growing aggression mounted against him and Khaled. However, given that the latter lacked any kind of substantial support network, including one that went beyond the usually necessary *wāsṭa*, he became increasingly the target of physical abuse that, at times, reached towering levels. In effect, Khaled was physically threatened and beaten on numerous occasions by seemingly random people he barely knew. The constant fear of violence made it more and more impossible for him to live in Lebanon. Of equal importance is the fact that his fame became a liability for his own family, who, soon enough, started encouraging him to leave the country.

Leaving Lebanon was anything but easy in the decade following the end of the country's civil war, especially for a young male Palestinian refugee with no particular academic or professional skills. Despite these impediments, Khaled succeeded in traveling to the United Kingdom, where he applied for asylum, arguing his case and foregrounding his countless violent experiences with homophobia in Lebanon. However, the matter of his case was dragged through the British courts for a period of more than ten years, during which his expulsion seemed many times to be imminent. Finally, he was allowed to stay in Glasgow, the city to which he had initially moved. However, without the complete settlement of his legal situation that would have permitted him to receive the necessary paperwork, he could not legalize his status. Such a step would have also permitted him to travel, notably for a visit back to Beirut to see his family, whom he had not seen since leaving Lebanon.

In the meantime, Ramzi twice visited his friend in Scotland. He was stunned to see Khaled in a state of perpetual anger and despair, due in large part to his volatile status as a refugee, a wretched legal category that had followed him since he was born. Although he had finally embarked on a career as a hairdresser and was in a relatively stable relationship with a young man from Poland, Khaled had started to drink. Regardless of how things turned out for Khaled, Ramzi kept in touch with him. They e-mailed and, on occasion, phoned each other. During these conversations, Ramzi would always update his friend about every detail concerning Beirut's *tantāt* (effeminate gay men), even though many of the social and spatial parameters to which Khaled was accustomed "back home" had completely changed over the years he lived in Scotland.

But many people still remembered him in Beirut. For instance, I will never forget the highly entertaining incident on a Sunday afternoon when Ramzi and I were walking on the Corniche on the level of the Pigeon Rocks in Raoucheh. Suddenly a car-honking concert started next to us. We almost automatically expected some act of potential harassment under such circumstances, but it turned out that, in this case, it was Françoise sitting behind the steering wheel of a borrowed car. Françoise, whose actual name was Fāres, was one of the celebrated *barbāra* drag queens who performed regularly in different venues around town. Another young Palestinian man from the camps, he was mostly known outside the queer circuit because of his infamous brother, who was an illegal immigrant and quite a ruffian drug dealer in Berlin. When Ramzi shared the newest news about "Khulūd" (the female version of Khaled) and his life in Glasgow, Françoise retorted in a high-pitched voice: "Tell me, ya Zara, wasn't this one in *Eskimo* or somewhere in those places?" On hearing Françoise's confusion between *es-scotland* (Scotland in Lebanese Arabic) and *Eskimo*, Ramzi and I burst out laughing, and ever since that comical episode on the Corniche, the two of us often talk about the day we will don our swanky kilts and tartans and go to *Eskimo*.

As for drag performances, Ramzi never found another partner quite like Khaled. He nevertheless continued to perform alone whenever he was hired for a gig at any nightclub on Rue Monot or elsewhere. He also danced at special private parties organized by groups of female friends who would hire him for bachelorette events. Thanks to these performances, Ramzi earned a little money over the years, which he mostly spent on the extension of his wardrobe and other accessories. It probably also helped him, to a certain extent, deal with the otherwise impossible situation of finding a regular job in either journalism or the television industry.

I accompanied Ramzi to a number of shows at clubs considered trendy at the time. He would arrive around 9:00 p.m. with a huge duffel bag containing all his clothes for the night. We would be ushered into a tiny antechamber with dim lights and a mirror where Ramzi could dress, put on makeup, and ready himself for the show. But before that, he was given brief instructions about what to do and shown around the performance space. Generally, the venue would already be crowded with men and women dancing ecstatically to the DJ's music selection. Resilient as he often was, Ramzi was accustomed to the noncommittal way of doing things in those places. As far as I could see, he was hardly ever treated with much respect and never more than with a minimum of courtesy. After all, he was just one item on the entertainment list, and he was expected to enhance the instant pleasure requirement of the cash-paying audience. Impatient and ignorant as I was regarding the way in which the art of drag was actually being practiced, I always thought Ramzi's preparation time took an eternity. While he was busy layering colorful blusher, eye shadow, foundation, powder, and mascara, I had to keep the conversation going for what seemed hours. It took Ramzi at least sixty minutes, if not more, before completing the work of art. Then everything moved very quickly. Either the club's manager or an intermediary would call Ramzi onto the dance floor.

Notorious among intermediaries in Beirut's entertainment business was the local drug dealer Rob Abou Tannoura (who had changed his name first from Rabih to Robbie and then to simply Rob). Manifestly always in the middle of an extended cocaine session, Rob made sure to squeeze his various protégés, leaving them with a minimum of what they duly earned on any given night. Although a fixture in the shady parts of Beirut's eclectic nightlife, Rob regularly vanished altogether. Once, it was rumored that he was in major trouble because he had upset one of his powerful clients. But soon after his disappearance, Rob resurfaced unexpectedly, and the gossips maintained that an even more powerful client had bailed him out of jail.

By the time Ramzi began his drag performance, it would be at least 11:00 p.m., if not well past midnight. As soon as he finished one part of his act, the music would abruptly change to the cheesy tunes of either Mariah Carey or Kylie Minogue. Now in full gear, including his high heels, called *kaʿb* in Arabic, Ramzi would begin the lip-syncing routine he had rehearsed at least a thousand times. The audience, many of whom were completely drunk, would start yelling obscenities and try to grab whatever they could of the drag queen's apparel. Sometimes the level of commotion in the club would be so high that it made it impossible for Ramzi to perform his routine in a way he deemed meaningful. I was present on two occasions when the hour-long preparation resulted in a performance that could not have lasted more than fifteen minutes. Shortly afterward, Ramzi would return to the dressing room, take off his costume and makeup, stuff everything into his duffel bag, and prepare to exit the venue, often without being paid by Rob Abou Tannoura. The latter would often claim that, due to some "unforeseeable situation," he would only be able to come up with the payment some other day. The dealer-cum-impresario did so sometimes, but there was always a case in which the "unforeseeable situation" would translate into a perpetual lack of cash.

Tired but not entirely exhausted at this fairly advanced hour, Ramzi and I would roam along Rue Monot, a street that in the early 2000s was lined with innumerable bars that, on weekends, were still packed around 2:00 a.m. In addition to the people walking from one bar to the next, scores of cars would be "stop-and-going" while carrying four and sometimes six passengers. Wrongly, I assumed their drivers were looking for a parking space as they drove down the popular street, which, by 2003, had been paved from top to bottom with concrete "cobblestones." Yet, given the almost certain impossibility of finding any free spot on or around Monot into which one could squeeze a car, there must have been another reason why all these people sat in their vehicles. Perhaps because they intended to just drive down a narrow one-way street that was not only a mere five hundred meters long but also in a perpetual state of repair. What puzzled me most was the fact that the cars stayed put, bumper-to-bumper, sometimes for more than an hour, without moving a single centimeter forward. At its best, this was "Stop and Go on Monot!"

Ramzi expressed amusement at my bewildered reactions and pointed to the obvious nature of the scene before us. He commented on how merry all the car passengers seemed to be (and indeed they were!) and evidently not at all in a hurry to move faster down a street, which was partly cut off because of continuous construction, in order to find a park-

Rue Monot sign, August 5, 2010.

ing place. On the contrary, what we were witnessing was the singular way in which some Beirutis went about enjoying their Friday or Saturday evenings. Being on Rue Monot on weekend nights guaranteed everybody present the complete spectacle of what was considered in the early 2000s to be one of the hippest and trendiest social scenes in Beirut. Moreover, anyone sitting in a car, preferably the latest model of some fashionable European brand, at 1:00 a.m. with a couple of friends wearing silk shirts and Ray-Ban sunglasses, was assured the night's best views. In effect, this setup provided the respective gazing protagonists with a perfect means to see and be seen by virtually everybody parading on the narrow leisure strip that was Monot for a relatively short period at the turn of the millennium.

Thus, sitting in a car that barely moved down the street was undoubtedly an end in itself—especially for those many young Lebanese who could not afford the occasional cover charge at several of the clubs on Monot, let alone the sometimes exorbitant drink prices at the various bars lining the then-celebrated street. However, the driving crowds also included homegrown representatives of the well-to-do classes for whom spending money for an excellent but expensive mojito cocktail at a place like the Pacífico restaurant-bar could not have been a major impediment.

For a multiplicity of reasons that had to do with the intricate local celebration of *maẓāhir* (the practice of "keeping up appearances"), sitting in a car at a standstill never turned out to be such an intentional large-scale performance in any other part of Beirut. But, at the time, it was a central performance on Rue Monot.

Rue Monot: A Street with a Convoluted History and the Importance of Sectarian Space

More than anything else, what fascinated me about Rue Monot was its complex history. Located only one block east of the former *khaṭṭ al-tamās* (Green Line), the street was adjacent to what had been until the year 2000 the main campus of the Université Saint-Joseph de Beyrouth, the city's Francophone Jesuit institution of higher education. USJ, as people in East Beirut called it while pronouncing the letters in French, moved most of its campus operations to Church-owned land in neighboring Rās al-Nabaʿ on the western side of the old demarcation line and next to a large compound that included the French Cultural Center, as well as the heavily guarded new French embassy. Yet, despite this major move, the university's social sciences faculty remained on Rue Huvelin, one of the streets perpendicular to Monot and a stone's throw from the many leisure-oriented venues that turned the street's name into a synonym for entertaining weekend outings. One surely wondered what the remaining fellows of the Society of Jesus thought about all this. As it happened, their main residence stood defiantly at the bottom of the ever-changing Rue Monot.

The Université Saint-Joseph had been founded in the early 1870s in obvious contrast to the Syrian Protestant College, the competing school that had opened its doors only a few years earlier and that would become the American University of Beirut.[5] Protestant missionaries from Massachusetts developed a large and previously empty area into an opulent modern campus in the western part of Beirut. In the mid-nineteenth century, what would become the capital of Lebanon seventy years later was a town with a growing strategic importance, which reached an initial peak during the regional civil war of 1860 and the arrival of the railway network. The great irony in the French vs. Anglo-American imperial battles surrounding educational institutions in nineteenth-century Lebanon is a remarkable detail that not many people remember today. What would locally become the most prestigious French-dominated school had been founded not with money from France, but rather with funds raised in the United States by American Catholics.

As opposed to the vibrancy that characterized most of the area around the American University of Beirut throughout the twentieth century, the narrow streets to the immediate west of the neighborhood of Ashrafieh, where USJ was located, had been, by and large, quiet and residential, posing no challenge to the Ḥamra district's status as the city's cultural nucleus. On the contrary, while Ḥamra, after the 1950s, was turning into the main socio-cultural focal point for the country at large, if not to say for an entire region, the neighborhood surrounding *al-yasūʿīyyeh* (the Jesuit university) could have been described as completely dead.

All this changed with the end of the Lebanese civil war. Even if the Ḥamra district remained a vibrant neighborhood, where commerce and entertainment had partly survived the skirmishes of the war, its former status as *the* place at the forefront of what was considered fashionable and exciting was undoubtedly lost—but then mostly recovered after 2006. As detailed earlier in this book, in the mid-1990s it was the northern suburbs of East Beirut and their burgeoning nightclub scene that attracted large throngs of mostly young people. Many were from the western part of the formerly divided city and therefore eager to discover places they had only heard about from their parents. Yet, nobody could give me a convincing answer as to why, shortly after Zouq and Kaslīk began to be written off the major clubbing map, bars started to pop up here and there in an urban area that, only a couple of years earlier, had been almost a no-man's-land—and an extremely dangerous one at that. I suppose that it had to do with an intricate spatial reconfiguration that the newly reunited city was undergoing, even if—as in the case of Monot—it was a reconfiguration that lacked any particular plan or strategy on the part of the authorities.

During the civil war, the area close to Rue Monot was of prime strategic importance for the various Christian right-wing militias, among which the *Katāeb* (Phalangists) were the most prominent. This significance had to do with the actual location of the neighborhood, namely one in the immediate vicinity of downtown Beirut and, therefore, next to the very front that divided the country. Situated directly north of the SODECO roundabout, south of the small Tabaris Square off Avenue Charles Malik, and east of Bechara al-Khoury Avenue, the area around Rue Monot did not lose its relevance after the fighting ceased. This time, however, the focus was not on war, but on leisurely activities.

In the 1990s, the area initially returned to its pre-1975 state of relative oblivion. But this changed quickly toward the end of the decade. Dozens of bars and restaurants rapidly emerged, taking over a neighborhood otherwise entirely populated with upper-middle-class Christians. The original causes for this change had to do with the proximity of Monot to everything else in central Beirut and to the fact that, by the time it had become fashionable to spend nights there, *ḍownṭown* had not yet been fully refurbished. Importantly, the Ḥamra district had temporarily lost the luster it had held throughout the 1960s and 1970s (although it would recover it shortly thereafter), and, apart from a few suburban outlets, no area within Beirut quite managed to attract the masses the way Monot did. As described previously, in the mid-1990s clubs like Amor y Libertad in Kaslīk began to draw a lot of revelers from West Beirut and other parts of the country. The war had prevented them from moving freely in areas considered enemy territory. However, with the growing attraction of Rue Monot, the number of these revelers increased. These numbers included those for whom it was much easier to access places within the city rather than driving to unfamiliar suburbs located at least half an hour's drive north.

Compared to its immediate western neighbors, Basta and Bachoura, Monot was also considered a somewhat licentious place. The local "party spirit" had relatively free range, not only regarding drag performances like Ramzi's, but also with respect to the consumption of alcohol and the generally relaxed dress code. During the civil war, marginalized Shīʿī refugees from the rural south occupied many buildings located on the "other" side of the Green Line. With this shift in population, a stark contrast emerged between Shīʿī Bachoura to the west and mostly Maronite and Greek Orthodox Monot to the east. Also, an upper-middle-class atmosphere distinguished Monot from the lower-class surroundings to the west.

Despite the ostensible spirit of tolerance experienced on Rue Monot, it always remained clear that this was Christian territory. In the midst of all these bars, there stood at least two big Christian altars on the street, decorated with statues of Mary accompanied by no fewer than two or three saints (preferably George with his huge sword drawn). Aside from the strictly religious iconography, the party offices of the local Katāeb branch conspicuously filled an entire building halfway down the street. The walls of the edifice were plastered with pictures of Bachir Gemayel, the political leader who was assassinated in 1982 by the Syrian secret service shortly before he was to be sworn in as president of the Lebanese Republic.[6]

The sheer number of pictures of dead politicians stuck to the walls of buildings everywhere in Lebanon is fascinating. While the scholarly

Photos of Bachir on a building in Ashrafieh, January 19, 2012.

focus has often been on the visual representation of the Shīʿī commemoration of martyrdom in Lebanon and elsewhere, the images of Bachir, as one and all called him, were—without any doubt—special when it came to celebrating the assets and virtues of the male body.[7] I knew countless young gay men who, irrespective of their sectarian background, developed erotic fantasies based on the numerous photographs that depicted Bachir, a hunky man in his thirties, wearing a pair of fashionable Ray-Ban sunglasses and looking fierce and, at the same time, munificent. He was only one of the omnipresent Christian "martyrs" whose images lined East Beirut's streets, but Bachir was certainly considered the sexiest, especially with his attractive looks and his rather developed biceps protruding from under the top of his sleeveless shirt.

As the newly elected president of the Lebanese Republic, Bachir Gemayel had died in an explosion in late summer 1982, not very far from Rue Monot, at the Ashrafieh headquarters of his political party-cum-militia, the Lebanese Forces (L.F.). *Al-uwwāt* (The Forces), as the movement is called, traced its political base partly back to the Katāeb Party, founded by Bachir's father. Pierre Gemayel modeled the party, including its internal structure and name, after Generalissimo Francisco Franco's Phalange. On his way back from the 1936 Berlin Olympics, Pierre Gemayel decided to found a political movement in his native Lebanon. This movement would be organized according to the Fascist and Nazi ideals to which he was introduced during his journeys to Mussolini's Italy and Hitler's Germany. Over the decades, what had become a political party after Lebanon's independence on November 22, 1943, quickly developed into one of the country's most important Christian organizations. In the early 1970s, when only a few voices warned of the looming possibility of a civil war, the Katāeb Party had already armed itself and was in the process of becoming the militia for which it would commonly be remembered.

The death of his son, Bachir, triggered the massacres in the Sabra and Shatila Palestinian refugee camps in West Beirut.[8] In the wake of the Israeli invasion that began in June 1982, West Beirut was cut off from the rest of the world in order to put pressure on Yasser Arafat's Palestine Liberation Organization (PLO) to leave Lebanon. Arafat, AKA Abu Ammār, and his men were escorted to Tunis at the end of the summer, leaving the refugee camps mostly defenseless. All parties involved in the conflict had pledged to refrain from entering them. As the anthropologist Julie Peteet puts it, the summer of 1982 was the end of an era, or what the Palestinians who departed called *ayyām bayrūt* (the days of Beirut), a "community that had felt itself proud, increasingly self-sufficient, and protected was now vulnerable, humiliated, and anxious as to its fate."[9] All these sentiments were partly confirmed in early September 1982, after the anger set off by Bachir's assassination was channeled into a livid rage against the then-sworn enemy of the right-wing Christian militias: the Palestinians (especially since it was impossible for them to harm the Syrian regime, the actual perpetrator of the death of the newly elected Lebanese president). With the help of the Israeli army, which at the time occupied most of Lebanon and encircled nearly all the country's Palestinian refugee camps, a heavily armed group from the Lebanese Forces, under the command of the young Elie Hobeika, was allowed into Sabra and Shatila by the orders of the Israeli defense minister, Ariel Sharon. Over the course of three days, Hobeika and his men rampaged through the camps, killing, according to official UN estimates, two thousand people.

After the civil war ended in 1990, the *Pax Syriana* required the interdiction of the Lebanese Forces, whose serving head, Samir Geagea, was imprisoned for more than a decade in the notorious Roumieh prison. Elie Hobeika, in contrast, quickly changed his allegiances and became a deputy in parliament and later a minister—of refugees!—in his country's postwar, pro-Syrian government. This was not the end of the story, however. In late January 2002, a bomb exploded in the East Beirut suburb of Ḥāzmieh, killing the former mass murderer-turned-politician Hobeika. Although no one officially claimed the assassination, many indications pointed toward Israel. Indeed, at the time of his killing, Hobeika was to testify in Brussels against his former mentor, Ariel Sharon. The day before he was killed, he had actually met with Belgian judges who went over a testimony he would never formally deliver.

As for Samir Geagea, the L.F. leader was later freed from prison. He was released in the wake of the so-called Cedar Revolution, following the assassination of the former prime minister Rafik Hariri on February 14, 2005, which later that year put an end to the Syrian military occupation of Lebanon. Shortly after having reinstituted his party within the landscape of official Lebanese politics, Geagea became one of the main political figures of the March 14th Alliance, which backed the then-pro-American government of Fouad Siniora.

The intention behind this historical synopsis, and its juxtaposition with the images and other kinds of visual representations that accompany virtually every exercise in Lebanese identity politics, is to engage with the knotty character of this particular portion of Lebanese history. It is a history that stretches from the early 1980s to 2005 and includes a succession of major events that have demarcated the chronological sequence in an overall convoluted political trajectory, which as yet has not ended. Moreover, I intend to assess the political iconography and the graffiti that accompany such a *histoire événementielle* for it can shed light on dynamics that are equally illuminating.[10] In other words, even if the Lebanese Forces had been forbidden from being part of the official political landscape for more than a decade, any astute observer would have been unable to ignore the numerous iconic crosses that were at all times sprayed on walls around strategic places in East Beirut and that symbolized unmistakably the continuously looming—albeit banned—presence of *al-uwwāt*.

The Iconography of the Hunky "Martyr" and the Symbolism of Space

Aside from the (homo)erotic dimension of the images of Bachir Gemayel, the almost omnipresent depictions of the handsome "martyr" were even more powerful than the numerous L.F. crosses sprayed on walls around

Beirut. The reason for this powerful effect was the commanding aura of the pictures. This distinctive impression defiantly evoked a past that was officially unrecognized before 2005. However, the display of the images alongside the fascist rendering of the generally sanctioned geometric Lebanese cedar symbol of the Katāeb made what was decidedly forbidden allowed, and thus celebrated, as an act of perpetual insubordination. As my friend Ramzi put it, "Bachir had become a demi-god in the Christian community. He had lost nothing of his symbolic power, being at once a political, social, religious, and sexual icon." According to Ramzi, Bachir was, for many Christian *shabāb* [male youngsters], the ultimate "bad boy" who rebelled against his father, created his own "clique," eliminated all the others, then became a *rayyes* [chief], and had all the women he wanted thanks to his "good looks" and his charisma. This was a combination every one of those *shabāb* probably dreamed of. His posters have never stopped adorning almost every street corner of Ashrafieh, and one still hears from time to time his voice blaring out of car radios at full volume with excerpts from his "historic" speeches.

Needless to say, the Christian altars, graffiti L.F. crosses, triangular green Katāeb cedars, and Bachir pictures disappeared as soon as one walked two blocks west of Rue Monot. Still, I was always stunned at how Bachir also had supporters among many non-Christian Lebanese of all sexual orientations. On the visible surface of places like Bachoura, Basta, or the neighborhood of Zoqāq al-Blāṭ, it was the green flags of the Shīʿī Amal Movement and the yellow banners from Ḥizballah that unquestionably dominated the local streetscape, along with hundreds—if not to say thousands—of pictures of their own *zuʿamāʾ* and *shuhadāʾ* (leaders and martyrs), functioning as steady "symbolic sites of struggle."[11]

Interestingly, to the north of both parts of town, the situation was completely different—at least before 2005 and the political stalemate between the opposing March 8th Coalition and March 14th Alliance, which formed separately shortly before the Syrian military withdrawal. Sometimes, when Ramzi and I left one or the other Monot club after he had performed his drag show, the two of us—carrying the duffel bag—would walk across Avenue Charles Malik and Martyrs' Square to check out the late-night scene unfolding *ḍownṭown*. This was before Martyrs' and Riād al-Ṣolḥ Squares became respectively the spatially inscribed symbolic battlegrounds of government and opposition that would haunt Beirut's city center for a number of years after the assassination of former Prime Minister Rafik Hariri in February 2005. Back then, an all-too-evident political iconography was nowhere to be found in what was called *ḍown-*

ṭown, the area between ʿAyn al-Mraisseh to the west and Gemmeyzeh to the east.

Yet, the lack of explicit political banners or pictures did not signify the absence of sectarian identity politics. Architecturally, the might of *ṭā'ifiyya* (sectarianism)—or what would be called confessionalism in a more French-influenced setting[12]—manifested itself through the presence of a dozen houses of worship, including those that catered to most of the many local Christian groups. Moreover, there were a couple of Sunni Muslim mosques in the downtown area, as well as one synagogue in disrepair. The conspicuous absence of a specifically Shīʿī mosque was striking, however, not only because of historical settlement patterns but also because of the marginal political role that had been played by this particular community since the formation of modern Lebanon. In the new downtown, Lebanese sectarianism was also exhibited by building owners who advertised their religious identities, either by hanging a huge Christian Orthodox icon at the edifice's entrance or by posting verses from the Qur'ān in a conspicuous place.

For some time after the turn of the millennium, the most poignant battleground of competing religious architecture was to be witnessed on the western edge of Martyrs' Square at its intersection with Emir Bachir Street next to the 'Azzarieh buildings. After the Maronites had rebuilt their Italianate Cathedral of St. George, roughly facing the Belgian embassy, Prime Minister Rafik Hariri, a Sunni Muslim, commissioned the construction of an immense mosque next door. The non-vernacular design of his commission overwhelmed in height and width every other structure in *ḍownṭown*. Even before its completion, Al-Amin Mosque looked like a combination of a reinforced concrete version of Istanbul's Sultan Ahmet Camii and a spaceship in full architectural attire. One may have thought that this was just another round in Maronite Christian-Sunni Muslim competitions, a consideration that is partly justified because the Sunni *waqf* (religious endowment) land on which Al-Amin Mosque was erected had never before "hosted" a house of worship this extensive in size. But as it turned out, the then big man in Lebanese politics, Rafik Hariri, outdid himself in the construction of the mosque, not so much in defiance of the neighboring Maronites, but rather as a sign of supremacy over a potential rival within his own sectarian ranks.

That rival was the Saudi Arabian prince and building magnate Walid bin Talal, who, at the time, had political aspirations in Lebanon. The Saudi billionaire held Lebanese citizenship, although, technically, that was impossible according to a Lebanese law dating back to the French Mandate, which allows one to inherit Lebanese citizenship only through the father. (The prince's mother was Lebanese, the daughter of the country's first post-independence prime minister, Riād al-Ṣolḥ.) What in the eyes of many Lebanese disqualified the prince further was the fact that he had not spent any significant time in Lebanon. To the dismay of his rivals, he spoke *khalījī* (Arabic with a "Gulfi" accent). However, the fear that preoccupied Hariri was the inherent power of what both he and his competitor knew best, which was money.

At the end of the 1990s, Walid bin Talal embarked on a series of prestigious construction efforts, one of which was the strategically located and Swiss-sponsored Mövenpick Hotel. Advertising an "East meets West" architecture and beach sand shipped from the Egyptian Sinai peninsula, the hotel was erected near the very tip of Rās Beirut, a location that made it possible for everybody to see. Part of the propaganda surrounding the building of the hotel was that the prince "loved" Lebanon so much that he was ready to invest a share of his considerable fortune and hire local laborers to work on his high-profile construction sites. As if out of nowhere, his *ḥaṭṭa*-adorned face (a mustachioed visage topped by a headdress) appeared on huge billboards on the way to and from the airport. The fireworks that marked the extravagant opening of the officially Swiss-managed Mövenpick Hotel could be seen and heard throughout the Beirut metropolitan area, reminding everybody in the most uncanny ways of the fighting that took place during the civil war. Traumatic memories notwithstanding, Prince Walid's fireworks were meant to rival New Year's celebrations in major world capitals. Given the ostentatious context, rumors spread to the effect that "His Royal Highness" was actually backed politically by the Syrians (a couple of years later he would be commissioned to build a massive Four Seasons Hotel in the center of Damascus). Since the Syrian military occupied two-thirds of the country at the time, one does not wonder about why Hariri worried.

The prime minister therefore had to act quickly. He decided to monopolize a construction project already underway *ḍownṭown*. Sunni religious leaders had planned all along to build a mosque on empty *waqf* land situated between the St. George Maronite Cathedral and Martyrs' Square, but without the enormous dimensions that would dwarf all other buildings in the area. Rafik Hariri personally took up the project, pumping millions into it in the hope that, by doing so, he would be able to visually outmaneuver Walid bin Talal on the phallocratically inspired religious front. From a historical perspective, he certainly managed to get the better of his potential competitor. In 2002, however, Hariri could not know that

Battle of the phalluses in *ḍownṭown*, June 18, 2011.

three years later his remains would be buried in a plot on the same strategically located *waqf* land, and this even before the full construction of the Mosque of Al-Amin would be finished.

These personal rivalries may have been forgotten. However, the Maronite Christian-Sunni Muslim competition remains part and parcel of spatial contestation in Beirut. Shortly after the Al-Amin mosque was finished, the Maronite Archdiocese of Beirut decided in 2010 to add some sort of *campanile* to the St. George Cathedral, and this in an obvious attempt to defy the quadruple phallocracy of its neighbor. Apart from corruption and a notorious disappearance of cash that delayed the completion of the church tower for years, it did not take long before the four thin minarets were visually met with a single—but massively thick—bell tower, a clear visual representation of a quintessential phallocentric cockfight, Lebanese style.

In advancing these examples of spatial and architectural symbolism in a city like Beirut, I do not want to overemphasize the importance of physical space over the ways in which it is perceived and later contested—as well as actively appropriated—by a range of people whose forms of identification are multiple. There might be the fine politics of sectarian demarcation, as engineered by powerful politicians, which bestows meaning to particular places before exploiting it according to personal advantages. There might also be large-scale sectarian identity politics that are mobilized and then inscribed through all kinds of visual projections onto the urban fabric. But there will also always remain practices of spatial appropriation and contestation that actively transcend—without necessarily cutting completely with—political identities otherwise imposed staunchly on everybody else by the countless ideologies of group-based solidarity. In the years following the 2001 "opening" of *ḍownṭown*, such an appropriation could be noticed best by observing closely the various people who came from all over the city—and the country at large—in order to congregate in a place that, within a relatively short period of time, had briefly become the nation's social and political stage par excellence onto which countless dreams, yearnings, and desires were relentlessly projected.

Yet, as I have tried to show, a particular physical place such as *ḍownṭown* can be ordered and, therefore, very much controlling as far as the individuals inhabiting it are concerned. It can impose a whole series of constraints, but despite these characteristics, physical space, more generally, can also be enabling, especially when it comes to the many zones of encounter within the larger urban fabric that foster attempts at transcending spatio-temporal fixities. For that matter, the purported exclusivity of a particular place such as *ḍownṭown* or the area around Rue Monot might be difficult to contest. The respective spaces are nevertheless appropriated by those whose inclusion is regularly dreaded by society's dominant strata. As discussed previously, the established bourgeoisie is in apparent command of local normativities. It sets the wider influential tone in terms of what it deems to be fashionable or not. Moreover, sectarian tension is played out along the lines of architecture and design, of which the particular (re)construction of churches and mosques is a case in point. In addition, there are more ephemeral examples of visual representation, such as posters of "martyrs." These posters capture their various sectarian agendas in more circumlocutory ways, of which posted photographs and political graffiti are just the most obvious examples. But there are also individual encounters, off the map of controlled space, that challenge all sorts of boundaries and their associated fixities. Mostly, these encounters are to be found in locations in and around Beirut that enable different kinds of individual representations, as exemplified by the range of non-normative bodily performances, be it Georgette's, Elio's, or Ramzi's. These representations arise from a dialectic relationship between a controlled and ordered space, on the one hand, and one that is always actively appropriated and lived in by the various seemingly marginalized people I write about, on the other.

Every so often, however, instead of being directly challenged, social boundaries become asserted and (sometimes) reinforced. Their ensuing reproduction often helps to maintain collective relations in a deceptive state of uncontested cohesion and coexistence. Within this contradictory reality, where the status quo is challenged and asserted, social space in Beirut continually incorporates a range of social practices, namely those of commonly shared, as well as those of individual, content. These varied social practices, be they individual performances or collective group dynamics, come into being and die, while their protagonists act out and—sometimes—suffer their consequences. Within this subtle context of what I will analyze next as underlying homophobia, practices of latent or manifest homoeroticism have their altering impact (explicit some moments and at others rather concealed) on the overall production of queer space in Beirut.

In the following chapter, I look closely at some of the different practices of spatial appropriation and contestation that persist despite all normative impositions. Occurring within what I call the "homosexual sphere," these practices are never completely disruptive, yet they are dynamic and can pose a fierce challenge to the larger order of things, which in Lebanon, for the most part, is channeled through a convoluted sectarian and class identity politics.

CHAPTER 5

The Homosexual Sphere between Spatial Appropriation and Contestation: Collective Activism and the Many Lives of Young Gay Men in Beirut

It can be analytically misleading to apply the social category of "community" to gay men in Lebanon. Thus, it becomes all the more pertinent for the anthropologist to look for an alternative and suitable concept that comes close to assessing the complexity of queer daily life experiences in and around Beirut. Therefore, in order to grapple with the frame in which gay social practices, along with their various representations, take place in the Lebanese capital, I choose to talk about a "homosexual sphere" instead of a "community."

"Homosexual Sphere" Versus "Gay Community"

I define such a sphere as a semi-amorphous space that is fluctuating and every so often ambiguous. This sphere is mostly a realm that consists primarily of gendered as well as sexual symbols in relation to which queer space is perpetually produced, be it at a particular social venue or a seemingly random street corner. Yet, the fluidity of the homosexual sphere in Lebanon aside, many gay men, almost as a rule, fall constantly back onto the insidious politics of social fixities and categorization that are frequently associated with their individual demeanor or their bodily posture.

Similarly, space deemed as queer needs to be understood physically as much as it has to be read in non-architectural terms. Queer space in Beirut designates the geographical, along with the socio-cultural and mental, fields in which various homoerotic practices take place and are being integrated into the respective lives of different individuals. For the same reasons I privilege the concept of a homosexual sphere in Lebanon, as a theoretical category, I prefer to subscribe to the adjective "queer," even if its equivalent, the English word "gay," is actually more widely used in and around Beirut, and this regardless of the spoken vernaculars locally used. In choosing the adjective "queer," I follow the particular connotations attached to its German counterpart *quer*, on which I elaborate at the beginning of this book. I thus call attention to the potential challenge and rupture that queer space may pose to any number of social normativities in a country such as Lebanon, as well as to the large array of copious social conformities that are attached to them.

Moreover, the integration of homoerotic desires and practices in Lebanon has for a long time been a foreclosing mechanism as to the local emergence of what has been termed a "gay community." This presupposes, of course, that one perceives such a community as being a somehow coherent and comprehending group of individuals who share corresponding, although at times competing, convictions and aspirations, and where the various erotic and sexual inclinations transform into a fundamental concern regarding the many social convolutions that affect identity formation. From the early years of the new millennium, there have been limited and quite timid efforts to come up with such a category in Lebanon. However, for the most part, the young gay men with whom I interacted did not have an active role in these efforts. They rather formed anything but an externally—let alone internally—uncontested social entity. Some, like Ramzi and Elio, self-identified as gay; others—for instance, Khalil—did so ambiguously (although that changed in later years). Those who self-identified as gay did not express any particular group solidarity, neither one based on a perceived common sexuality or one informed by a mutually embraced political cause. The initial difficulties in engineering a widespread social solidarity in Lebanon based on a common sexuality may thus be one of the factors explaining why there have been scarcely any effective spaces in the immediate post-civil-war period that managed to demarcate activities of an inclusive community, one that socially identified itself with its particular (homo)sexual orientation.

These difficulties notwithstanding, I certainly do not intend to overlook the precedent attempts, generally quite composite in their convictions, of various groupings that have emerged over the years in order to reach out into what they started referring to as a "gay community" in Lebanon. In 2002, for instance, a socializing network of lesbians and young gay men, most of whom were part of relatively affluent Beiruti families, formed a group semi-officially. They christened it "HELEM," which is Arabic for "dream," but the term is also an acronym for *ḥimāya lubnāniyya lil mithliyīn wal muzdawijīn wal mughayirīn*, which translates into "Lebanese Protection for Lesbians, Gays, Bisexuals, and Transgenders." The historical interplay worthy of note between political events, on the one hand, and some of their socio-cultural repercussions, on the other, illustrates well the ephemeral nature of queer spaces in the early 2000s and their perpetual contestation in Lebanon. In other words, queer spaces and those who appropriate them can benefit from particular situations, but they can also be on the receiving end of a range of detrimental repercussions, including latent homophobia and outright physical violence.

The aftermath of the so-called Cedar Revolution, following the assassination of Rafik Hariri, the former prime minister, on February 14, 2005, led not only to the withdrawal of Syrian troops later that year, but also to an increased self-awareness and self-empowerment of large parts of Lebanese civil society. This development included the partial reimagination of local queer identities. Despite the violence generated by the Syrian military retreat, the brief moment of perceived liberation was equated not only with a general shaking-off of fear, but also with a concerted "coming out" by HELEM, the local lesbian, gay, bisexual, and transgender (LGBT) group. The group's nascent community activism became institutionalized around the emblematic Zicco House,[1] which had been the address of countless local NGOs since the early 2000s, in Beirut's Ṣanāyeh neighborhood and was increasingly reported on by international media.[2] Moreover, the devastating war unleashed by the Israeli military against Lebanon in summer 2006 propelled many advocates for "gay causes" to the forefront of more general humanitarian aid. This activism transformed them into relief workers organized with other civic groups in an effort to help scores of refugees. Given the knowledge in public relations accumulated over the few years since its formation, HELEM and its supporters were able in summer 2006 to capitalize on their commitment to general humanitarian causes during a national disaster. With it, they also hoped to further their own particular agenda, one that reached beyond the armed conflict with Israel and was more closely focused on gay issues and other related matters of concern.

However, all this changed a few months later after the resignation of the Shīʿī ministers and their allies from Prime Minister Fouad Siniora's cabinet and the ensuing stalemate between the government coalition (March 14th Alliance) and the opposition with its various allies (March 8th Coalition). In the spirit of appropriating symbolic spaces all around the city, the opposition—Muslims *and* Christians who were organized around Ḥizballah's ideology of "resistance"—went *ḍownṭown* in order to assert a physical presence intended to emphasize its own "right to the city" and, by extension, to the country as a whole. Thus, *ḍownṭown*, Beirut's central district, which had been completely refurbished after the end of the civil war in accordance with the late Hariri's dream of a prosperous and exclusive Lebanon, saw itself overwhelmed precisely by those citizens the established bourgeoisie was anything but keen on having around. Yet they came, and in throngs, setting up camps in open spaces surrounding the area around Maarad Street, the main pedestrian artery of a previously fashion-conscious city center that, by then, had almost been deserted by the members of the local establishment and those many who, only a few months earlier, wanted desperately to be a part of it.

The demarcation of political power and ideology was not limited to the drawing of mere emblematic boundaries. For the first time since the end of the civil war in the early 1990s, barbed wire was put up within the downtown district, this time demonstratively on the streets to and from the elevated Grand Sérail. Set up by the Lebanese Army, these fences were intended to protect the seat of Prime Minister Siniora's government, which the Ḥizballah opposition sought to topple. Although they did not manage to do so, the "*ḍāḥiya*'s presence *ḍownṭown*" and its various sociopolitical ramifications made its mark on countless Lebanese, regardless of their respective political convictions, culminating in a polarization between ever-shifting government and opposition alliances. This polarization prevented *ḍownṭown* from continuing to be a leisurely parading ground and, therefore, led many of my interlocutors to claim, "*Baṭṭal ḍownṭown!*" (Ḍownṭown is no more!)

Crucial for my purpose here is not whether *ḍownṭown* ceased to exist, but the general sentiment of uncertainty that permeated the Lebanese political landscape in the aftermath of the 2006 Israeli war, from which Ḥizballah emerged anything but vanquished. It was a landscape where physical violence erupted regularly and where the total destruction of the Palestinian refugee camp of Nahr al-Bāred in northern Lebanon a year later was but one major pitfall in a series of near and full-fledged disasters. This daunting situation cast a shadow on large parts of the population, including some of the groups that had organized around issues relevant to their vision of a functioning civil society. The vigorous *élan* that these various groups—who had organized around matters pertaining to democracy, women's rights, and LGBT activism—experienced during the Cedar Revolution of 2005 and the 2006 war transformed into a state of pervasive ambiguity that pushed many of them away from the forefront of their activist work. This uncertain situation thrust an organization like HELEM into a limbo that was followed by a semi-conscious retreat into limited, albeit temporary, invisibility.[3]

Some of the young gay men involved with HELEM stopped being politically active. Those who defended the rights of homosexuals in regular columns for major Lebanese newspapers all but vanished from the surface of a media landscape, which not all that long before had showered them with attention.[4] Others were utterly disillusioned, despite the obvious difficulties of admitting it. Those who could sought physical and mental refuge in provisional—and, at times, permanent—emigration, preferably to Canada, and pledged to continue their activist work from the distance of, what they perceived to be, transatlantic safety.

To prevent any misunderstandings, I wish to clarify two things related to what I have stated above. For one, I do not intend to argue that the various extra-governmental groupings in Lebanon (and here I am not talking about conventional NGOs) have been linked unanimously with the particular political effervescence caused by the so-called Cedar Revolution. There have all along been many grassroots social movements in Lebanon that catered, and continue to do so, to those whose political inclinations are anything but inspired by the euphoric wave generated by the March 8th Coalition and March 14th Alliance.[5] Second, when referring to the temporary retreat of HELEM activists, I do not have in mind a total eclipse from the larger social platform, let alone a necessary failure, on the part of their work as advocates for what they saw as gay and lesbian causes in Lebanon. More than being interested in quantitative or qualitative achievements, I want to look at—and assess—the delicate rapport entertained between the visibility of usually marginalized groupings, on the one hand, and the particular political situation at hand, on the other. It is, furthermore, the visibility of queer space that alternates with its invisibility depending on the socio-political climate of the day that is significant.

Thus, by examining the historical interplay between specific political events and their socio-cultural repercussions in Lebanon, I can best analyze the ephemeral and difficult-to-pin-down nature of what I have here called "queer spaces," as well as the various ways in which such spaces are perpetually contested by a multiplicity of subjects and subject matters. As for my various remarks concerning HELEM and its activism, they are mostly informed by the dynamics of the early years. Even if a group like HELEM manages to capture permanently positive attention on the part of Lebanese society and politics, the encouragement would still be coming from that precise historical interplay to which I have been referring. Within such interplay, political effervescence, based on its particular context, can either mean life or, as an alternative case in point, it can indicate death *tout court*.

This presence of two opposing possibilities is essentially the main reason why I am hesitant to haphazardly use the term "gay community" in Lebanon. The phrase also reminds me in part of a concerted effort by some community builders to establish spatio-temporal fixities not everybody can—or wants to—abide by. The reasons why some individuals have difficulties conforming to these fixities are legion. Sometimes, they are motivated by a mere lack of interest: the issues of some are not inevitably those of others. Sometimes, however, they are informed by a willful act of exclusion on the part of the organized group itself. The act of excluding somebody from the group—be it in terms of formal membership or in matters concerning specific incidents of homophobia on the street—is generally inspired by a perception on the part of certain group members that the excluded person does not fit the overall model set by those who otherwise wave banners for the universal liberation of gays and lesbians in Lebanon. The reasons behind a possible exclusion can range from an individual's class behavior being deemed inadequate to somebody else's reluctance to play by the rules of political correctness imposed by the larger group. Notwithstanding the complications attached to the organized formation of a "gay community" in and around Beirut in the early 2000s, I do not intend to dismiss the general belief in LGBT activism in Lebanon. Despite an ideological influence emanating in part from the global West, the activism in question is an entirely local one and informed by a complicated mechanism of circulation and translation of ideas that always receives its share of home-based content. In the face of justified caution and criticism, it remains too soon, I would argue, to sum up and fully assess the impact the formation of HELEM has had, and may continue to have, on Lebanese society at large.[6]

For now, let me shift my attention from the various attempts to form and categorize an activist LGBT movement in Lebanon to the numerous spaces, physical and mental, of intersecting and corresponding borderlines that amount to those ephemeral queer spaces. In doing so, I stress my interest in the individual lives of young gay men in Beirut, who are very diverse in their specific experiences and larger socio-cultural affiliations, as well as in their social status and economic concerns. These young gay men, many of whom use the English word *gay* as an individual qualifier, irrespective of the language they actually speak, entertain distinct, albeit heavily charged, relations with each other, as well as with society in general. I want to focus on the physical but also the mental space of these relations in order to consider the varied and, at times, conflicting aspirations these individuals embody in their attempts at approaching and coping with their very own lived realities. More than by an actual space, these relations are informed by what I specifically define as a "homosexual sphere," a continuously fluctuating area lacking manifest order and control. But for now, let me begin by advancing another ethnographic vignette that will introduce my theoretical concerns.

While I focused earlier on parts of the life stories of Elio, Sal, and Ralph to illustrate the multiplicity of relations that young Lebanese gay men have with each other and with the various worlds and spaces they respectively inhabit, I now offer an additional ethnographic example, along with a further description of the urban landscape in and outside Beirut. Both are intended to demonstrate what I mean when I refer to the mental space some of these young people try to appropriate in order to cope with the different realities they confront in their daily lives. The same thing applies undoubtedly to the anthropologist himself, who, as a *Querdenker*, advances his critical attempts at what Pierre Bourdieu termed "participant objectification." In this capacity, he cannot disassociate himself from the convolutions of space as well as their human consequences.

The Way to "Paradise": A Story of Hadi

It was again on Jbeil's Paradise Beach at the beginning of the 2002 summer season that I was approached by a very young man whose animated eyes could not hide his inherent enthusiasm. At the time, Hadi was eighteen and looked like what the French call a *gros bébé*, especially with his apparent baby fat, which he carried with juvenile confidence in and out of the shallow waters of the sea. There, he kept trying to grab, somewhat awkwardly, a big inflated red plastic ball, as if the bulky sphere would save him from an oversized wave, which during the month of May was still anything but a rarity on the eastern Mediterranean. Coincidently, it was on a weekday that I met Hadi for the first time. I had decided to take the day off, pack my bathing suit, and leave my shared apartment in the Ḥamra district. Instead of taking a service or a micro, I walked up Bliss Street, turned left and went all the way down until I reached the Corniche. I truly loved walking on the Corniche in the morning, especially at the beginning of the summer, when it was warm enough to wear shorts and a t-shirt. There was always a pleasant breeze that reminded me of the days before the cold, northerly Mistral wind would hit the coast around the Marseilles of my childhood.

Before noon on weekdays, the area in and around *ḍownṭown* was generally empty, at least in comparison to the masses that invaded the same place on Friday or Saturday evenings in the early 2000s. Whenever I was around Nejmeh Square during the day, I rarely missed the opportunity to grab at least three scoops of the excellent ice cream sold in the café/restaurant facing *al-sāʿa*, the big clock, located next to the Lebanese parliament building. I would then cross Allenby Street before turning right and continuing to the desolate and totally barren area of the so-called Normandie landfill, where parts of the war rubble of the former downtown were shoved into St. George Bay. The original rationale behind the enterprise was to claim solid terrain to be ostensibly used for the construction of a state-of-the-art financial district that was never built.

Behind the desolate land—where I always wondered what exactly the occasional hoist was lifting—stood BIEL (Beirut International Exposition and Leisure Center), like a fortress on a manicured plot. The road access to BIEL was, for pedestrians, a virtual impossibility as it was devoid of any kind of sidewalks. This bleak wasteland could not have formed a starker contrast to the rest of the city or to the island of seeming serenity that the couple of acres surrounding BIEL were supposed to represent to their various visitors. At the back of this circumscribed area began Beirut's port authority. The harbor was completely cut off from the rest of the city, a fact of urban planning I lamented each time I remembered how, in my childhood, I took immense pleasure in watching the countless ships and longshoremen from the beautiful exposed urban promenade in Algiers. No such thing in Beirut, for one could only see the various port activities from a distance, where the elevated terrain of some parts of the city allowed for relatively unrestricted views.

The Charles Hélou Bus Station faced the main entrance of Beirut's Port Authority. It was named after a former president of the Republic and located in a space that was underneath a speedway bridge. From this strange place, one could board a bus or share a taxi bound for comparatively faraway cities like Damascus, Aleppo, and Amman, or closer municipalities within Lebanon, such as Tripoli in the northern part of the country. The ride to Tripoli took usually a little more than an hour, depending on the traffic, which was sometimes excruciating, around the Bay of Jounieh. Many travelers, however, preferred to catch the bus going north along the coast at Charles Hélou, otherwise called by locals *al-būr* (an Arabic corruption of "port"), because it usually did not stop before it reached Jbeil, roughly forty minutes north of the capital Beirut.

And this is precisely what I generally did, providing I was coming from the Ḥamra district in the far west of the city. On my way back from the beach, I liked taking the smaller micros that drove along the old coastal road, only meters away from the Mediterranean. But getting to Jbeil was much more expedient on the *autostrade*, a more recent construction corresponding in parts to a modern highway. After leaving Beirut, passing the Dora roundabout in Burj Ḥammūd, one drove on a huge business strip that seemed endless before reaching the Kesserwān region. There, municipalities such as Zouq, Kaslīk, and Jounieh followed the northern Metn region suburbs of Ḍbayyeh and Zalqā. The last two were located on a wide commercial span where all the country's local and international franchises had established stores that catered to a composite clientele.

The area was evidently located in the "Christian heartland." However, like its "Muslim" counterpart, the road past Khaldeh and the international airport south of Beirut, it almost functioned as the equivalent of downtown Beirut's Maarad Street. To promenade and be seen was a high-priority routine for large parts of the population, regardless of sectarian background. The *autostrade* through Ḍbayyeh and Zalqā was, of course, not the complete equivalent of Maarad Street. One did, evidently, not walk on the *autostrade*, but drove, preferably by speeding as much as possible, past the numerous chain stores, outlets, and restaurants with the occasional stop here and there. This particular practice drew all kinds of people to specific places on the business strip, which they would appropriate and contest for a variety of reasons. Most notable among these places was the so-called ABC mall in Ḍbayyeh, where one did not go only to shop, but also to have an informal *gazdūra* (stroll) through the different boutiques that included the checking out of the local scene. For the young gay men with whom I interacted, there was, of course, also the Dunkin' Donuts in Zalqā, referred to earlier in this book. Moreover, the rather empty area around the new Ḍbayyeh marina, with one of the best views of Beirut, functioned for some as a cruising ground, especially during and after sunset. As far as the highway itself was concerned, however, it was a point of general reference—and, sometimes, of a pride that was difficult to understand, given the complete ugliness of the place—namely one that uncritically embraced an unapologetic capitalism *à la libanaise*.

Going from Zouq to Jounieh, one crosses Nahr al-Kalb (Dog's River) with its numerous monumental inscriptions of foreign and domestic armies that conquered the place starting with the ancient Egyptians a few millennia ago. One must pass through a short tunnel that, up until the early 2000s, prominently featured in large Arabic letters the local political household name, namely *al-katāeb al-lubnāniyya* ("The Lebanese Phalange"). Once in Jounieh, Christian religious insignia are omnipresent, beginning with the larger-than-life Jesus statue and ending with the many cross-topped churches and monasteries, including, at the very top of the hill, Ḥarīssa, along with the cathedrals dedicated to Lebanon's Christian patron saint, the Virgin Mary.

At the end of this continuum of local commercial and religious architectural expression, and at the northern tip of the Bay of Jounieh, is the notorious Casino du Liban, perched above the pleasure haven of Maameltain. Considered by locals to have been the biggest gambling place and spectacle venue in the world when it first opened in the late 1950s, the Casino was refurbished after the civil war to reopen in 1996, entertaining the rich and famous at home and from abroad with, for example, ballet performances by Maurice Béjart, as well as mass entertainment competitions such as Miss Bikini International.

If traffic was slow on the *autostrade* around the Bay of Jounieh, it usually cleared up around Ṭabarja, behind the Casino du Liban. It was then a comparatively short ride to Jbeil. Apart from its final destination, the bus to Tripoli had no scheduled stops on the way. However, it was always possible to let the driver know that one wanted to get off at an earlier point in the journey. Whenever I went to Paradise Beach with my friends, we tried to go to downtown Jbeil first. We would inevitably stop at Restaurant Rock, owned by the Kaddour family, where the staff recognized me every time I showed up to have one of the best *shish-ṭaouk* (marinated and grilled chicken) sandwiches around, along with a mixed fruit juice with raw peeled almonds served at the café next door. Armed with a light meal in one hand, a big plastic container full of fresh juice in the other, and my beach towel in a rucksack on my back, I would walk with friends from Jbeil's main street to the picturesque old town with its little fishing port at the bottom of the street. We then generally sat on the harbor's concrete promontory, ate our chicken sandwiches, and contemplated the back-and-forth movements of the small vessels that carried names like *Carine*, *Florence*, or *Bisous*.

To get to the stretch of sandy beach south of the fishing harbor, one could either go back up into town or stay next to the water and walk on a little path alongside big rocks. The trail, right below the fenced-off area that contained the excavated Roman ruins for which ancient Byblos was famous, was regularly washed away by the sea's fierce winter waves. By the time I finally reached the northern tip of what back then constituted Tam Tam Beach, I could not stop to be perplexed by the sight of so many people who regularly spread out their camping chairs and towels in the midst of waste debris that the Mediterranean swept ashore. Later, after friends of mine pointed it out to me, I recognized the strategic location of the place. The beach's northern tip was a bit elevated, and thus advantageously overlooking the entire area, a welcome location for those seeking good views.

The day I met Hadi, Tam Tam Beach was relatively empty. It had not yet vanished to make room for the construction of two exclusive beach clubs only a few months later. Those clubs, Voile Bleue and Eddeh Sands, were built to attract a high-end clientele. For now, it was still the semi-*shaʿbī* (popular) coastal stretch where lower-middle-class families gathered on weekends, along with groups of youngsters—including all genders—who turned the beach experience into their main summer entertainment. Everybody shared a stretch of sand that, although not always the cleanest beach, was relaxing to most. The relative proximity to Beirut, as well as the lovely landscape with its comparatively copious greenery, made it the perfect destination for almost anybody intent on enjoying a pleasant time in or near the sea. As mentioned before, Paradise Beach formed the very southern point of the sandy stretch, and it was traditionally occupied by dozens—even more on summer weekends—of gay men and some lesbians. And there, in the very back, was Labiba, the godmother of them all, ruling the realm in front of her cooking shack and ensuring that none of her queer subjects were harassed by the occasional homophobic outsider.

Atypically, Hadi seemed to be alone on the day he approached me on the beach. There was always the occasional oddball—including myself—who would show up and spread out his beach towel without necessarily facing the ostensible social problem of solitude. I came to know the relatively small crowds very well and very quickly through regular visits. Many of those "queens of Paradise" turned the individual skill of ignoring others into a performance of utmost collective art. For a young man like Hadi to show up on Paradise Beach, without an inner circle of friends, was quite a rarity that even the nineteen-year-old Rachid would not have attempted when he initially came to neighboring Tam Tam beach with his cousin. I was thus quite intrigued by Hadi, although his juvenile playfulness was not exactly what I had expected to find when I initially embarked on my journey to Jbeil.

Hadi had obviously come alone to Paradise Beach. I never really found out if that was his first visit. In retrospect, I have the strong feeling it was his first time on the famed stretch of sandy beach. He knew that Paradise Beach had, for many years, attracted queer crowds from all over the country, mostly men with the occasional woman whose sexual orientation was not always readily ascertained. Before he interacted with me, I watched Hadi try to start a conversation with almost everybody present. The responses were mitigated, however, with a general reaction that seemed to lean toward indifference. This relative unresponsiveness vis-à-vis his various attempts at engineering a meaningful communication did not deter the enthusiastic Hadi from trying to chat up somebody. Thus, he did not fail to notice that when I arrived at the beach, I was without evident company. It did not take him long before he actively sought to capture my attention.

I was returning from a swim that had taken me far out into the bay, when Hadi commented on the distance I had left behind me with a big smile on his face. He asked me whether I came often to the beach. This question was probably prompted by the fact that it was a pre-summer season weekday, when "normal" people actually went to work. I replied that I came relatively frequently and that, whenever I could, I also enjoyed Paradise Beach in the middle of the week, the relative emptiness of the place being a welcome change from the hustle and bustle of my daily life in Beirut's Ḥamra district. Curious, Hadi inquired about where exactly I lived and what I did for a living. I told him that I lived in Ḥamra and that I taught social sciences, leaving out my specific affiliation with the American University of Beirut. When it came to introducing ourselves with our names, however, Hadi was expectedly puzzled by my first name because it is distinctly non-Lebanese. I duly explained that I was Algerian and that *sufyān* in Arabic was far from an uncommon name in North Africa. Little did I know that the disclosure of this part of my identity would trigger further enthusiasm on the part of Hadi, especially since it rarely did with my other fleeting interlocutors in Lebanon, unless I completed the disclosure by acknowledging my German heritage and—even more so—citizenship.

This was the prime reason why I generally avoided the subject altogether with casual acquaintances. For most of them, I was either an "odd" Lebanese—an identity that, in all probability, was based more on my accent and less on my physical appearance. The latter did not match in the least the imagined collective self of a people with "naturally pale skin." Sometimes, I was assumed to be Palestinian, the ultimate "internal Other" for many Lebanese. On numerous occasions, I was even alternatively perceived as Egyptian. This last identity surprised me most because, at that time, I had never even been to Egypt and my various linguistic intonations were unlike the familiar accents on the ubiquitous *musalsalāt* (TV series) coming from the land of the *byramids*. More than anything else, it was the combination of an "obvious" Arab identity and a dark complexion that put me into the largely imagined wastebasket of an alleged Egyptian identity.

For Hadi, the issues were a bit different, however. It was so at least on the day we met. By telling him I was Algerian, Hadi realized that I could potentially be a Francophone interlocutor for him. "Ana French-educated" (I'm French-educated), he told me with a strong rolling *r*, using typical Lebanese sentence structures intended to stress the presumed cosmopolitanism and symbolic capital of the interlocutor. It turned out that his French was not bad at all, even if it was clear that he had not really mastered the language. He told me that he had grown up partly in Lyons, France, and that he was educated at a Catholic school. At the beginning, I took all of what he told me at face value. Months later, however, the background Hadi had constructed for himself started to crumble bit by bit, which in turn shed an oblique light on a whole series of lies that he carried around wherever he went. Even now, I do not fully know his exact story, but he was certainly not the only young gay man I met in Lebanon who entertained whole edifices of deliberately created false statements and impressions. These façades were meant to cope with a reality that was believed to be unbearable if confronted with clear-cut truth and honesty.

For what I think is that Hadi is the youngest son of a poor Shīʿī family from the historically marginalized Hermel region in the northern Bekaa Valley. At the time, both his parents were elderly. He has many older siblings, although I have never known exactly how many. A year after I met him, Hadi transformed from a witty—albeit harmless—boy into a drama queen of substantial notoriety within queer circles in Beirut. He also started rumors—true or false, I do not know—that one of his brothers was a member of Ḥizballah and was intent on cleansing the family's shame by killing his gay little brother. Once again, the story, as gruesome as it was, might have been accurate, especially as far as hostilities directed toward him were concerned. Whether they included serious death threats from a family member, however, was something I could not ascertain. But in the general light of a widespread practice within certain circles of cultivating the art of *kizib* and *tifnīs* (lies), I always met the possibility of false statements or half-truths with a mixture of deception, fascination, and—almost always—complete powerlessness.[7]

Hadi's knowledge of French had apparently something to do with his attendance at *madrasat al-ḥikmeh* ("The School of Wisdom"). The school was one of the long-established Christian Maronite institutions of primary and secondary education that, in its branch located in West Beirut's Kanṭāri neighborhood next to the city's downtown district, catered to a sizeable number of Muslim students. Whether he actually went there—and if so, for how long and in what exact capacity—remained a mystery to me. But to clear up such mysteries, I readily realized, would ultimately not add or remove anything from Hadi's attention-grabbing life journey. In early summer 2002, I largely perceived Hadi as this endearing *gros bébé* of whom I rapidly grew fond. For that entire summer season, I saw him regularly on Paradise Beach and chatted with him in *franco-libanais* while I rolled my *r*'s as much as I could with that Levantine-French accent I very much loved to imitate.

Despite his initial difficulties, Hadi soon became Paradise Beach's new social butterfly, interacting pretty much with everybody, including some of those gay men who had shunned him at first. Now one might have thought that he had been their best friend for quite a while. Then, in fall 2002, I completely lost track of Hadi. I never saw him at any of the social venues I went to in and around Beirut. Albeit anything but inclusive, these venues catered to a broad range of queer-identified individuals, some of whom, I thought, he would have easily identified with. It was not until winter that Hadi's smiling face appeared before me once again, this time in the company of a few members of HELEM, some of whom I had been introduced to a year earlier.

In the early days when I hung out with Hadi on Paradise Beach, he would not tell me much about his life. Instead, he inquired about mine. Sensing his general reluctance to unveil anything revealing about himself, I refrained from asking too many questions. He mentioned, however, that he lived with some members of his family (not including his parents) somewhere near the Sin al-Fīl and Dekwāneh districts of East Beirut, a neighborhood otherwise referred to as "Nabʿa." Again, whether this was the plain truth, something totally different, or a version in between, I do not know.

Parts of the Dekwāneh district exemplified the broader segregated spatial sectarianism operating in a city like Beirut. While East Beirut had become almost entirely a Christian area during the fifteen years of civil war (as opposed to the much more mixed western sector of the city), there remained a couple of Muslim pockets in the midst of the all-pervading sound of church bells and the ever-present display of saints' shrines and graffiti crosses. In contrast to the rather affluent lower western part of

Ashrafieh, where some notable Sunni families lived around the Baydoun mosque, Dekwāneh was a sizable lower-class neighborhood of Shīʿī Muslims, whose residency in the area predated the beginning of the civil war. When walking in that neighborhood, I was always struck by the sea of green Amal flags with an increasing, but still limited (at the time), number of yellow Ḥizballah banners.

Hadi claimed he lived in Dekwāneh with one of his brothers (the member of Ḥizballah?). Despite his regular visits to the beach during summer 2002, he would occasionally disappear and, upon his return, say he had been at his mother's, somewhere in the Lebanese south. I never asked too many questions about the overt discrepancies. For example, had he not informed me that his parents lived in Hermel, the very northeastern corner of the country where the Bekaa Valley meets the high plains of the Anti-Lebanon mountain chain? But I saw clearly that something was going on with Hadi, something I was not fully able to comprehend, not even by asking some of the other gay men who interacted with him, even though I suspected that he must have had an occasional confidant.

When I finally saw him again in the early days of 2003, Hadi was still his chatty and ebullient self. Something, however, had changed from the early days of our acquaintance. He had appeared to me then just like a jovial kid who was constantly exploring, with a goal I was not always able to figure out. In early 2003, Hadi was staying with a number of friends, some of whom were part of the nascent HELEM. Others were members of *al-khaṭṭ al-mubāshar* (Direct Line), a progressive political group invested in leftist politics and culture. It thus happened that Hadi was living with an older friend, Messoud. In his mid-thirties, Messoud worked full-time for a reform-oriented local NGO and was an activist with both *al-khaṭṭ al-mubāshar* and HELEM. How Hadi and Messoud met, I do not know. I only knew that Messoud shared an apartment with another left-leaning local gay activist in Beirut's neighborhood of Ṣanāyeh and was obviously having an intimate affair with Hadi. From the outside, it looked as if Messoud was indulging in the role of the "older brother" with the occasional sexual benefit. Hadi would talk about this setup with relative clarity, claiming an "open relationship" with the fifteen-years-older Messoud.

That spring Hadi's personality changed quite a bit—at least as far as I could see. Gone was the presumed juvenile innocence, replaced by a particular queer persona, with a transgressive emphasis. He willfully exhibited dramatic gestures and took on the specific role of a young social butterfly whose desire for everybody's attention became gradually more paramount. It was also at that time that I started noticing him at bars in the company of some of his gay leftist activist friends. Given their particular personalities and political commitments at the time, people like Messoud avoided gay-identified bars and clubs and instead patronized social venues known for their politically left-leaning clientele. There they could mix freely with men and women with similar political ideologies.

In the early 2000s, the main hangout for *le tout Beyrouth activiste* was Chez André, a bar located in a relatively small and rather hidden, old-fashioned city mall on Ḥamra Street. Ten years later, the entire shopping center became the site of numerous well-lit bars catering to leftists, gays, and lesbians, but in 2003, one had to know exactly where Chez André was in order to find it. Back then, the smell of cigarettes enveloped anybody approaching the venue, which attracted a number of rugged intellectuals and the self-declared acolytes who worshiped them unabashedly. In addition, many Western expatriates—whether students at AUB, journalists, or a disavowed spy in residence—frequented Chez André. This most idiosyncratic of Beirut social venues was a den of presumably unambiguous political commitments. Its walls were plastered with pre-civil-war local newspaper clippings featuring photographs of people as diverse as Ché Guevara and Georgina Rizk, the only Lebanese Miss Universe (1971), whose first husband's notoriety as a Palestinian political activist may have added to the prestige the "national beauty" enjoyed among many of the patrons of Chez André.

Oddly enough, it was within these walls decorated with journalistic memorabilia of a distant past that Hadi embarked on his social début. Glamour aside, Chez André was still a dark, smoky tavern where the flow of Heineken beer accompanied plates of *ma'ānak*, the small, grilled Armenian lamb sausages. The heated political discussions were to exclude religious talk, according to a discreet and, given the city, almost capricious sign posted next to a huge rack that held everything from local arak to Scotch whiskey.

The owner of this widely known joint was Vartan, a local middle-aged Armenian. Three years after the Lebanese civil war officially ended, Vartan had recuperated his inherited business from hostile militiamen affiliated with the Amal Movement. Considering the generally positive mood prevalent in the mid-1990s, it did not take Vartan long to transform Chez André into a locally famous meeting place. Although a bar in essence, Vartan's tavern would on occasion shift from an exclusive place for political debate to a dance hall. By playing Arabic dance music late at night, Vartan provided those less inhibited among the "reasonable" crowd a platform to indulge in all kinds of hip and belly motions that added to the common effervescence regularly unfolding on the premises.

As far as I know, Hadi was the first avowedly gay young man who would, on a regular basis, get up on a table at Vartan's joint and gracefully move his stout body to old belly dancing tunes. Despite his early successes at Chez André, however, Hadi had not yet matured at that time into the semi-professional performer he would become just a couple of months later. For now, he was trying out the terrain. In other words, he was testing the possible ways in which to appropriate spaces that were physical (i.e., the bar) but also mental, inasmuch as his testing had to do with a concerted effort in (re)configuring an identity of somebody who would eventually emphatically assert: "Ana shāb gay!" (I'm a young gay guy!)

In these early days, Hadi's apotheosis as a belly dancer accelerated when Vartan opened Regusto in spring 2003. The new café/restaurant/bar was intended to attract the same clientele as Chez André (which would close its doors some years later), but the setup was totally different. It was located, mostly outside, on the gallery of the Ḥamra Square business center only a couple of blocks away. Gradually acknowledging the attention Hadi attracted whenever he "made the moves," Vartan hired the young prodigy for a meager tip on weekday evenings in order to entertain the crowds whose conversations would have otherwise been limited to regional social justice—or the lack thereof—and the fantastical possibilities of overcoming Lebanese sectarianism. It was also at that time that it became clear that Hadi had stopped interacting directly—let alone sharing living quarters—with anyone in his family. I even suspected that he refrained completely from visiting his old parents who lived in the isolated Hermel region. Instead, he moved in officially with Messoud and his gay leftist roommate, an arrangement that turned quickly into quite a bumpy enterprise.

After having been introduced to a twenty-five-year-old Syrian assistant fashion designer, Hadi moved into the designer's small apartment one block off Clémenceau Street. His name was Nadim and he agreed to welcome Hadi temporarily. It was a highly unusual living situation for a single young man to rent an entire apartment for himself, and Hadi felt validated in his decision to leave Messoud. What is important to note is that, at the time, he had hardly any money, so wherever he lived, he lived for free. He also let himself be treated to regular meals here and there. Going out further meant that he needed some temporary benefactor who would cover expenses for such a costly clubbing front as the one in Beirut. Despite occasional difficulties, Hadi seemed to juggle pretty well the different elements of his lifestyle, including the regular sexual intercourse with his host at any particular time.

While living at Nadim's, Hadi perfected his belly dancing skills. He spent hours in front of the fully mirrored wall in Nadim's apartment, relentlessly rehearsing all kinds of dance routines to music that he played at maximum volume, so that virtually everybody in a one-block radius could hear it. Although this made Nadim worry about possible problems with the neighbors, he had nothing substantial against Hadi's continuous presence in his apartment. They were not a formal couple, but they did many things together, probably also due to the feeling of obligation Hadi may have had toward his host. They regularly hung out on Friday nights at Mint, a "gay-friendly" bar on Rue Monot. On Saturdays, they went to Acid, the dance club in East Beirut's Horsh Tabet district for which Hadi seemed always to be able to come up with the necessary US$20 entrance fee. On Sundays, both would take the bus to Jbeil and spend the entire day on Paradise Beach.

It was on Paradise Beach that Hadi introduced me to Nadim, with whom I was soon to embark on an intense romance that lasted almost a year before it ended on a deeply ill-fated note shortly after I left Lebanon. In retrospect, I still feel a bit remorseful about the way in which Hadi left Nadim's Clémenceau apartment and provisionally returned to live with Messoud in Beirut's Ṣanāyeh neighborhood. Because of my emotional involvement with Nadim—which transformed into a committed and passionate relationship for quite a while—I moved into the very apartment that Hadi perceived as his personal safe den. In other words, the closer my intimacy with Nadim grew, the less room—in physical and mental terms—there was for Hadi. Moreover, the emotional attachment I had previously developed for Rachid, the former arts student from Tripoli, may also have contributed to spoiling Hadi's chances to get a gig at the TV station where Rachid worked for his partner, Khalil. Even though nothing substantial grew out of the attachment I had developed for Rachid, Khalil ended up building a vivid animosity against me. Worse, he started seeing anybody in my company as a potential threat to him as well as to the status he imagined himself to represent to the outer world.

Even though I did not see it at the time, the sense of remorse I felt later vis-à-vis Hadi did anything but fade away when I recognized how, after all, he did not hold a grudge against me. Following his move back to Messoud's place, we kept in touch and tried to interact the way we did before, although with noticeably less enthusiasm this time around. It was specific places—the beach, Acid dance club, and Regusto—that would continue to bring us together. Nevertheless, it became clear that my initial interaction with the seemingly innocent and chubby young social butterfly more than a year earlier had become something totally different. Part of that difference was due undoubtedly to my own romantic involvements. However, it goes without saying that Hadi had evolved as well. He had grown up, lost some weight, and become a character who inspired awe in some men in and around Beirut. Hadi had also found a way to cope with wide-ranging judgmental attitudes toward him that made dealing with the outside world anything but an easy undertaking. His particular way of dealing somewhat successfully with his difficult reality also liberated him from some of the constraints experienced by other young Lebanese men his age.

To me, Hadi changed a lot over the year 2003. Many factors contributed to this transformation. Apart from his personal investment in belly dancing at Regusto, he also worked part-time at Metallica, a store located near the Concorde movie theater in Ḥamra. The place catered to a wide range of young customers who shared an aesthetic interest in tattoos, piercings, and clothes considered highly alternative by Beiruti standards. Hadi's employment at Metallica was anything but stable; still, he soon began donning earrings and dog collars whenever he went out on weekend evenings. Despite this ostensible toughness, Hadi was a master in queering any individual performance. For that matter, metal dog chains and skull rings always complemented well-done eyebrows and, quite often, circumspect makeup. Yet, Hadi's queer heavy metal look was only one part of his new persona. The other part was firmly anchored in an almost stereotypical feminine sensuality that went beyond the occasional mascara. He would exhibit his personal pursuit of pleasure whenever he felt he was in accepting company.

Socially speaking, Hadi kept political company mostly with his friend and roommate Messoud and with Messoud's acquaintances, but he avoided taking part in a series of direct actions organized by *al-khaṭṭ al-mubāshar* (the Direct Line). His activist interests at the time developed more along the lines of those of HELEM, the local lesbian and gay group that had been founded at the same time he met Messoud. Thus, in March and April 2003, Hadi became part of the undisclosed queer contingent at demonstrations mounted against the then-looming U.S. war against Iraq. His personal dream, however, was to escape permanently from his family and Lebanon and into the imagined abundance of Western Europe with some gray-haired Prince Charming. Yet, as a result of his professional and activist involvement, Hadi also changed his demeanor, as well as the overall attitude with which he engaged his surroundings.

Knowing that for a substantial number of gay men in Beirut he had become prime acquaintance material, Hadi developed a latent, and sometimes quite manifest, sense of arrogance. It infiltrated his self-awareness, which made him relatively aloof to many young men he stopped perceiving as his equals. He continued to interact with me on friendly terms, but it had become plain that he had lost interest in me. Whenever we talked, he avoided looking into my eyes, relentlessly shifting his gaze toward potentially more promising human landscapes. For me, the most striking metamorphosis was his facial expression, especially with respect to his eyes. Initially full of a genuine and direct disposition, those eyes now had become the main instruments of his noncommittal search for instant gratification.

The development of his calculating and scheming skills notwithstanding, Hadi's juvenile fragility remained somewhat intact, and I would go so far as to contend that his persistence in exhibiting indifference and superiority, to an extent, had to do with his various attempts to protect a manifest vulnerability on his part. Even in times of emotional distance between the two of us, I tried to follow some of his intimate encounters with men in their forties to whom he would systematically feel attracted, but who, in response, would oftentimes deal with him as a mere toy for temporary personal enjoyment. Despite the inherent potential of deception, Hadi, in an evident search for paternal love and protection, always fell for men at least twice his age. His preference was for men with substantial gray hair ("*shaʿr shāyib*," as he put it). Only rarely though did any of these men take Hadi and his many aspirations seriously.

When I initially left Beirut to return to New York in early 2004, I had unfortunately all but lost contact with Hadi. On a following visit in the fall, common friends told me that he was not in Lebanon anymore and that a middle-aged German man, with whom he had passionately fallen in love, had taken Hadi to Istanbul to dance at a local nightclub. Again, I do not know whether this information was correct. However, one thing is certain: after a couple of months, Hadi suddenly resurfaced in Beirut, evidently still full of the youthful, resilient energy that he had displayed ever since the first time I saw him on Paradise Beach. Now, back in Beirut and an accomplished male dancer specializing in *raqs sharqī* (Oriental belly dance), Hadi decided, for a variety of practical reasons, to widen his repertoire by including routines featuring the music of Madonna and other Western pop idols. He began to diligently imitate the synchronized movements that experts like Ramzi used in drag performances. In so doing, Hadi made a concerted attempt to conquer, and thus appropriate for himself, the potentially very lucrative world of Lebanese post-civil-war "bachelorette" functions, much to the irritated, and at times fuming, chagrin of Ramzi and other established local drag performers.

I saw Hadi again seven years later. By summer 2011, he had mellowed considerably. He said that he had finally made peace with his family. Having secured a Schengen visa, he was on his way to an international gathering of gay youths in Barcelona. When I returned to Beirut six months later, Hadi was no longer there, and mutual friends confirmed his continued presence on the Costa Brava. No one could tell me how he was faring on the opposite end of the Mediterranean, but everyone was confident that Hadi would do fine regardless of where he lived, always finding his "way to paradise."

The Homosexual Sphere and the Formation and Contestation of Mental Space

The extensive ethnographic example surrounding Hadi and his particular early life trajectory is intended to convey the multi-layered nature of mental space and the numerous ways in which it is formed and contested. It is an ever-shifting area that Hadi and many other young gay people in Beirut have tried to appropriate in order to cope with the different realities they encounter in their daily lives. To follow the individual itinerary of somebody like Hadi, initially over a period of two years (2002–2004), permitted me to distinguish among the diverse and heavily convoluted relations he entertained with his family and peers, as well as with Lebanese society in general. Thus, much more than physical space, it was the mental space of these relations that became my prime focus. The reason for this was my intention to analyze the wide-ranging and, by and large, conflicting hopes and ambitions that Hadi and some of his like-minded peers embodied in their individual attempts at approaching and thus muddling through the particularities of their very own lived realities.

More than by any physical space, these relations that link a young person such as Hadi to his social world were informed by what I have characterized at the beginning of this chapter as a "homosexual sphere." Despite its spatial tangibility, it is a sphere that operates as a continuously unpredictable realm of sorts. It lacks clear-cut order and control but provides the possibility of dynamic identity formations, all supposed incomprehensibility thereof notwithstanding.

Moreover, due to the notorious—and typically overwhelming—need in Lebanon to categorize people by putting them into a socially convenient set of drawers, it becomes increasingly pivotal to consider a whole set of less predictable dynamics. In particular, specific details and motivations in gay practices are the tenets that go beyond any sort of fixities and that, for instance, in the case of Hadi, are often related to the individual minutiae of lived realities. These minutiae unfold precisely within what I have called "zones of encounter." Those—usually open—sites are part of the larger cityscape and do more than just manage to transcend fixities of a spatio-temporal nature. Through symbolic representation by some concerned individuals, they also manage to defy an overwhelming normative orthodoxy, on the one hand, and its socio-cultural correlates, such as unquestioned compliance and mimicry, on the other.

At first glance, this representation is a symbolization that dissimulates more than it shows. However, next to frontal, overt—that is to say, declared and codified—individual performances, this symbolization also encompasses relations that are hidden and clandestine. These relations are linked to relatively concealed zones of encounter, such as particular street corners, half-abandoned movie theaters, and beaches. They are locally reminiscent of sites of transgression, particularly those regarding sexual *jouissance*, and this together with their conditions and consequences. Yet, these social relations can also be linked to zones of encounter that are anything but concealed, where the overt access to a presumably heteronormative space can lead to outright homophobia as we will see in the following chapter. But, as in the case of the café/restaurant Regusto, zones of encounter can also mean the potential for queer appropriations, of which Hadi's regular belly dancing performances are but one fitting example.

CHAPTER 6

The Queering of Closed and Open Spaces: Spatial Practices and the Dialectics of External and Internal Homophobia

An urban environment such as that of the Lebanese capital Beirut contains all sorts of zones of intersecting encounters and correspondences, which different inhabitants of the city assign to specific places at particular times. In turn, these places, be they clearly marked social venues or partly hidden sites, become appropriated and varyingly interpreted by a range of individuals and groups, including, but not limited to, the young queer-identified men among whom I conducted fieldwork. My intent in *Queer Beirut*, and particularly in this chapter, is to show that in post-civil-war Lebanon, the representations of productive relations in spatial discourse do not only encompass relations of state and governmental power. They also always reflect a variety of alternative potencies that become crystallized within the larger context of their own dynamic representations.

The spatial setting of such representations is related, for example, to a presumably random road intersection, entire neighborhoods, or even a variety of particular buildings scattered around the city. Therefore, while the formality of frontal relations in Lebanon is often brutal and based not just on the state and sectarian power structures but also on an assortment of less easily distinguishable social authorities related to class and status, this formality never completely manages to prohibit individual activities that are remotely transgressive or perhaps even outright clandestine and underground. In other words, there may not be power without accomplices and without police, but there cannot be power without those who refuse, in one way or another, to go along with it either.

Appropriating, Contesting, and Representing Space in the Café Sheikh Manoush

In the aftermath of the Lebanese civil war, there were spatial practices in 1990s and early 2000s Beirut that were officially perceived and sanctioned by large parts of society. On the one hand, these practices included the production, reproduction, and destruction of entire districts of the city. This unique development is symbolized by the countless parking lots on sites previously occupied by all sorts of commercial spaces and individual dwellings, and this, with a few exceptions, regardless of the particular neighborhood in question. On the other hand, and despite an overarching normative urban discourse, there have also always been different representations—i.e., counter-appropriations—of space within and without the city.

For example, there are the various appropriations of the café or the nightclub where the clientele changes from day to night times, tuning itself in to the continuous flow of a spatial and temporal tournament of value. These representations are constantly shifting, and they convert those frontal relations of production and reproduction I mention earlier into informal signs and codes that are prone to being heavily contested and struggled over. Spaces of representation, moreover, like the social hubs along Rue Monot in the eastern neighborhood of Ashrafieh or *ḍowntown*, are the best incarnations of "lived spaces" for a more general, even if far from all-inclusive, public. Parts of these spaces, as we will see, also present complex symbolisms associated with the intricate social processes of ascertaining a queer presence in Lebanon.

Thus, by encompassing a carefully selected list of social venues, the practice of "bar hopping"—where one may start the evening at Ḥamra's Regusto, then move to a bar on Rue Monot, before dancing until the wee hours at Acid in Horsh Tabet—eventually becomes a kind of code shared by a specific group of people. It is not a mere appropriation of space, but rather of spaces of representation that include a reframing of these spaces in the form of a temporary displacement, as well as some kind of collective, albeit generally contradictory, social identification. Whatever its specific nature, the local contestation of values in Lebanon is not necessarily teleological in outlook. That is, the process, along with its impromptu results, can never be estimated in advance.

In May 2002, Café Sheikh Manoush closed its doors in a basement on Bliss Street, a mere stone's throw away from the campus of the American University of Beirut. A heedless observer may well have wondered why this bar/restaurant would cease an operation that, only a few months before, was a packed place of seemingly undisturbed homoerotic consumption. The anthropologist, providing s/he is lucky to enjoy the full presence of his or her activated senses, may read and thus decipher—in an almost Geertzian fashion—the always already-existing inter-text, one that is informed by countless local socio-political references. As stressed before, no contestation of values has a preset script, and the various practices such a challenge entails generally lack a clear-cut teleology that is all too easily attributed to them after the fact. As a result, this highly convoluted process, together with its impromptu results, can never be estimated in advance.

Thus, the answer as to why the Café Sheikh Manoush closed its doors, despite its early commercial success, has to do with the intangible nature of socio-political challenge and contestation in Lebanon. Moreover, the answer is located in the larger and often contradictory ramifications of a socially widespread homophobia in the country. Part of that contradiction is that, over the two years of its successful existence, the Café Sheikh Manoush, without doubt, managed to attract large numbers of local gay men. In fact, on Saturday nights until summer 2001, it became part of the local "bar-hopping" topography and something of a pleasure-seeking hothouse of coy male glances and stares. The locale found its legitimacy as a springboard from which people later in the night proceeded to enjoy themselves in dance clubs, notably (again) in the notorious and queer-identified Acid, which was located until its closure in 2010 in the eastern part of the capital.

Success frequently comes coupled with a heightened public visibility, so some predictable problems were already looming for the Café Sheikh Manoush. But before I engage in analysis, let me first describe what the place, with hours limited to the night, was all about at the start of a weekend. Following is an uncensored excerpt of my fragmented notes that I took on a Saturday night upon formally embarking on fieldwork in summer 2001. As with all things uncensored and fragmented, the ensuing paragraphs express a few of the methodological—but also simply human—flaws and weaknesses of the ethnographic novice. However, they further illustrate indirectly many of the theoretical questions that came to haunt me during many years of life and research in Lebanon.

The primary color of the locale is blue, as is the color of the menu, which has a cover outlining an oversized compass and suggestively reads in large English letters, "Café Sheikh Manoush: Where West Meets East," as if intentionally designed for the Lebanese version of a collectively sanctioned amour bleu. One enters the premises from Bliss Street by going some steps down in order to reach an underground lounge decorated in Orientalist fashion à l'arabe. In the middle of the restaurant stand a bunch of low wooden tables around which one can sit on pseudo-traditional chairs that face each other.

At the far left stands the bar where a group of men is sitting on high stools, two rather old fellows and two youngsters. One of the youngsters wears a muscle shirt that accentuates the developed lines of his gym-trained body. Despite the comparatively more mature couple at the bar, the rest of the customers seem to be quite young, mostly men in their twenties. The music is a concoction of 2001 Western summer remixes, but there are also moments when Arabic songs get played, thus enticing large parts of the audience into standing up and moving their trendy—but not always athletic—physiques to the tunes of the sheer zillions of local pop icons . . .

All of a sudden, a group of four male philanderers enters dramatically the Sheikh before deciding to sit in the far right corner that, alas, is situated immediately behind me. I'm facing a dilemma now. On the one hand, I hate sitting in corners myself, or rather with my back to walls, reluctant to hide plainly from my surroundings. On the other hand, I hardly appreciate it when presumably interesting things happen right in the rear of where I am.

Therefore, I have to weigh my own narcissism against my notorious curiosity. The other thing that bothers me is that I somehow recognize one of the two old men sitting at the bar. I must have encountered him in past years when the Sheikh was still in its old location above ground and somewhat less stylish, although still highly distinguishable by its intricate wood paneling taken from the old B018, that featured the names of famous, now defunct, singers, not just Arab, but also European and American. For some reason, I can't forget the Arabic letters denoting "Edith Piaf" and "Elvis Presley."

The old guy is looking at me with his squinty eyes. He actually looks freaky, I must admit. Perhaps he knows why his face looks familiar to me. I doubt it, though. To my right, there lingers a cute young male couple. To tell the truth, there is just one who looks winsome to me, the other embodies something quite rigid and is endowed, I have to say, with anything but a pleasing face . . .

Why is this waiter coming and going in my direction? Judging from his eyes, it's definitely not because of me or because of my empty glass, but rather because of the enticing bachelors in full commotion behind me . . .

Newcomers! And this is not all! It's intriguing to note that another familiar face has just stepped into the Sheikh. And this time, I can even place the person. It's a fellow I literally met in the water. It was while swimming in the waves of Jbeil's so-called Paradise Beach just about a couple of days earlier. Back then, the fellow primarily struck me as being the only one on that stretch of littered sand who actually knew how to swim, indulging his athletic body in sound and studied movements that clearly distinguished him from his drifting peers. After floating inconspicuously next to each other under the burning August sun for a while, we mutually broke the ice by talking about the sun's astounding reflection on the relatively smooth surface of the Mediterranean Sea.

He told me that he was originally from Beirut. However, he had been working in Saudi Arabia over the past couple of years. Having left Jeddah only four days earlier, he already started missing the city. Whether he preferred the Red Sea to the Mediterranean, I thus sheepishly inquired. "Not really," he replied. What he longed for was rather the greater freedom with which Lebanon was presently falling short to provide him. (Later he mentioned to me that his family was awfully eager for him to get married as soon as possible.) "In Saudi Arabia, anything goes and I don't feel looked after all the time like the way I'm being monitored here," he further explained.

Soon later, our conversation started to lose substance. He asked me where my towel was lying and, in stepping out of the water, offered me a ride back to Beirut, which I merrily accepted. But as the moment arrived to leave, I couldn't find him. Had he changed his mind or did something unforeseeable occur? I don't know. In any case, now he's at the Café Sheikh Manoush, standing just about ten meters away from me and ignoring his former fellow bather as best he can.

The waiter finally took my empty glass from which I had been drinking, under compulsion, a rather nondescript cocktail called "Tropicana." Whatever the exact ingredients of this non-alcoholic mix may have been, I wonder . . .

The old guy, along with his younger companion, just stared intensely at me. I'm probably making this one up by way of projection because the eloquent swimmer from Jbeil continues blatantly to avoid paying the slightest heed to me. Nonetheless, I remain intrigued by the fact that next to the fifty or so years-old bald and cross-eyed gentleman sits this attractive youngster with carefully fashioned sloppy hair.

In the meantime, there are two further couples of the older generation making their rather flamboyant and eye-catching entry into the lounge, which—by now—has become an exclusively male space. Such odds notwithstanding, I have to confess that, especially at this point, I'm anything but into the theatrics of these local sugar daddies. But look! One of them exchanges three kisses on the cheek with one of the shabāb[1] *sitting behind me . . .*

Why is the bald man squinting in my direction again? Possibly just in order to get a glance of what is happening at my back where two of the guys are leaving now, yet not before profusely saying "byyyye" to the small crowd sur-

rounding them. The attractive one brings them to the door, but comes back and proceeds with his distracted chat with the barman. In the meantime, the couple to my right is sharing some fruity cocktail. While sucking the proclaimed exotic liquid through their respective purple straws, they seem to be engaged in a balmy conversation.

The cute one's affluent economic background is very much noticeable. He is most certainly some spoiled ibn ʿayleh, *or "son of a family" in Arabic. He sports a thin goatee around his secretive lips. His looks are quite delicate, full of a certain grace. Some would later say that his demeanor has even a feminine touch to it. Whatever that is supposed to mean anyway . . .*

To my left sit two other male representatives of the older generation. As far as I'm concerned, they both appear like relatively square chubby hubbies. And, as it happens, some Greek god makes his way into the Sheikh and greets them. Is this for real or am I just imagining these particular patterns of an odd plot unfolding in front of my eyes? In this case, at any rate, we are talking about an T-shirted blond beauty with an aquiline nose, a tight butt, and significantly developed triceps, again . . .

It's getting too loud, and this annoys me because I have an increasingly hard time bearing, let alone appreciating, the blasting drums of the Sheikh's music in the background . . .

The "son of a family" (or shall I say "family son"?) to my right is at times pensive, nervously putting his purple straw in and out of his mouth . . .

It just occurs to me that I haven't mentioned yet the two TV sets behind the bar. Both are tuned to the locally very popular Fashion TV *and show the latest* tendances *worn by whey-faced super models. At this point, just about everything at the Café Sheikh Manoush looks to me all the more like an unmistakable parade of vanities of some sort that is vigorously being mimicked by the very reality in which I find myself tonight. Yet, at the end of the day, I find myself asking the unavoidable question, "What is fake and what is real in here?"*

I call for the check, and here he comes, the waiter, that is. I guess now the stud from "Paradise Beach" recognized me for sure (as if I have had tentative doubts about it). Still, there is no explicit acknowledgment on his part. Or maybe I'm just incapable of picking up the relevant signs.

For that matter of uncertainty, it always strikes me how much can happen within the apparently mere exchange of a glance. Besides, there appears to be so much of an implicitly assumed recognition that nothing needs to be explicit or even cheaply overt anymore.

No wonder that I find myself in the midst of some thriving pick-up scene. This being said, at the end of the play, there are moments in which I fool my-

self into believing that I can take equal part in this exacting kind of a covert game. However, there are other moments in which I simply can't, let alone go—undisturbed—along with these undoubtedly thwarting rules.

As for the lack of censorship of the above, I hope that the excerpt discloses the difficulties I initially had in approaching theoretical questions, often quite haunting in character, surrounding the tangled interactions among young and not-so-young gay men in Lebanon. Notwithstanding this disclosure, I want first to indicate briefly some of the conjectures that partly delineate the probing conundrum of the queer encounter in Beirut. This indication is necessary in order to tackle in some meaningful way the subject of homophobia and reply to the crucial question as to why, despite all commercial and social success, the Café Sheikh Manoush closed less than a year after I wrote down my first general observations. As becomes manifest in the excerpt, one of the striking aspects of that encounter is to be found in its inter-generational dimension. The category of age is again essential in assessing the dire politics of access and prestige in Lebanon. Thus, the seemingly undisturbed congregation of young men with their older cronies points to what I shall later examine as "paternalism" within the larger context of the homosexual sphere in Lebanon.

But for the moment, I will assess the complex politics of clothing and style as embodied by many gay men in Beirut. In this context, the wearing of muscle shirts—or of what in Lebanon are called "I-shirts" (i.e., a particular version of a tank top that is cut like a T-shirt around the neck but like a muscle shirt around the shoulders)—is primarily intended to display the more or less muscular upper extremities. Further, the willingness to exhibit a gym-trained body is presumed to reveal the sex appeal of the male protagonist. Along with the appropriate accoutrements, such as rings and the occasional designer wristwatch, this willingness underlines wider aspirations to compete for a place within the local realm of a compound process of cultural globalization.

Within such a process, the politics of ideals is often limited to the basic setting of certain fixed types that are collectively reinforced by shared patterns of global consumption. However, such an individual bodily exhibition is usually also a collective attempt to indulge in a global culture, where the major tenets revolve around the mundane consumption of globally circulating fashion and style. Similarly, music plays an important role in fostering the image of the smart and trendy. That being said, the cultural consumption of all things global can in no way be reduced to matters generally deemed as "Western" in form and content. The phrase

"Where West meets East" (and precisely not "Where East meets West"), prominently featured on the cover of the menu of Café Sheikh Manoush, may perhaps point in some cheap way to an essentializing cliché, but it is also a reference to the often contradictory politics of self-perception and self-definition that affects, among many other aspects, a majority of gay men in Lebanon.

Interestingly, however, since the 1990s, Lebanon and the rest of the Arab world have witnessed an important revival and popularity of Arabic pop, making it almost impossible for local dance clubs not to play the songs of the moment. Within the Beiruti homosexual sphere in the early 2000s, it would have been difficult to find somebody oblivious to the salient fact that on weekends—at 1:30 a.m., to be exact!—the DJ at Acid played *ʿarabī* (Arab[ic] dance pop). "Enframed" by the beating remixes of a Said Mrad and the catchy vocals of a Nancy Ajram, the flashy dance club became packed with belly-dancing aspirants trying to give the best corporeal performances. It is precisely this willful synchronization of fashionable bodies, rhythmically moving to synthesized tunes in an eclectic and stylish nightclub, that best captures local interpretations of global habits of consumption.

I expand on this note about dancing at Acid later in this book. For now, I strongly argue that the dominant aspiration for an individual place within the embattled local Lebanese realm of cultural globalization tends to translate into a politics of ideals that often limits itself to the basic assertion of fixed types drawn from the repertoire of a larger post-colonial predicament. Moreover, as becomes apparent in the above excerpt about my early experience in the Café Sheikh Manoush, the general appeal in terms of bodily aesthetics and sexual attraction is typically linked to the exoticism of a complex beauty ideal flourishing among the haunting ruins of a seemingly ageless colonial past. It is an ideal that, as an unfaltering social rule, has the tendency to privilege unabashedly light complexions over all darker ones.

Almost corresponding to a paradigm, I maintain that this ideal ends up being projected onto the blemished mirror of post-colonial haughtiness. Within the homosexual sphere of status-obsessed Beirut, the image of the "blond (and preferably blue-eyed) hunk" transcends in desire, admiration, and prestige the likelihood of all other homoerotic categories, thus discounting practically any kind of counter-currents. This peculiar projection of exoticized images, which are deemed as ideal, always remains, I am afraid to say, quite a pernicious one. To desire the admired "fairness" of the Other—and not the Other as such—by passing over any pigmentation that would be regarded as too "conspicuously dark" puts into perspective a latent and sometimes unapologetically overt racism, which tends to be rampant in Lebanon. It further uncovers the problem of a continuously colonized society faced with the perpetual and deceptive processes of identifying itself according to contrived ideals, all of which are primarily associated with some locally imagined and heavily essentialized Western world.

To assess, therefore, such convoluted processes of identification by dwelling in one's own social space within the homosexual sphere in Beirut is a delicate undertaking for any concerned individual. This includes, for instance, the queer-thinking anthropologist. The consequences that such a social challenge generate always go well beyond any sort of narcissism—whether latent or manifest—on his part. These consequences transcend any semiotic confusion, evident through the possible exchange of misunderstood glares and gazes that, for the most part, form an integral component of the researcher's interactions with his or her would-be interlocutors. These interactions are always potentially predicated on the impending incapacity to pick up relevant signs, which are themselves continuously displaced by all involved protagonists.

Moreover, the displacement of the interactions between anthropologist and interlocutor goes mostly hand in glove with generalized mechanisms of projection and defense, such as the exhibition of arrogance, indifference, and aloofness. All of these generally form an integral part of what I discuss later in reference to Jacques Lacan's "mirror stage" within the larger context of the socio-cultural repertoire of human interaction in Lebanon. Indeed, to recognize people—a happenstance hardly to be avoided in such a minuscule country—does not mean that person A has to acknowledge person B outright. Quite the opposite is de rigueur. As partly illustrated above by the behavior of the young Lebanese man working in Saudi Arabia, you can easily talk to a person at a particular time and in a particular place. However, once those temporal and spatial coordinates have shifted—the exact causes that may generate such a shift notwithstanding—the same person can refrain from looking at you altogether. Instead, "he looks at himself."

Visibility and Its Homophobic Discontents

Within the specificity of the moment and through a distinctive mobilization of covert gazes and gapes on the stage of the Café Sheikh Manoush, familiar faces are always screened first and evaluated by the respective party according to their particular relevance. If somebody happens to lack, for one reason or another, the attributes of a timely social significance, the person in question is generally met either with indifference or with some equivalent negative attitude suggesting that he barely exists. Nonetheless, if a young gay man manages, for better or worse, to entice the attention of his target audience, he will probably find himself at the center of some propitious interest. As a consequence, the ultimate question boils down to this: How is the young gay man to provoke the undisputed acknowledgment of his peers?

The answer lies partly in the strategic ability to display successfully one's own aloofness in the presence of others. Such an ability amounts to a collective power play of sorts where the presumably desired individual, in a stroke of conscious glamour, indulges himself by taking up the part of the unreachable icon. This individual is endowed with a number of social dexterities, from a deliberately short attention span to the capacity to forge false promises—or outright lies (*kizib*, or *tifnīs*), for that matter. These multifarious skills generally help him to get rid of his respective interlocutors in order to move on quickly to somebody—it is hoped—more becoming in appearance and benefit. In addition, such a protagonist, providing he is effective, rapidly assesses his own potential interest in his counterparts and acts accordingly. The question is always how to prepare a face for such a cursory world and how such a world may show itself in the resulting face. To play at being hard to get reflects the ideal of anonymity in encounters within the Lebanese homosexual sphere, which, for the most part, discounts the very idea of sustained relationships, let alone the identifiable commitment this would generate. Yet, the performance of this play also points to local ideals of anonymity in a very small country that is notoriously anything but anonymous.

At the same time, to play the aloof role highlights the deceitful determination to protect oneself. This determination comes in the shape of a covert—but sometimes quite discernible—denial of one's own ultimately non-normative sexuality. In this context, the denial "Ana mesh heyk!" (I'm not like that!), is commonly used by many Lebanese male homosexuals in order to demarcate themselves from those who, on the face of it, seem to carry the perceived lack of their own social acceptability too far. In turn, the production of desire and the resistance to it become a skill. It highlights personal characteristics that are created to be well received in most circumstances by one's own entourage. This creation includes the particular looks of a given man and the various ways this same person is capable of physically mobilizing in order to exhibit actual—or oftentimes made-up—material wealth. Here, the aforementioned complex issue of "paternalism" comes into play. For younger men, generally, the purported prestige associated with any older or mature man is linked, whether directly or through the tangled ramifications of a psychoanalytical projection, to that person's socially perceived status.

In an arrestingly patriarchal setting such as Lebanese society, a social configuration that is so much predicated on the fallacies of categorizing people, the phallic figure of the mature and seemingly affluent male—generally, a locally perceived heavyweight—remains central. This centrality is anything but simple, however. From it, and beyond the local obsessions of relentlessly labeling individuals, originate large webs of complex individual and collective desires and dependencies, as well as a conformist acquiescence that equates male maturity with the opportunities of a prevalent power that occasionally wants to be defied, yet ends up being reinforced all the same. The result of all this is a paradoxical equation that perpetually shifts between defiance and reinforcement. It makes evident the pitfalls of a mainly ordinary situation, one where structures of oppression are adamantly reproduced by precisely those individuals who are understood to be suffering most from their repercussions. Yet, despite everything, these same individuals indulge in the deceitful comfort of normative conformity—as well as in the volition of looking and acting alike—that is generated from thinking and "performing" in a socially acceptable and generally expected way.

This presumption—albeit, certainly, incomplete—coupled with the paradox alluded to above, points directly to the subject of homophobia in Lebanon, which can be traced back to external—and internal—visibility and its resulting homophobic discontents. Thus, despite all commercial and social successes, the Café Sheikh Manoush closed its doors for reasons that are to be found in the conflicting ways in which a collective raison d'être, discounted as "conspicuous behavior" by Lebanese society at large, becomes gradually visible only before it becomes a subject of external—and internal—suppression. On a trivial level, it would have been possible to limit my analysis to the purely factual, for example, in simply stating that the café's owner suddenly did not want a queer-identified crowd as his primary clientele before closing the place. In part, it would even be pertinent to hint at the post-civil-war alacrity of the Lebanese in catering to a home-grown culture of excessive consumption that tended to be predicated on a social craving for immediate gratification. This craving, in the long term, could hardly be satisfied by just one venue, regardless of whether it was queer-identified. Hence, the ubiquitous practice of opening and closing innumerable restaurants all over Beirut. Yet, in the case of the closure of the Café Sheikh Manoush, all of the above reasons alone cannot do justice to the totality of the different shapes that the various knotty processes of homophobia take in a country such as Lebanon. As a matter of fact, these processes are anything but clear-cut in character. Rather, they are marked by bumps and hitches.

By early summer 2001, the Café Sheikh Manoush had not only become one of the main hot spots within the highly contested topography of Beirut's homosexual sphere, it had also started to attract a male queer-identified crowd that, at the time, was in a vigorous process of asserting its social visibility. As illustrated by the above excerpt from my field notes, the place had quickly converted into a stage of ostensibly alternative appropriations, where the intricate interplay of social pressure and individual resistance materialized into a succession of competing encounters and skirmishes. In the end, these contestations remained cautious and rather feeble. They rarely crossed the line in potential defiance of an ultimately overpowering conformist normativity. The display of what would later be denounced by a whole range of detractors as "conspicuous demeanor" provides an example of the contesting of conformist normativity. Such behavior was deemed as inappropriate by men who set themselves above their peers due to what they perceived as a disturbing fact, namely that "men acted like women."

Not that such a conveyed "femininity" had ever been foreign to gay men, or even to society at large, in Lebanon. Socio-historically speaking, quite the opposite is true. Despite its limited and officially unacknowledged nature, an understated—yet effective—local permissiveness had generally allowed for socially marginalized identities in Beirut and elsewhere in the region to prosper—up to a certain point, that is. However, when the corresponding intersections of visibility were perceived as becoming all too excessive and potentially threatening to the order of all things social, as in the examples advanced in previous chapters, suppression made—and still makes—itself manifest as the almost inevitable answer. Suppression, however, can be spelled out in many different ways. What interests me here is not so much state suppression per se. This kind of suppression is a mechanism that continues to be potent and pivotal by way of official persecution, traditionally legitimized by Article 534 of the Lebanese Penal Code that outlaws all "sexual activity that is contrary to nature."[2] Rather than seeking properly external factors, I am much more concerned by the complex dynamics of what I wish to call here an *inter-*

nal, as well as a perpetually *internalized*, homophobia in Lebanon. It is operative and very much present within, and not merely without, the homosexual sphere in and around Beirut.

Odd and trivial as it may appear, the closure of the Café Sheikh Manoush must be explained by the notorious drop of excess that caused the glass of micro-social contingencies to spill its presumed transgressive content. In this context, an increasingly asserted "feminine behavior" on the part of some young male customers not only started to antagonize the normative mental comfort of the café's owner, but also irritated and provoked the hostility of many male homosexual customers eager to demarcate themselves from any kind of potentially incriminating conspicuousness. This eagerness to be different from—i.e., better than—the effeminate *tantāt* leads to a peculiar kind of homophobia that, I would argue, is internal to, and therefore part of, the homosexual sphere in Lebanon. Moreover, the urge for superior distinction within a potentially inferior context is successively internalized by a great number of protagonists who otherwise commonly operate in an undisturbed fashion. It is a demarcation that bears at its core a complicated apparatus of disavowal.

For that very reason, the widespread and emphatic proclamation "Ana mesh heyk!" (I'm not like that!) includes the general rejection of any alternate idiosyncratic differences that may characterize the Other, regardless of whether external or internal. Coupled with particular interpellations denouncing such an effeminate Other, the categorical claim of not being what one actually is, points, by extension, to a convoluted act of projection with a mental—and, at times, physical—violence that cannot be underestimated. The result is that the Other (always with a capital *O*) remains consigned to a position of transcendence. It is a spatial arrangement that separates people perpetually in space, time, and character. Instead of being acknowledged as a coeval referent, the Other becomes associated with some anachronistic representation that prevents him or her from being engaged by all potentially concerned individuals as an equal and, therefore, respected counterpart. Such inability to interact with the Other leads to a neurotic and awfully frustrated performance that clearly privileges the mimicry of the normative over a common recognition and acceptance of difference. The ultimate consequence is the implication of xenophobia in its most literal sense.

This, at first, somewhat hesitating, then violent performance, one that is so strange to the observing eye, bears a frightening potency and increases horror to the realm of social tragedy: If you are not like me and if you do not share similar ideals and compatible desires, you cannot possibly be part of the world I inhabit. Therefore, if I look at you at all, I will look *through* you and ignore your very existence. The underlying neurosis of such a performance may, paradoxically, be based on a profound individual urge to actually express oneself. Yet, this urge tends to mutate into a conformist mimicry that coerces the person into acting out a projected ideal image in which s/he wants to partake. Often enough, the material affluence in personal backgrounds is all but pretended. The lack of money, together with the opprobrious compulsion to look physically like the normative rest, is another instance where relations of paternalism come into play. It is an instance that turns more than a few young gay males to various relations of patronage, where special favors (sexual ones, for instance) are exchanged for particular material means.

To stage this unbridled mimicry in front of television screens, all tuned to the Fashion TV channel, which is committed to the latest designer trends from Europe, establishes a parade of vanities. Here, the anthropologist as general observer, in his relentless attempts at a Bourdieusian "participant objectification," struggles in vain to distinguish between what is fake and what is real. It is precisely this interplay between phantasm and perceived actuality that best characterizes the lived reality within the homosexual sphere in Beirut. There, the conceivable human comedy of the ensuing encounters, ones that are reckoned as public and where challenge rapidly mellows into a melodramatic cliché, ends up covering certain tragic realities that haunt contemporary Lebanese society. In this instance, the structural poverty of individual opportunity forces people, such as young gay men, to surrender before the potent and fortified walls that are perpetually erected by almost everyone in order to protect and preserve the normative social order of things.

In addition, tensions between the personal quest for long-lasting attention and the contradictory display of arrogance toward others are always part of the daily realities in Beirut, of which many are quite tragic. Repression and disavowal, as well as the conceptual divide in the propagation of ideals that exoticize the fair and flaxen-haired by proclaiming its occasional representative as the epitome of beauty—a proclamation predicated on a post-colonial sense of inferiority—often result in an individual suffering that is founded on the collective effort by many gay men in Lebanon to accommodate impotence. I would further argue that the particular conjectures, ranging from the larger context of paternalism to the notorious politics of aloofness and the rampant internalization of homophobia, partly delineate the probing conundrum of the homosexual encounter in Beirut. To a great extent, it is precisely these conjectures that were ultimately responsible for the closure of the Café Sheikh Manoush. This being said, to display a demeanor generally understood as "feminine," or "effeminate" for that matter, is far from having to be interpreted as a detrimental transgression per se. At specific times and in certain situations, transgression may even be welcome by many social protagonists. Yet, the event of a favorable circumstance notwithstanding, such potentially transgressive behavior, providing it is perceived as increasing in visibility, will undoubtedly turn into the declared target of a mentally and sometimes physically violent internalized homophobia.

The always looming potential of violence is based on a deep-seated sense of uneasiness that runs through the various strata in Lebanese society. This is to say that an intensifying visibility of what may challenge social normativity invites, in many cases, the tendency to conflate what is visible with the possibility of a consequential threat to the patriarchal order and, therefore, the protected ideal of male—i.e., masculine—supremacy akin to the locally normative concept of the *'abadāyy*, which roughly translates into a group's self-declared "big man." Accordingly, this is the main reason why any protagonist of potential deviance must be chastised by all possible means.

As mentioned earlier, the more the Café Sheikh Manoush evolved into a prominent hangout for gay men in Beirut, the more economically successful it became as a business enterprise. However, as I also indicated, this success also meant the increased visibility of individuals who were regarded as behaving "conspicuously" and, therefore, in inappropriate ways. As a result of this perception, a double backlash followed. On the one hand, the initial stages of an internal permissiveness gradually mutated into hostility, not only on the part of the owner of the establishment, but also among those homosexual customers who saw their normative social comfort challenged. In several ways, both opted for the deceitful safety of auto-censorship instead of confronting a challenge they sensed would perhaps compromise their presumed undisturbed status—or social reputation—commonly referred to in all local vernaculars as *prestige*. Ultimately, such an option was predicated on affliction and the fear of being socially disparaged. Yet, to censor oneself only became possible after the concerned individuals managed to separate themselves conceptually from the people whose "conspicuous" behavior they exalted in denouncing.

On the other hand, the resulting ramifications of an internalized and outwardly perpetuated homophobia—one that always takes various forms of latent as well as manifest aggression and bellicosity—prompted the majority of the clientele, in an almost ironic turn of events, to a progressive withdrawal from the café. Finally, after staying empty for a couple of months, the formerly lucrative Café Sheikh Manoush was forced to close its doors in May 2002. Before and even during the pivotal 2001 summer, the café had, of course, never been the sole Beirut social venue that, for one reason or another, welcomed homoerotic encounters. My motivation to draw on this specific example is informed by my realization that it is crucial to illustrate some of the many complications that producing queer space in Beirut forcefully entails. What happened at the Café Sheikh Manoush encapsulates all these different dynamics.

After the closure of the café, the general visibility of a male and queer-identified crowd in Beirut on the image-wary surface of Lebanese society did anything but decrease. Neither did the enduring presence of the potentially "conspicuous" detractors I have mentioned here all along. Instead, substantial parts of the local homosexual sphere started to contest and appropriate a multiplicity of what they saw as alternative spaces, some of which were characteristically closed (semi-private), while others were specifically open (mostly public). This process of spatial appropriation created a tangled series of actions that remains to this very day inherently mocking of the easily scandalized. These are also actions of perpetual violent contestation, antagonism, and human suffering.

Psychological Aggression and Physical Violence: Another Story of Ramzi

To give further ethnographic credence to the various homophobic practices of violent contestation, antagonism, and human suffering in Lebanon, I offer a concrete example of violent homophobia, where psychological aggression and outright physical violence form a deceitful pair. In speculating on the possible motivations behind this particular event, I focus on the receiving end of an instance of homophobic violence in the wider context of compound understandings of masculinity that idealize the concept of the *'abadāyy* and include the sheer actuality of xenophobia.

Times of internal political crisis in Lebanon have often led certain individuals and groups to search for easy scapegoats, among whom gay men have historically formed an unfortunate target group. Generally, one or several men who were identified as gay would be accused of having broken the law, an allegation fully separate from the men's supposed or actual sexual orientation. An imagined felony—such as theft, for example—would be brought up, a crime far removed from the actual causes behind the charges filed. This sort of search for—and indictment of—somebody who could be unjustly blamed for causing a social affront targets mostly those who dare to challenge, symbolically as well as practically, otherwise heavily contended normativities. This is one of the main reasons why many gay men in Lebanon have been historically afraid of being overly visible within the larger public realm and have felt obligated to avoid the appropriation of certain urban spaces, some of which are exceedingly pivotal and contested by Lebanese society at large.

I cannot emphasize enough my observations of how the politics of homophobia in Lebanon is a highly complicated issue. Many—not necessarily uncritical—voices would argue that the country is replete with gay men who have no more difficulties in living their sexual orientation than their brothers on the northwestern shore of the Mediterranean. However, the expressions of homophobia are multiple, to say the least. In Lebanon, they intersect with expressions of gender, and their strength—or weakness, for that matter—must always be understood in correlation with the particular socio-political situation of the moment. This situation is one that can change from one day to the next. Moreover, when they are strong, homophobic expressions in Lebanon tend to be directed toward individuals whose behavior is subjectively perceived as being socially inappropriate. The causes that prompt such a perception are commonly due to an uneasiness triggered by a non-normative gender behavior in the eyes of many social conformists. This behavior, in turn, is interpreted as a major danger that, from the perspective of the powerful, must be fought off by all possible means.

This regrettable reality is no random occurrence, however. It is exemplified in numerous hateful incidences I came across in Beirut, the most notable happening to my friend Ramzi, who had been exposed to much homophobic violence over the years. Ramzi's personal experiences with such violence can primarily be traced to his apparent "difference," a social variation of sorts based in part on his bodily demeanor identified by some as "effeminate" and, therefore, out of place by the perpetrators of this violence.

Within a period of only a few months, Ramzi was aggressed and beaten at least twice in the middle of the street, not far from East Beirut's Sassine Square close to his home, purportedly because of his "effeminate gayness." The first incident involved a "psychotic" service driver who, as soon as he saw Ramzi's "difference," began to act in an explicitly hostile manner, mimicking his customer's speech and bodily gestures in the most distasteful way. It should be noted that Ramzi was no complete stranger to such reactions, but he definitely was unaccustomed to the shift from passive-aggressive "mental violence" to actual eruptions of physical brutality.

I distinctly remember occasionally being the target of antagonistic verbal comments when I walked the streets of Beirut with "visibly effeminate gay men" like my friend Ramzi. Not that this was a rule in any meaningful way: he and I, after all, had roamed the alleys of working-class neighborhoods such as Barbīr and Burj Ḥammūd without ever having had a single negative experience. Yet, mounting tension could be felt at specific moments and in certain places in and around the Lebanese capital. This tension would mostly manifest in "open" spaces and at relatively exposed locations—major crossroads, for example—and generally in confrontation with a group of young men, but never with lone individuals. In these uncomfortable situations, I always felt that an unruly crowd best characterized many hostile expressions in Beirut. In fact, I never witnessed anyone display homophobia without the apparently necessary backup of at least two other individuals. Oftentimes, this would translate into the individual manifestation of an *'abadāyy* who, in front of "his" crowd, would put on an elaborately performed show of orthodox—i.e., normative—masculinity intended to impress everybody present, reassert his own status within the group, and, of course, thoroughly intimidate the person on the receiving end of this game. Yet, one of the game's rules, it always seemed to me, was that the same individual who in a group performs the role of a lion, is the most docile animal when caught alone.

At the time Ramzi became the target of physical aggression, he was unfortunately alone, leaving *ḍownṭown* for home. But instead of walking the relatively short distance, he decided to take a service to Ashrafieh. The trip from Martyrs' Square up the hill to Sassine Square is quite short and generally does not take more than five minutes if there are no huge traffic jams. There were not many cars on the road when Ramzi flagged down a service, which was headed eastward and already carried a young male passenger on the backseat. Ramzi joined the other customer and instantly felt the gazing eye of the driver staring at him in the car's back mirror.

In a mere few seconds, the driver showed Ramzi that he disapproved of him. He asked, using the grammatical feminine in Arabic, "Kīfik al-layleh ya ḥelwa?" instead of "Kīfak al-layleh ya ḥelū?" (How are you tonight, my [female] dear?). Ramzi did not answer, which prompted the driver to address his other customer: "ʿAmm t'kebbar ḥālha al-ḥelwa" (She's arrogant/aggrandizing herself, the [female] cutie). In response, the young man began to giggle offensively. Not long after, the service reached the upper end of Rue Monot, near the SODECO roundabout, and the snickering customer got out. At this point, Ramzi definitely should have exited the car as well, but for some reason, he remained seated, alone with the hostile driver, who started a series of angry rants against his still silent—albeit heavily agitated—customer. When the service reached the heights of Sassine Square, Ramzi said, "ʿAmul-maʿrūf law samaḥt" (Please have the kindness, if you don't mind, [to let me off]).

By this time, the driver was calm, yet he asked Ramzi for a taxi fare of LL 5,000 (US$3.33). The amount usually required for a service at the time was LL 1,000 (US¢67). Ramzi finally snapped; asking for a taxi fare for such a short ride was a clear act of provocation on the part of the driver. Apart from that, Ramzi had not only flagged him down as a service, but the car already had a customer, an obvious sign that the vehicle was intended to be publicly shared with others for rides within the city limits of Beirut.

However, the driver would not have any of it. Rather, he became increasingly aggressive while remaining steadfast in his unwarranted demand for *khamstalāf* or five thousand Lebanese lira. Sensing that the situation was hopeless, Ramzi dropped a LL 1,000 bill on the front seat and exited the car as quickly as he could. Unfortunately, he was not fast enough. The service driver got out of his car in order to chase his customer. When he caught Ramzi, he threw him on the street and started to beat him up. Ramzi retaliated by hitting the driver with his cell phone.

As it happened, Ramzi struck the driver's head, which resulted in a small cut that began to bleed. The cut was nothing major, but it enraged the driver even more. He cursed Ramzi, using all kinds of epithets that would have made any thug blush. People in Sassine Square, the heart of upper-middle class Christian Ashrafieh, started gathering around the scene. To them, it looked as if a "ruffian faggot" had attacked an innocent cab driver, who had not been paid the appropriate fare. It did not take long before the *darak*, the local police or gendarmes, arrived. They took both Ramzi and the service driver to the nearby station. There, reports were filed that clearly stated that Ramzi was the foremost aggressor. The driver, judged to be a mere victim of a "pervert's criminal principles," was released almost immediately. Ramzi, however, was put into the police station's secure unit, and his family was contacted and informed of the "official version" of the incident.

Thanks to some high-placed contacts from the days when Ramzi's father worked as a civil servant, he was able to secure an early release for his son. Already worried about Ramzi's lifestyle, his parents began to grow even more anxious about his safety. In turn, Ramzi, who had been physically assaulted and utterly traumatized, did not leave his family's house for many weeks. Further, it took him several months to partially reclaim his former social life for which the appropriation of countless closed *and* open spaces in and around Beirut had been of pivotal importance. Moreover, Ramzi never found the justice that would have somewhat redeemed the physical and psychological horror he had experienced. He filed a second report at the police station, but it never led to anything but an encounter with a cynical officer on duty whose own homophobic attitude reminded Ramzi of his friend Georgette's "egg treatment." Unfortunately, the media were not more receptive. Ramzi contacted the main Lebanese newspapers, none of which wanted to run his story. The exception was a relatively new daily funded by the state of Kuwait. It printed an article written on the subject by a journalist whose framing and overall tone was of no help either.

Strangely enough, even HELEM, the newly founded Lebanese lesbian and gay advocacy group was not able to back up, and thus officially validate, Ramzi's unfortunate story. He never understood the organization's lack of interest. Did the responsible counselor at the time think the matter was "too political"? Was it a lost cause, as far as LGBT activism in Lebanon was concerned? Or could it be that he was turned off by Ramzi's personality, which was a mixture of intellectualism, strong-minded determination, and campy effeminacy? I never managed to find an adequate answer to these questions.

Alas, the service episode was not the only violent homophobic incident experienced by Ramzi during the time I knew him. He was attacked once more on Sassine Square. This time, however, not by a "straight" homophobe, but rather by a gang of young local men whose homosexual hustling activities were known beyond the narrow limits of Ashrafieh's main plaza. One can only speculate about how Ramzi, who had to flee the place to a chorus of laughter and bawdy remarks, was perceived by his tormentors. Here was a relatively successful local drag queen, who also appeared to be highly educated. At the same time, people knew that Ramzi frequented places where anyone with the social potential to *shūf ḥālu* ("to look at himself" is the Lebanese Arabic equivalent of "to be arrogant," discussed later) would never consider spending time. In other words, Ramzi could not easily be put into one of the many drawers Lebanese society seems to provide for its constituents. And this was extremely unsettling to some. He incited jealousy and, consequently, blatant anger.

Ramzi's perceived ostensible effeminacy, which many equated with emasculated weakness, led to verbal attacks by the gang on Sassine Square that, soon enough, became a physical assault. He found himself in immediate confrontation with half a dozen male hustlers, who were indirectly backed by countless disaffected, upper-middle-class citizens. Their unwillingness to help a bullied victim was motivated by a mixture of indifference, fear, and an underlying negative judgment toward a group of people whose very morality was put socially into question. With upsetting irony, the group of bystanders equally and negatively looked down upon the hustlers-turned-mob and their victim, Ramzi. Their undiscriminating negative moral judgment made Ramzi's cherished daily perambulations in the streets a real torment.

The momentary hostility exhibited by the examples above is, without any doubt, motivated by the "here and now" and the particular situation at hand. However, I would also argue that the (almost) "structural danger" that somebody like Ramzi generates—whether in the eyes of the hustling mob, the disaffected onlookers, or even the "psychotic" service driver—prompts, to a large extent, the above-mentioned escalations of violence. Importantly, in the relative short term, I maintain that this danger has to be understood within the context of the general political instability that has been affecting the country since the end of its civil war. In the long term, however, one cannot dismiss an almost constant underlying aggression prevalent in Lebanon within the broader experience of conflict and war that the country has been living through for times seemingly immemorial.

Moreover, I would assert that it is this highly politically explosive state of affairs, whether short- or long-term, that, beyond the many structurally homophobic social problems already to be reckoned with, tries to marginalize a homosexual presence as such. It is a marginalization that, for a variety of reasons, is brought into existence in part by some gay men themselves. Note that the well-heeled, arrogant fellows sitting at the Café Sheikh Manoush are gay, as are the working-class hustlers roaming around Sassine Square. This state of affairs renders difficult, even if not impossible, any individual attempts in Lebanon at living the unharmed life, physically and mentally speaking, of a self-identified gay man. Within that structural impasse, there are some people who are made repeatedly unhappy—if not miserable—by others who, to begin with, have been coerced into irrevocable sorrow themselves.

As a poignant paradox, such condescending pretense is often itself based on a profound individual—albeit hopelessly aborted—urge to express oneself. The secret desire for difference notwithstanding, which is akin to a desperate cry that bears no recognizable acoustic discharge, the results of this urge tend to mutate into a social coercion where implicated persons—such as the mob, the bystanders, and the service driver—are made to believe that once they are no longer protected by the imperial garments of social conformity, their lives are bound to collapse. Thus, they are compelled to act out ad infinitum a projected and fictive ideal image that, fearing exclusion, they feel obliged to uphold and actively partake in. As we will see in the following chapter, by providing the stage for an interference of gazes and stares, where different actors, the public, and the text, along with its author, meet, the various spaces of individual and collective performances are—despite all social prohibition—appropriated in a multiplicity of ways by the homosexual sphere in Beirut.

CHAPTER 7

The Gay Gaze and the Politics of Memory: A Stroll on the Corniche and a Walk through Zoqāq al-Blāṭ

Beirut's eventful seashore promenade, known to everybody by the French word *corniche*, is situated below the Ḥamra district in the western part of the city. Over the years, the Corniche has managed to retain a sort of timeless social substance. In many ways, the promenade embodies a perpetually enacted microcosm within the clashing context of the macrocosmical social theater of one of Beirut's main stages. During its rich and conflicting urban history, the Corniche has, by and large, remained a twenty-four-hour-long experience. Its various sections, each different in character, stretch from ʿAyn al-Mraisseh in the city's northeast to Ramlet al-Bayda in the southwest. And in each, the bustle of urban life is always present, day or night. Despite the manifest enactment of a larger social macrocosm within the spatial confines of a parading ground, the Corniche today is also the socio-historical product of a post-civil-war society widely obsessed with the importance of hierarchies and haunted by the sore politics of class-based and ethno-religious segregation.[1]

The Queering of Open Spaces in Beirut: Strolling on the Corniche

In this light, it is only to the idealistic and uncritical observer that the Corniche is one of the few places in Beirut where almost everybody congregates. However, the truth about Lebanese patterns of congregation is also that, despite all limitations, there are always individuals who manage to contest and appropriate certain spaces that go far beyond the social confines of a lived normative conformity. Similarly, the impediment of spatiotemporal fixities does not stop at an active production and appropriation of what I have been calling "queer space." According to the particular time

Life on the Corniche, June 23, 2011.

of day or night, and the particular part of the Corniche, even the most fleeting partaker manages to encounter *shabāb* (young men) of all sexual persuasions who congregate mostly in groups, but also sometimes wandering alone. If alone, the young man in question would unfailingly lean on the railing of the seashore promenade and gaze selectively at virtually everybody who happens to pass by.

Although there are always people present on the Corniche, the seashore promenade becomes crowded for the most part in the evenings—weather permitting, that is. By the time the setting sun finally disappears in the waves of the eastern Mediterranean, the Corniche is jammed with people. In fact, the more temperate the evening during the months of May to October, the more people indulge in either a brief or longer *gazdūra* (stroll) on the city's generally action-packed Corniche. All of a sudden though, the blackness of the night makes itself known. Because of enduring electricity problems pertaining to the larger and long-lasting crisis of the local energy sector, some of Beirut's streetlights often remain turned off. Oddly enough, it is precisely this lack of visibility on the Corniche that allows for a heightened social activity that is closely related to the numerous sociable undertakings in this place of bustling urbanity.

Considering that during the day Beirut is a haven for flings and flirtations of multiple kinds, it is easy to fantasize that in the dark anything goes. But this remains a fantasy, even if some occasional lived reality sometimes appears to come close to it. What a bitter irony it is, therefore, to recognize how even the city's electricity shortage may be converted into a social happening or even a personal adventure where the appropriation of space challenges the contestation of personal dispositions and identities. But this, of course, always remains highly liminal and limited to specific sites and areas that can sporadically defy order, authority, and convention. Such spaces, however, may be, to some degree, prone to ultimately reconfirm what they initially set out to challenge.

In order to provide a tangible example of some of these sites and areas along the Corniche that manage to provide a broad stage for the occasional transgressive act and, in so doing, circumvent the otherwise endorsed order of general respectability, I embark on an epigrammatic stroll along Beirut's main promenade. While this walk is reminiscent of the queer urban stroller's traveling practices delineated in chapter 3, it is also an effort to activate once again the *flâneur*'s sensory system, thus providing his alter ego, the anthropologist, with the ability to engage in what Bourdieu calls "participant objectification."

If, after midnight, one abandons the immediate area closest to *ḍowntown* and strolls toward the sea, one leaves behind the newly furbished Zeytouna Bay Marina with its glitzy pretense of an imagined St. Tropez to the right. This is the eastern end of Beirut's historical hotel district and the very site where a huge bomb destroyed the convoy of the former prime minister, Rafik Hariri, in spring 2005, killing him and almost everybody else in his entourage. The haunting place between the rebuilt and expanded Phoenicia Hotel and the still intentionally dilapidated Hotel St. Georges gives way to a promontory where, over the next couple of meters, the entire acoustic ambiance seems suddenly to change. The babble of supposed socially permissible activity that stirs men's and women's voices against the Corniche's background transforms into an altogether different universe, further west and across the street from the mosque of ʿAyn al-Mraisseh. Within the labyrinth of shadows stretching westward in the direction of the new towering lighthouse, some canonical magic is taking forceful effect.

The construction of the new *manāra* (lighthouse) at the very tip of Rās Beirut was finished in 2003.[2] The main reason for a new lighthouse was the uncontrolled building boom in post-civil-war Lebanon. This unrestrained growth made it relatively easy for all sorts of local potentates

The Phoenicia Hotel with the old Holiday Inn behind it, June 24, 2011.

to put up high-rises wherever and whenever such an enterprise happened to satisfy a momentary business whim. Such was the case with the new *manāra*. The old—and substantially smaller—lighthouse, located slightly uphill from the Corniche, had been partly eclipsed by an illegal high-rise apartment building in its immediate vicinity. Quite a few cynical voices speculated in 2003 about how soon the new lighthouse would become a nuisance for a new generation of influential builders. At the time, however, little did these cynics know that it would not at all be builders as such, but rather strategic destroyers who would soon leave their unquestionable, disparaging mark on one of the new symbols of Lebanon's architectural pride.

In July 2006, an Israeli missile destroyed parts of Beirut's new lighthouse barely three years after its inauguration. The violent attack on the new *manāra* was only one part of the devastating Israeli onslaught unleashed on the entire Lebanese territory during that summer. While virtually all of Lebanon fell prey to the bombings of its southern neighbor, the area around the Ḥamra district, of which the quarters of Rās Beirut and Manāra were the western extension, remained mostly untouched. The notable exception was the new lighthouse, for its strategic and symbolic

The old *manāra*, June 22, 2011.

value turned it into an almost necessary target for the Israeli forces. Strategic and military significance aside, the *manāra* interests me because of the larger symbolism emanating from its very structural nature. It is a three-dimensional piece of architectural overstatement with an imposing stature that can hardly be dismissed within the wider realm of Beiruti representations of power and potency. To jump a bit ahead in my deductions, I would go so far as to argue that, even more important than its strategic significance in military terms, Beirut's new lighthouse was bombed in a further symbolic attempt on the part of the Israeli state to emasculate its imagined northern adversary.

Let me explain this further. By the very nature of its architectural imposition and casually intimidating character, which is not unlike the new Mohammad al-Amīn mosque *ḍownṭown*, *al-manāra al-jadīda* (the new lighthouse), as the concrete structure is commonly called, not only takes the material shape of an omnipresent watchtower, it also appropriates the unmistakable meaning of the urban phallus par excellence. This is the foremost reason for why one need not speculate much about the dire consequences of a castration—or emasculation—complex that has been engendered by the 2006 Israeli summer onslaught, including a number of

The new *manāra*, June 20, 2011.

socio-cultural and psychological ramifications that have to be assessed on multiple levels.

For now, let me go back to my stroll on the Corniche and the numerous ways in which the new *manāra* had been perceived and appropriated shortly after its inauguration in 2003 within the various mental spaces produced by many inhabitants of Beirut. In the shadow of the lighthouse, the strolling *flâneur*-cum-anthropologist, after activating all his senses, becomes the observer—if not to say the self-conscious voyeur—of multiple forms and physiognomies in the almost all-encompassing night. Through the lenses of *flânerie* as a form of intimate and purposeful observation, one realizes how faces of all shapes and colors gaze with feverish intensity at each other. The only continual assertiveness is the cacophony of car noises but also of different intonations and dialects that resound at all hours from every possible back corner.

When passing the *ḥammām al ʿaskarī* (military bath) at the end of the Rās Beirut promontory from June to August, one easily distinguishes the privileged acolytes of Lebanese army officers as they—men, women, and children—enter the heavily protected premises on weekend mornings and afternoons. It is easy for the outsider to imagine them sunbathing on their martial chaises longues while being watched and "protected" by physically over-endowed soldiers, whose most coveted and highly visible equipment is—apart from their ubiquitous machine guns—their professionally developed triceps. The less fortunate, however, are denied access and thus proceed on foot toward Beirut's effervescent Luna Park. At the park on weekends, people mostly from the capital's southern suburbs indulge in the humble but popular joys of riding a slightly decrepit Ferris wheel while listening to the blasting sounds of overly recycled tunes sung by one of the countless Lebanese pop divas, such as the barely tolerable Najwa Karam.

Moving slowly away from these acoustic discharges and up the only real hill that shapes the topography of the Corniche's otherwise relatively horizontal landscape, one reaches the area of Raoucheh, a section of West Beirut that was originally famous for the Pigeon Rocks, formations that to this day define its coastal line. Even from the outside, the chichi atmosphere of such restorative places as the so-called Petit Café and its "Grand" counterpart imposes itself on anybody who happens to walk by. Between the indistinguishable aesthetics of "small" and "big," the "Orient," and whatever its current globalized incarnations may yield in terms of postmodern consumerism, is near its best in blatantly Orientalizing itself. On this particular stretch of Beirut's seashore promenade, the restless spirit of hollowness is successively reinforced the farther south one walks. While what for some time was called the "Palm Springs complex," with its always-packed Starbucks, could not look phonier in its painful imitation of Floridian hacienda-style architecture (itself a brazen fake), it is best equipped to rival the unusually large, yet equally bursting, Burger King next door.

If you ask at this point whether you have seen it all, the response would be a simple but emphatic "no." The Arabian phantasmagoria of the Mövenpick Hotel, built in 2002 with money provided by Walid bin Talal, more or less on the opposite side of the street from Burger King, tellingly flies the flags of Lebanon, Saudi Arabia, and Switzerland in the Mediterranean sun. This luxury hotel features a huge white entrance-driveway in the shape of an oversized Arabian tent and beats everything else along the Corniche in providing a mirror, even if a largely unnoticed one, for many a fair of local vanities that pose as breathing the air of the world while in fact choking on the self-imposed rules of conformist mimicry.

Yet, it would be ultimately misleading for the anthropologist to limit his or her observations to the overtly phallic manifestations of normative power, regardless of whether these manifestations are in the form of architecture or within the intransigent frame of social hierarchies in

Lebanon. Again here, the anthropological importance of looking beyond these fixities applies especially in light of the practitioner's relentless attempt at "participant objectification," one that is ultimately intended to gain a reflexive distance from an oftentimes despair-provoking subject matter where the sheer proliferation of self-indulgence can easily make anyone weep. This particular kind of anthropological despair, coupled with the occasional urge to reach for a tissue, feeds not only on the many individuals for whom, for a multiplicity of reasons, access to the illusory heights of an earthly paradise of high-end consumerism is denied, or at least made extremely difficult, but also on the potential violence, physical and mental, such denial entails. Thus, everywhere on these sections along Beirut's Corniche, next to those individuals suffocating from the ramifications of their inimically performed privilege, there are always these countless others for whom this type of suffocation is not even a remote option.

Even if the margins have the general tendency to be adamant in asserting their potential for facing any sort of dominant current, within the nervous context of post-civil-war Lebanon, the quietest transgressions often tend to be engulfed by the powerful whirlwinds of social conformity. As I have argued before, the actual lack of belonging to certain locally promoted ideals not only results in gawky wannabe-bourgeois mimicry but also, ultimately, in a widespread suppression of socio-cultural difference in such a contradictory place as Beirut.

In a variety of ways, the Corniche provides the stage for this very upsetting paradox, one that becomes more and more physical from one stretch to the next. At the southern edge of Prince Walid bin Talal's pompous Mövenpick Hotel, for instance, one passes the construction site of another of these seemingly random and nondescript luxury high-rise apartments. Yet, what displays manifest randomness and active amnesia can be the hidden site of memory. So it is in this case, for one is facing the location of the now-vanished but to this day still-famous Hotel Carlton, itself a tourist resort of yesteryear. Rare are the locals who do not have a personal story to tell about the Carlton with a past glory that is incidentally not only associated with the ostensibly undisturbed hedonism of the pre-civil-war era but also with the highly entertained homoerotic joys of its late mayoral owner from the Lebanese mountain district of Kesserwān, the notorious Antoine Medawar.

Despite the singularity of a past deemed "glorious" by many, the Hotel Carlton, fifty years after its construction, was no more. Even the promontory rock on which the edifice was perched had been dynamited away to make room for the new apartment building, the so-called Carlton Resi-

The location of the former Hotel Carlton, June 27, 2011.

dences. In the new millennium, chain entertainment complexes like the Mövenpick Hotel took over completely from a long tradition of family-owned establishments that dated from the first part of the twentieth century. Apart from major shifts in the Lebanese tourism industry after the 1975–1990 civil war, the poor condition of the Hotel Carlton shortly before it closed had as much to do with the violence unleashed in its vicinity during the war as with the results of the varying strategic alliances that the Maronite owner was able to successfully negotiate in order to keep his property out of the way of the then-ubiquitous shots and bullets.

Ten years after the end of the Lebanese civil war, the Hotel Carlton bore haunting witness to a scarred and painful past. The building that had stopped welcoming visitors in 2001 was, until its demolition seven years later, still full of its early seventies-era furniture with its psychedelic colors and designs that were reminiscent of a quite defunct and unrecoverable past. I often wondered about this past, especially as symbolized by the old hotel. Granting that a good portion of misplaced nostalgia accompanied my deliberations back then, I could not but imagine all the possible implications stemming from a setup where a bygone world, in the shape of the Carlton in near ruins, looked down upon the deterring animations

Ramlet al-Bayda, June 27, 2011.

of the present world, as manifest in the Mövenpick and its surroundings. Informed by such a pondering state of mind, I continued on my journey along Beirut's long and winding Corniche. I often wondered about whether there was the slightest chance that the city's past and present would ever reconcile. After all, Beirut was an urban setting forever full of twists and turns that kept its occasional observer in an almost permanent state of bewilderment, fascination, and rage.

For better or worse, the next actual turn on my journey was not far away and comparatively close to Rue Chouran, the famed address of the former Hotel Carlton. Ramlet al-Bayda, the urban beach stretch, euphemistically referred to in Arabic as "White Sands," can be spotted as soon as one looks away from the immediate vicinity of the Carlton. The general perspective is also eased because of the physical features of the terrain itself. The area around Raoucheh is comparatively higher than its surroundings and, therefore, permits an almost unimpaired view of that particular part of Lebanon's capital city.

Leaving the Hotel Carlton behind, I make a slight descent on the Corniche, which, at its southern end, turns into a boulevard. On the left, a row of luxury apartment high-rises borders the boulevard, and, on the right, Ramlet al-Bayda. From a distance, one could almost mistake this part of the city for some sort of local Ipanema. However, as with many things in Lebanon, an up-close view reveals vistas that are quite different from the initial fantasy. These days, the sands are far from white, but rather widely littered and washed by a sea afflicted with a rotten smell and a color that frequently tends toward a questionable green. Still, the beach retains popularity among those crowds who cannot afford the high entrance fees to the trendy resorts outside the city. The contradiction could not be more straightforward. On one side of the street, the rich and beautiful sit high above the boulevard on their large balconies while sipping the most exotic cocktails under the Mediterranean sun, and on the other, down (t)here, one encounters the "noise" of crowds trying hard to have their share of a summer diversion.

Male Cruising and Homoeroticism: A Story of Ali

The blatancy of spatially fixed and fixing social hierarchies is evidently not limited to this particular site, nor are its human representations reduced to manifestations that occur in daylight only. On the contrary, Ramlet al-Bayda is one of the foremost zones that facilitates the initiation into male homoerotic encounters in Beirut. Nights tend to transform the boulevard into a parading ground for anticipated sexual gratifications, but occasionally also for yearning—albeit often aborted—romantic desires. One can walk at any time during the night on the sidewalk of Ramlet al-Bayda and encounter a variety of men, young and old, walking or sitting in their cars, waiting for something to happen. The confrontation with suggestive gazes, and sometimes evocative bodily postures, makes it clear to the observer that the apparently blasé dude leaning on the railing *khasso* or *fāyit bil-jaw* (respectively, is concerned with or is part of the [gay] atmosphere), according to the elaborate local vernacular.

In fact, this inherent state of suspended intentionality very well summarizes what kind of activity homoerotic cruising is within the parameters of an "open space" such as Beirut's Corniche. Before any kind of direct interaction involving speaking takes place, let alone one that includes physical contact, the ubiquitous exchange of gapes and stares respectively assesses and categorizes the potential object of desire. There is always a certain shared familiarity to this demeanor, and everybody who is part of it seems to abide by some set of informal codes and criteria that regulate what takes place on this particular stretch of seashore promenade.

As persuasively portrayed by the first pages of Nabil Kaakoush's photomontage, "Hey Handsome" ("Ya ḥelū"), the visual registering of the presence of somebody who "is concerned"—*khasso*, that is—is usually followed by a supposedly credulous, yet highly calculated, verbal interaction, intended to confirm the respective protagonists' motives.[3] Following the never-failing inquiries about the exact time or about borrowing a cigarette, a rehearsed, yet only seemingly disinterested, and sometimes even indifferent, dialogue ensues about the contrived coincidence of being in the same place at the same time.

Let me give an ethnographic example to clarify the pivotal role played at night by certain stretches of the Corniche as zones of encounter for all sorts of gay men, regardless of whether self-identified. It was in late summer 1999 that I initially met Ali, a teenage boy from the southern suburb of Ghobeiri. The two of us finally engaged in a conversation weeks after I first saw him strolling around and paying attention to some of the cars parked conspicuously next to the sidewalk. Ali had definitely checked me out—and I had checked him out—on the very first night that I walked down the relatively steep slope from the Hotel Carlton all the way to where the stretch of sandy beach started. I distinctly remember the balmy breeze of a late August night that was a welcome relief from the excruciating heat of the day. When I arrived at around 11:00 p.m., there were already about twenty or so men on the boulevard of Ramlet al-Bayda. Some were strolling on the sidewalk and others were leaning on the iron railing that separated the road from the adjacent beach. A third group of slightly older men was sitting in cars parked next to the boulevard's sidewalk, and it was with great interest that I watched the many highly studied, and almost ritualistic, interactions between those who sat and those who walked, or those who merely leaned on the Corniche's balustrade, manifestly waiting for something to happen.

Ali was one of those who tended to wait and see while leaning patiently on the iron railing. With its light blue, peeling paint, the railing bordered the entire stretch of Ramlet al-Bayda. Since I had already seen him about half a dozen times before our first direct interaction, I knew that he occasionally responded to certain calls that emanated from one of the cars parked next to the sidewalk. But, in contrast to some of the other protagonists who were around his age, Ali was a rather reserved fellow, possibly enjoying the human scenery unfolding before him much more than actually partaking in it. However, despite the shyness, he approached me, wondering why I did not smoke in a place where the high consumption of cigarettes seemed to form an integral part of the progressing ritual of walkway courtship. I immediately realized that Ali must have observed me well, for I had indeed been confronted countless times by the occasional night cruiser requesting a Marlboro from me. Since I rarely smoked at the time, carrying a pack of cigarettes was not part of my daily routine, which was unfortunate, for it made me lack any kind of "capital" in the eyes of some of my potential suitors.

It turned out that Ali was no more of an actual smoker than I was—at least, he did not have cigarettes of his own, perhaps an intentional lack that enabled him to talk to others. Nonetheless, he borrowed the occasional smoke in situations for which he thought the question "ʿIndak sigāra?" (Do you have a cigarette?) would start a conversation with whomever he fancied at the moment. I think, more than anything else, Ali was a bit puzzled by my regular nightly presence on Ramlet al-Bayda, although I was by far not the only man who showed up with a certain consistency. Even though I tended to chat with many young males, I must have struck him as not completely fitting into a scenario with a plot I apparently had not fully mastered. Despite this, Ali approached me and started a conversation that I found, in retrospect, to be greatly instructive.

After an hour or so of small talk, I concluded that Ali was no ordinary young man. Even though he seemed to lack formal education, his overall demeanor was highly eloquent. In addition, his politeness startled me quite a bit, especially given the rarity of general graciousness among the overwhelming majority of the men who frequented Ramlet al-Bayda at night. While we chatted, sitting like roosters on the balustrade, with our feet firmly planted on the lower bar of the iron railing and our buttocks moving uneasily on the upper one, at least twenty men cruised us, either in pairs or alone. They walked by with a performed lack of "concern," yet not without intensely scrutinizing the two of us from the corners of their eyes and with an unmistakable interest.

Partly acknowledging the commotion unfolding around us, Ali told me that, a couple of years earlier, when he initially started patronizing this particular stretch of the Corniche at night, he felt curious and, at the same time, guilt-ridden. He felt like a child who had lost his parents on an extended walk in some strange city far away from the hustle and bustle of the Lebanese capital. "I always wanted to travel to a foreign land," he added. "Have you ever been afraid to venture out here and hook up with the wrong people, getting in their cars and so on?" I somewhat obliquely inquired. "Not really," Ali asserted sharply, saying that, over the years, he had become more than a regular cruising customer at Ramlet al-Bayda, solicited by a few car-owning sugar daddies who sat silently but always alert in their vehicles. "On the contrary," my young interlocutor later replied, "I have never really been scared of what is going on here at night, apart from maybe, on occasion, the Syrians and their *mukhabarāt*" (Intelligence Services).

To my question, Ali responded that "even if I have been at times abused by those guys, deep in my soul, I detect a profound sentiment of affinity that draws me to these many individual faces who are not that bad after all. They may be strange (*ghurabā'*) but certainly not foreign (*ajānib*)." (I was not sure whether, by "those guys," he meant the regular cruising customers or the Syrian Intelligence Services. As for the words *strange* and *foreign*, they referred to people from different Beiruti neighborhoods or Syrians, but also to the occasional Westerner.) It did not take me more than a couple of nocturnal field trips around Ramlet al-Bayda to figure out that the "affinity" (*ulfat*) Ali was talking about had a little, albeit crucial, material, and sometimes even political, twist to it. Whereas the majority of pedestrians like Ali, and myself, were more or less between fifteen and twenty-five at the time, the other cruising contingent—that is, the men who sat nonchalantly in their cars—was at least twice our age.

Given this larger human configuration, it is certainly quite easy to set up a dichotomy that posits an apparently affluent maturity against young men whose pecuniary means were highly limited. One could even go so far as to argue that what I had stumbled upon on Ramlet al-Bayda was a clear case of male homosexual prostitution, where destitute young male hookers were parading before a potential clientele that was characterized by status and prestige based on the simple ownership of a car, with the occasional brand name further distinguishing—or not—its particular driver. Of course, all of it is not altogether far-fetched. If one defines prostitution by the exchange of a sexual favor for a material one, be it in the form of money or something else, then prostitution was definitely part of the whole social picture on and off the sidewalk at Ramlet al-Bayda. Although tolerated by the local power structure, what was happening on Ramlet al-Bayda was, strictly speaking, not "legal," as in the case of Samir Khalaf's pioneering sociological study on the socio-economic factors that drove female prostitutes at the height of Lebanon's age of insouciance.[4] When it came to the general tone of power relations in the context of my study, conducted some thirty-five years later, the reality of an undeniable paternalism linking young "hookers" and older "johns" in a hierarchical fashion typified many of the interactions I observed regularly on my nocturnal outings on the Corniche.

However, the general sense I gathered from my fieldwork was that the different rituals of courting that were unfolding before my eyes on Ramlet al-Bayda were of a much more complicated nature. First, the projected affluence of the men sitting in the cars parked along the boulevard remained very much circumstantial. Everybody present knew that the likelihood was quite high that the BMW in which the imagined potential sugar daddy was sitting was actually not his own, but rather "borrowed" from God knows where. Second, not all the young men "lounging" on the sidewalk were from destitute backgrounds, although many were. To my understanding, only a fraction was clearly after money. Others, like Ali, congregated on this particular stretch of the Corniche, a mere stone's throw from the Raoucheh Pigeon Rocks, because they could not afford to do anything else on a Saturday night. Hanging out at any café around Raoucheh, on Rue Monot, or *ḍownṭown* amounted to a financial impossibility. At the same time, Ramlet al-Bayda guaranteed entertainment, regardless of the night's particular form and content. As Ali would put it to me, "Hown, mannī zah'ān" (Here, I'm not bored).

For those, however, who otherwise could have gone to any of the many social venues the Lebanese capital had to offer, but who still decided to "go down to Ramlet," their reason to stroll on the sidewalk echoed the one given to me by Ali. Being there was, for most of the men present, a thrilling experience full of latent excitement. Even though new faces were almost always part of the human landscape on any given night, I saw circles of conjectural friends form over time. These acquaintances met up regularly and engaged in extended gossip sessions, all the while surveying the larger scene for a potential encounter that might yield sexual gratification. Moreover, when Ali told me about the profound sentiment of affinity (*ulfat*) that drew him unequivocally to the crowds assembled on Ramlet al-Bayda, I quickly assumed that that "affinity" had not only a potential material twist to it, but also one that was outright political. Although I did not notice it at first, it did not take me very long to start to wonder about the black Mercedes limousines, which at irregular intervals at night were parked next to the sidewalk.

Whereas the connection was initially anything but obvious to me, I was unsure about how to interpret it. The relationship between the tinted windows (*gzāz fumées* in French-inflicted Lebanese Arabic) on the luxury vehicles and the almost constant presence of markedly mustachioed men who roamed the sidewalk at night for purposes that seemed to transcend the strict character of a cruising scenario was too blatant to be ignored. This feeling was confirmed and reinforced when I saw that these men in no way appeared to be at odds with the overall homoerotic atmosphere of the place.

I should have known it, but I simply did not at the time. One of the main headquarters of the Syrian *mukhabarāt* (Intelligence Services) was located in a luxury high-rise on Ramlet al-Bayda. As I learned later, the phrase *Ramlet al-Bayda*, from the civil war until the complete withdrawal of Syrian troops in 2005, also stood as a euphemistic synonym for the notorious presence of "our Syrian brothers" in Lebanon. I spoke to many people in the 1990s and early 2000s who said that they saw the ominous Ghazi Kanaan, longtime head of Syrian intelligence in Lebanon, jogging early in the morning on the very sidewalk on which, only a few hours earlier, some of his colleagues indulged in homoerotic shadow plays that sometimes became serious games of trafficking prostitution. For the Syrian general, such serious games irrevocably ended with his assassination some years later, and this by his very own cronies.

I did not follow up on the exact nature of the thorny business that was manifestly part of what was happening before my eyes during my nighttime visits to Ramlet al-Bayda, nor did I ever see Ghazi Kanaan, the local chief of the Syrian security services (who allegedly committed suicide on October 12th, 2005, in the wake of the killing of Rafik Hariri and Syria's military pulling out of Lebanon), jog there in the early hours of the day. Both activities would have posed a potential danger, for which I was not ready to be challenged at the time. Apart from that, I found myself already so fascinated by what I saw happening on the blurry surface, that a thorough look at the bottom of the issue of occupation, state corruption, and prostitution would have diverted my attention away from my initial research questions, which focused on the bodily performances of Ali and the other young men I observed and interacted with on the sidewalk of Ramlet al-Bayda. This being said, there were times along the nondescript railing, with its light blue, continuously peeling paint, when I felt I was standing in some laboratory of pleasures. Occasionally after midnight on weekends, a kind of voluptuous labyrinth would erupt, and it was then that I would witness an upsetting of what I perceived to be local practices of strolling homosexual prostitution. Young men would approach the ostensibly random black Mercedes, open its back door, and disappear behind the tinted windows for a number of minutes before reemerging again onto the nearby sidewalk.

In these instances, Ali would only say to me in a distinctively dismissive tone, "These are Syrians!" But I was never really able to figure out whether he only meant the *shakhṣiyyāt* (personalities) sitting in the back of the parked limousines or whether he also included in the category of "Syrians" the young men who would purposefully walk toward their potential customers as if they were performing the most natural thing in the world. Maybe they were. For all I know, the contingent of young males who most likely received money in return for the somewhat limited variety of sexual acts possible in the restricted space of a car was quite diverse in its composition. Some were Syrian laborers, who, according to Ali, were coerced into sexual activities in exchange for menial work their patrons promised to provide. Others were undoubtedly Lebanese from the whole panoply of ethno-religious backgrounds the country had to offer. Some of them had in common a relatively low social status, which turned them into a prime target group vis-à-vis the powerful.

It goes without saying that I was greatly intrigued by what was going on in terms of the decidedly illegitimate and "illegal" attempts by some to gain advantage over others through an elaborate display of unrestrained superiority. However, I did not want to discount the importance the other cruising men represented. For them, after all, money was no priority. Yet, they showed up regularly on this particular stretch of Beirut's Corniche in order to *shamm al-hawwa* (smell the air, which, in Lebanese Arabic, means to "have a stroll"). They did so while making eye contact with other men at Ramlet al-Bayda. These visual contacts would sometimes lead only to a mere conversation, but other times, they translated into a sexual encounter for which space and time needed to be arranged first.

Before continuing my discussion about the diversity of the men who congregated at Ramlet al-Bayda on almost a nightly basis, I want to turn my attention once again to the very space that enabled the encounters in the first place. This perfect example of a "zone of encounter" is a straight-running beach boulevard named in the 1990s by and after the late prime minister, Rafik Hariri. In historical and material terms, the businessman from Saida was the most powerful man in the country before his assassination on Valentine's Day 2005. Why he chose this particular road to be named after him is a mystery to me. Perhaps it was the road's exposed and affluent character, which could have attracted the attention of someone as ostentatious as he.

Al-jāda rafīq al-harīrī (Avenue Rafik Hariri), otherwise known as Ramlet al-Bayda, stretches more or less from the Mövenpick Hotel compound in the north to the Summerland Hotel and the Emirati and Algerian embassies in the south. As noted, Ramlet al-Bayda transforms at night into an informal strip, where the commodification of homosexual desire becomes de rigueur. This transformation occurs despite, and sometimes because of, the regular patrols of local gendarmes and, up to 2005, Syrian Intelligence Services agents, some with their own dubious stakes in apprehending the individuals they decided to "watch closely." The ensuing overt commodification of homosexual love and desire at times involves young men who are materially and often socially marginalized, but not always. Depending on one's perspective, of course, one could say that these young men tend to be on the receiving end of a micro-social dynamic that is based on a highly complex bodily performance of local hierarchies and a politics of class differences that makes counter-performances a most difficult, if at all possible, task.

Although not an active participant in the strolling prostitution involving parts of the Syrian Intelligence Services that I witnessed on Ramlet al-Bayda around the turn of the millennium, Ali was still a case in point. He illustrated marvelously the micro-social dynamics always immanent in Lebanese society. A son of Palestinian refugees who grew up in one of the many southern suburban shanty neighborhoods of Beirut, he rarely saw his family at the time I met him. After a number of relatively brief interactions, he informed me that his single mother had repudiated him a couple of years back. As I understood it, the parental repudiation was mostly based on the many critiques by key members of the family who accused Ali of being a *ṭobjī* (a "faggot") and her for being mainly responsible for it.

Ali told me half-jokingly that, as a result of a personal family situation involving economic and physical hardship, he became partly a *sharmūṭ*, a male prostitute. Yet he vehemently denied that he had exchanged sex for money with one of the Syrian officers behind the tinted windows of their black Mercedes, which, for him, represented one of the worst things he could possibly do. Ali was less reluctant to admit that he had "occasionally met" a wealthy Arab from the Gulf. In the summer months, this tourist would cruise the boulevard in the luxury car he brought with him from Riyadh, searching for a suitable young man to satiate his sexual urges. However, Ali's presence on Ramlet al-Bayda was not solely focused on a sexual gratification achieved by pecuniary means only, especially since I had never seen him enter one of the parked cars with tinted windows. As mentioned earlier, there was no viable alternative as far as entertainment on weekends was concerned, so he simply enjoyed being on this specific stretch of the Corniche. He manifestly loved to interact with some of the men who patronized Ramlet al-Bayda at a late hour—including myself. As if he needed to justify himself before me, Ali exclaimed, "After all, the entire world feeds on cocks! *ma heyk?!*" (No?!)

I do not recall what I said in response to his slightly suggestive exclamation, or whether I said anything at all. I do remember that Ali winked at me, as if to say, "Stop asking all these questions and see for yourself if you are *that* interested in what goes on over here." Needless to say, I was actually tempted on occasion to reach for one of the car doors, step inside, and see what would happen without considering whether the windows were tinted or whether the person inside was one of the *shakhṣiyyāt* or just a random driver who needed a temporary release on his way home. Had I dared to go ahead and reach for the hypothetical car door, perhaps I would just have had a stimulating ethnographic conversation with the person inside, or I would have been surprised by an encounter I was only able to speculate about in retrospect. Instead, however, I willingly stepped back and contented myself with observing the wealth of human details unfurling before my eyes. In so doing, I was too apprehensive, I suppose, to uncover layers of a frustrated male homosexual desire that I was—simply and frankly—not ready to confront at the time.

The inherent state of suspension that tends to characterize the homosexual sphere in and around Beirut, as well as the very practice of cruising within the risky, even if sometimes thrilling, parameters of a particular open space such as the sidewalk of Ramlet al Bayda, begs the question: Who exactly is gazing at whom and, for that matter, why? Is Charbel glancing at the marvel of Ali's bodily contours, or is Ramzi staring at Paul's attractive anatomy? On an urban platform like Ramlet al-Bayda, the archetype of the gaze is of pivotal ethnographic relevance. Despite its cultural specificity, this archetype always assumes its powerfulness because it projects the common terror, as well as the ostensible fantasy, that is represented when we dream about being naked in a public place. It reminds us that what we normally think of experiencing as the solidity and comfort of ordinary life—coupled with the whole insidious set of social expectations, ranging from heterosexual normativity to the maintenance of hierarchies and parochial principles—is actually a deadly abyss, one that is terrifying and enticing at the same time. To that generalized dread of spheres and places, where passages are open to nostalgic moments challenging public morality, one can always distinguish, beyond the barriers of black doors and tinted windows, a corridor that gives way to bedrooms with doors set ajar. Yet, it is usually in a concocted bathrobe of conformist mimicry in which a long-rehearsed song is sung to the syncopated rhythm of a well-known tune. In the eagerness of incipient transgressions, fingers unlace themselves and an overcoat comes instinctively down, leading the way to the semi-anonymous journey of physical executions. Yet, despite all transgressive promise, eventually, the protective layer almost always goes up again, thus restoring the never totally jeopardized land of supposed social respectability.

The Politics of Memory: Zoqāq al-Blāṭ and the Story of Charles Ingea

Before elaborating further on the intricate relationship between transgression and conformity in Lebanon, let me continue my stroll by providing another ethnographic vignette intended to describe Beirut's urban landscape and the various human ramifications unfolding in its streets and alleys. Leaving Ramlet al-Bayda altogether and shifting one's direction all the way back to the east, the strolling observer, in returning to the other end of the Corniche, has to pass first through the labyrinth of ʿAyn al-Mraisseh's shadowy streets where most of the *ḥārat al-sharāmīṭ*, the local female "whores' quarter" is to be found. The place is also known as the "Hotel District" because, as I mentioned earlier in this book, it was there that Beirut's first lodging facilities were built in the late nineteenth century. Seventy years later, establishments like the St. Georges and the Phoenicia gave the neighborhood its glamorous edge, despite the fierce battles fought there during the civil war—notably around the Holiday Inn, which today casts its haunting shadow over its immediate surroundings.

Behind this ever-so-fascinating quarter of ʿAyn al-Mraisseh was the now totally vanished pre-civil-war red-light district, the Mutanabbi Street along with the legendary Zeytūna, a name that would almost certainly make any North African shudder. Its still recently battle-inflicted lunar landscape, by now turned into a surreal real estate utopia, must be crossed whenever one wants to go eastward toward Bāb Idrīs, the part of town that harbors the historic—and now completely lost—Jewish neighborhood of Wādī Abu-Jmīl.[5] But before getting there, the new "Zeytouna Bay Marina" imposes itself with its ostentatious cafés and restaurants that welcome to their tables an equally brazen clientele.

Whenever I stroll through the area, I remember the scent of the wild mimosas in springtime. Solidère planted the trees in the early 2000s below the post office in the lower part of Zoqāq al-Blāṭ to feign a sense of garden

Zeytouna Bay Marina, December 30, 2011.

atmosphere in a place that, only a couple of years earlier, was decidedly off limits for virtually everybody. The peculiar relationship between the devastation of the past and the created garden atmosphere of the present made it clear to me that I needed to pay close attention to the various absences in the urban landscape of Beirut and to look at what exactly functioned as a substitute for something that manifestly once, but no longer, existed. With a queer stroller's eye, I keep considering the many parking lots that are to be found all over the Lebanese capital.[6] They range from those built where apartment houses had stood before to others that substituted temporarily for former official buildings. One such building was the old American embassy located on the Corniche on the western end of ʿAyn al-Mraisseh: an unspectacular lot with a spectacular history that hardly anybody seemed to remember.[7] Later, even the parking lot would vanish, and in its stead emerged one more of the countless empty luxury apartment buildings that, after the turn of the millennium, covered large parts of Beirut.

Meanwhile, selective memory is part of a larger local picture with a panoramic frame that willfully excludes a number of details.[8] Yet, in following the conspicuous scent of the wild mimosas, a mix of light green and fluffy yellow lost in the soon-to-be filled empty lots of the past, one can still see many things that even the ravages of the post-civil-war period were not able to fully obliterate. In Wādī Abu-Jmīl, it is possible, for instance, to make out Beirut's only distinctly visible synagogue. The yellow building is one more of the many "preserved" ruins within this downtown pantheon of built carcasses where, as the Lebanese urbanist Jad Tabet tellingly writes, "the war-torn city [clashes with] the memory of the future."[9] Such a "disoriented" memory becomes manifest after virtually every step in and around *ḍownṭown*. Thus, in the middle of the site of this previously almost totally annihilated urban center stands the ugliness of the Starco Building, a revived modern concrete structure that, over the postwar years, sheltered Lebanon's Ministry of Culture; Strange Fruit, the charged moniker of a cabaret-bar; and, for many years, the former branch of a quite defunct Planet Hollywood.[10]

This highly intricate mixture of a "marked space" calls attention to the very meaning that such a space has for the inhabitants of Beirut, as well as to the unyielding connection that history and geography entertain with each other. Marked space in Beirut points to external and internal bound-

Where the American embassy once stood (a former longtime parking lot on which a luxury high-rise was built), June 18, 2011.

aries, as well as to the mental construction that provides any astute city dweller with the general idea of the concept of urban landscape. Every aspect of that landscape is a space of memory that is engaged in a perpetual relationship with its multiple readings of history, which are often competing and contradictory.[11] To paraphrase Italo Calvino's remarks in *Invisible Cities*, as waves from memories flow in, the city soaks them up like a sponge and expands.[12] In Beirut, however, the memory of a violent past, and sometimes present, tends to get obliterated all too often and, in its stead, a repressed version of times gone by emerges. But this emergence never occurs without betraying a future where the potential for bearing disaster always haunts the present. This version is captured in an idea of a future that is perpetually projected without ever becoming manifest. It holds Beirutis as hostages once more, as they form part of an expanded sponge. As Jad Tabet puts it, this time around, the inhabitants of the Lebanese capital are caught between the disrobing mirror of the past and the idolatry of an imagined present that is shaky at best.[13]

But reality, regardless of how deeply repressed, always resurfaces in one way or another. Behind the Starco Building, the queer stroller quickly reaches the neighborhood of Zoqāq al-Blāṭ with its ruined palaces that once housed European and American consulates during the Ottoman Empire. Today, Union Jacks and Stars and Stripes are anything but visible on top of these palaces, which were converted during the civil war into makeshift shelters for refugees from the south. Instead, the favorite colors of the day are the green of the Amal Movement and the yellow of Ḥizballah, both symbolizing the current Shīʿī protagonists within the highly contested Lebanese political arena.[14] To be sure, the neighborhood of Zoqāq al-Blāṭ ("Cobblestone Alley" in Ottoman Arabic) is known for being a borough of vanished official splendor where old bourgeois family residences, like the Ḥneineh and Ziyādeh Palaces, now await destruction in order to make room for the new, and increasingly ubiquitous and car-infested, highways that have been intensely promoted inside the city of Beirut by successive post-civil-war governments. However, Zoqāq al-Blāṭ is also a neighborhood that features within its jurisdiction the intricate wealth of Lebanese cultural history, past and present combined.

Numerous were the former mansions in Zoqāq al-Blāṭ that, at the beginning of the twentieth century, formed the *barrio alto* of the then-emerging Lebanese capital. As far as architecture and physical space in post-civil-war Beirut were concerned, the German Orient-Institut was one of the few still-intact Ottoman structures that, for almost an entire century, had characterized this privileged neighborhood. However, most

Ziyādeh and Ḥneineh Palaces, June 3, 2011.

other buildings were in disrepair, including the house in which the famed singer Fairuz had grown up in the late 1930s and 1940s and such important historical sites for the advent of the late nineteenth-century *nahḍa* (Arab[ic] Renaissance) as Boutos al-Boustani's National School, the iconic *madrasa al-waṭaniyya*, now lying derelict behind countless banners and posters of the Amal Movement.

The importance of historical sites is, of course, a topic full of contestation and divergent historical readings. To explore this contestation a bit further, I shift my attention to an ethnographic vignette that manages to bring together many of the ideas about how past, present, and future collide in post-civil-war Lebanon. In October 2002, I went to Zoqāq al-Blāṭ with a German female friend who was researching the history of the neighborhood in order to conduct an interview with a man who, at the time, was seventy-three years old. I will refer to this most eccentric of hosts by the pseudonym "Charles Ingea." I had seen Ingea on a couple of earlier occasions. His stocky, slightly hunchbacked physique was rarely absent from ballet performances or concerts of Western classical music at either the Baalbek or Beiteddine Festivals. Ingea did not miss any of the numerous diplomatic cocktail parties around town, be it the yearly extravaganza on July 14th at the Résidence des Pins, the French ambassador's opulent residence near Beirut's Hippodrome, or the reception hosted by the German ambassador on October 3rd at the Roman baths located *ḍownṭown* immediately behind the Fascist-era buildings of Bank Street (where Elio and his pals congregated on hot summer nights). More informally, I had seen him at a leisurely get-together his long-time friend, the late owner of the Hotel Carlton, had organized in the courtyard of his Kesserwān mountain villa after a conference on Ghazzal (Arabic love poetry), held in the summer 1999 at the Orient-Institut.

Charles Ingea was the epitome of a Beiruti high society *passe-partout*. He loved to mingle with the *grandes dames* of the Lebanese bourgeoisie as well as in diplomatic circles that made him think of a lost cosmopolitan age that the Levant of his youth was supposed to have been all about. Whenever I saw him, especially in the company of one of the countless face-lifted, middle-aged "beauty queens," I had visual flashes of the old Truman Capote, who was certainly not busy socializing with the faces behind redone noses, but happily dancing with Marilyn Monroe. Yet, oddly enough, instead of residing in the vicinity of Lady Cochrane on the affluent Rue Sursock in East Beirut's Ashrafieh district or in suburban Rabieh, the avowedly Roman Catholic Ingea lived alone behind the high walls of a mid-sized mansion in the neighborhood of Zoqāq al-Blāṭ. In that unusual locality, the self-declared "sophisticated glitter boy" of yesteryear was surrounded by poster after poster featuring Shīʿī martyrs who had died for the causes of Amal and Ḥizballah.

When my friend and I arrived at the Ingea residence, Salim, the homeowner's Sudanese servant, let us in through an automated iron gate. When I saw Charles Ingea and Salim, standing next to each other, I was reminded of E. M. Forster and his servant-cum-partner ʿAbduh, living their lives on the ambiguous margins in "cosmopolitan" Alexandria.[15] I thus wondered what exactly was going on in this large and strange house, where the ground floor was completely packed with all kinds of antiquities, books, paintings, and bibelots.

As quickly as Salim had appeared, he vanished. Ingea, who was looking intently at my tall, blonde female friend, totally ignored me. However, he made sure we understood that we should sit down on the leather couch in the drawing room, but not before he made clear that he wanted our conversation to be conducted in English "to challenge my old man's wit," as he put it. For Ingea, who considered French to be his mother tongue, Arabic—"well, Arabic!"—had never even been under consideration to be spoken on "serious occasions" such as that unfolding around us on that late October afternoon in one of the numerous microcosms of Zoqāq al-Blāṭ. My friend and I barely uttered a word. It was, rather, Ingea who asked and responded to his own questions. He told us that, after a childhood spent in Beirut's Clémenceau district, he had moved with his mother to the house in Zoqāq al-Blāṭ in the 1960s. Apparently, his mother, a native of Damascus, refused categorically to set up quarters in Beirut's eastern districts. She argued that the "authentic Beirut" was to be found in no other place but west of *al-burj*, the pre-civil-war city center that, by now, almost everybody was calling *ḍownṭown*. Interestingly, the son still concurred with the mother's verdict some forty years later.

Born and raised in Beirut, Ingea studied in post–World War II Paris, where he later settled in an apartment near the Arc de Triomphe on a side street of the Avenue Foch, working as a banker in one of the city's more prominent institutions. By the early 1970s, however, he had mostly returned to Beirut, continuing to work in the banking sector. At the same time, he was following, with many "single" men his age and status, a busy schedule on the social front that included the entire range of high entertainment follies that the imagined pre-civil-war "Switzerland of the Middle East" had to offer the world. Ingea's mother died in 1980, and, as eerie as it might have appeared at the time of our visit, there was some hint of Norman Bates in the air. Our host told us proudly that nothing had been touched in her second-floor suite since the day of her passing, some twenty-two years earlier. He showed us around his large house, including his private bathroom, prominently featuring a toilet seat decorated with dollar bills that he had purchased during a visit to New York, but the tour excluded the mother's quarters.

In terms of Lebanese identity politics, Charles Ingea was a complicated candidate. He distanced himself from his fellow Christians who lived in East Beirut, making sure we knew that he was a *Roman* Catholic who went to the weekly French-language mass at Ḥamra's St. Francis Church and decidedly not a Maronite *montagnard* (mountain dweller). He could also have gone to the English service, but there were "too many Sri Lankan maids" with whom he did not want to mix. Never mind his unapologetic xenophobia, Ingea also appropriated a non-Lebanese identity that he thought ennobled him somehow vis-à-vis the rest of his fellow citizens. When I finally overcame my inhibition and asked him whether he had ever thought of settling in Paris for good, Ingea looked at me and candidly responded in French, rolling his *r*'s with this most distinguishable of Levantine accents: "En France je me sens oriental" (In France, I feel Oriental).

Needless to say, given the circumstances, I was not at all surprised that

Ingea appropriated the identity of an "Oriental" and not that of an Arab, which would have run against his own self-image. During the four or so hours that my friend and I spent within the walls of this most eccentric residence, I got the distinct feeling that Ingea was almost yearning for the restoration of the Ottoman Empire, a projected social space within which he saw himself as a seamless bridge between what he considered East and West. To accentuate this nostalgic note that played on the peculiar mixture between a long-vanished Mediterranean high-end cosmopolitanism and the "edifying" constituents of Western colonialism, Ingea informed us that he was actually descended from Italian noblemen and that acquaintances addressed him as "Sir Charles." Moreover, he proudly declared that his family had all along been the "humbled" owners of British overseas passports, as if "the Empire" still played a formal role fifty-five years after the Union Jack was for all time lowered on the Red Fort.

In a way, I would have understood this resilience coming from Lady Cochrane, the doyenne of Greek-Orthodox Christian East Beirut who sat in her Orientalist fantasy of a palace on Rue Sursock and longed for the days under the Ottoman Empire, what she thought history had mistakenly understood to be "the sick old man of Europe." But Ingea had been living his entire life—save the years he partly spent in Paris—in an urban space dominated by its Muslim inhabitants. Yet, as if anticipating my question, he said in a categorical voice: "In case you wonder, I have nothing to do with all these Alis around me. We respect each other's presence, but we don't interact." Even though Ingea was a devout *Roman* Catholic (he had even shown us his private collection of about three dozen antique crosses hanging in one of his bedroom closets), what became more and more apparent to me during his endless monologues was that he was not at all a Christian supremacist. Rather, he was a social elitist, distancing himself equally from Maronite *montagnards* and from what he perceived to be the largely underprivileged Shīʿī "Alis" surrounding him in Zoqāq al-Blāṭ.

Just as I was coming to this realization, the *azān al-maghrib* (the call for the Muslim prayer at sunset) enveloped us with its overpowering acoustics. "That's for you from my friend, Abdelrāḥman Pavarotti!" declared Ingea with a huge mischievous grin on his face. Given that this particular call for prayer was coming from the nearby *aḥbāsh* mosque, a Sunni group locally known for its reactionary reading of Islam, Ingea did not have to elaborate on his stance toward the religious splinter group. He only said with a performed indifference in his tone that he woke up every morning at dawn when his "friend, Abdelrāḥman Pavarotti" called for people to wake up and "leave their lazy lives behind" unless they wanted to "burn in hell."

By the time the sun finally set, it seemed as if Ingea had not left out anything from his personal repertoire of grand-bourgeois entertainment, ranging from cultural sophistication to social stereotyping, all the way to underlying flirtations directed at me, the person he initially ignored. He reminisced about how he wrote poetry, some of which had appeared in the 1980s in French (of course!), but that he was reluctant to publish it again lest the *NRF* (Gaston Gallimard's preeminent literary magazine, *Nouvelle Revue Française*) offer him a contract. Whenever he could, he played the religious card. For instance, he juxtaposed my alleged Muslim Sunni identity to that of his servant Salim, but not without an explicit sexual undertone and an exoticizing reference to both our comparatively dark complexions.

By the end of the evening, I had increasingly become the object of his flirtatious deliberations. While Salim had disappeared shortly after our arrival—with the exception of when he duly served us tea and *maʿmūl* pastries from one of the Ḥallāb outlets in Tripoli—the assumed servant reappeared for the scheduled house tour, opening one door after another for us. In moving from one overly decorated room to the next, I could not avoid noticing how Salim stared at me while moving his tongue lasciviously from one corner of his mouth to the next. He did this with the apparent encouragement of his "master," but made sure my female friend would not notice anything of what was going on around her.

Apart from touring Ingea's private bathroom with the dollar-bill toilet seat, we almost climbed the stairs to the roof. Our host told us, squinting at me first, that he went there every morning to sunbathe naked, hoping to heal a chronic skin condition. But, given the late hour, and our sheer exhaustion after four hours spent in the company of this fat old man, who grew more excited and energized as time passed, my friend and I refrained from going up to the roof and decided instead to bid farewell to Charles Ingea and his servant Salim. Ingea told Salim, whom he referred to as his "valet," to drive us home in his car. He also said that my friend (but not I) should come back and pay him a visit if she had any further questions—an ironic statement given our host's penchant for indulging in seemingly never-ending monologues. My friend and I politely refused the generous offer of a ride. We shook hands with the person we felt had ethnographically challenged and overwhelmed us. As soon as we were out of sight, we looked at each other and shook our heads. We might have thought we would either burst out laughing or break into an avalanche of comments and remarks. But we were mostly silent. I took my friend to her apartment in the Zarīf neighborhood and continued my journey westward toward the Ḥamra district, musing silently over all the incredible things I had just experienced in this strange house in Zoqāq al-Blāṭ.

In retrospect, what fascinated me so much about Charles Ingea was the fact that, at the time, he was one of the surviving figures of *un Beyrouth bleu d'antan*, "a vanished gay Beirut" of sorts, which had long since disappeared before that October afternoon at his extravagant residence in Zoqāq al-Blāṭ. The term "gay Beirut" was not, of course, part of Ingea's vocabulary. He was the perfect example of a "tacit subject" for whom the elegant bourgeois motto applied: *on ne se prononce pas!* (one does not declare oneself [publicly]!).[16] However, *le tout Beyrouth* of old times, and what was left of it in the new millennium, was all about "tacit agreements" that draped reality in the velvet of its projected imaginations. It knew about his, as well as his peers', sexual orientation. To be sure, however, nobody spoke about it overtly. Even Ingea himself, despite his relentless, overt sexual hints directed at me, refused to even remotely thematize the subject of homosexuality during our visit. Although this pointed omission must have been in part due to the presence of a woman, I doubt that Ingea would have addressed the topic in a more direct way even in the exclusive company of homosexual men.

Charles Ingea might not have uttered the words *gay* or *homosexual* (or, for that matter, any term that would have suggested homosexuality), but whenever he talked about his "glorious past," he made sure to refer to all his previous friends and mentors, who had all been known in Lebanese high society circles for their homosexual orientation. In listening to him talk about this past, I visualized a world of wealthy and influential men who were either successful businessmen (like Ingea himself) or high-placed politicians like the notorious former minister Henri Pharaoun (1898–1993). Ingea mentioned Pharaoun several times during our visit. Apart from significantly shaping Lebanese independence, the minister, born at the turn of the twentieth century as the son of a wealthy Melkite Catholic merchant in Egypt, had designed Lebanon's flag. Throughout his life, he remained a staunch Mediterraneanist, opposed to the very idea of Arab nationalism. In retrospect, however, what made him notorious in the eyes of his compatriots was his homosexuality, and a dramatic death, which remains to this day subject to all kinds of speculations, including the story that he was killed in 1993 (at the age of 95!) in his bed at the Hotel Carlton in the presence of one of his male lovers.

I later discussed Henri Pharaoun with my friend Ramzi, the "drag queen from Sassine," as he would jokingly call himself. Ramzi described the assassinated minister as "one of the big figures that shaped Lebanese independence after the French Mandate." Ramzi added that Pharaoun was a famous philanthropist: "He used to help a lot of students. And, my father mentioned once that in the 1960s he was given financial funding by Pharaoun, along with a group of his friends, so they could attend a conference in Switzerland." For Ramzi, it was the first time he had heard his father speak about *tantāt* in a positive way. Perhaps it was thanks to Pharaoun that his father was more or less accepting of his homosexuality. Yet, Ramzi said, "The old minister was known for his promiscuity too, and a lot of young boys saw their 'services' remunerated." Much of this "remuneration" happened in his beautiful mansion, which he had bought and renovated before the war with money from his banking enterprises. It not only faced the Orient-Institut on the other side of the crossroads in Zoqāq al-Blāṭ, but also Charles Ingea's eclectic residence. At the turn of the millennium, Pharaoun's mansion had been transformed into the Mouawad Museum, highlighting the already existing Orientalist interior with an impressive collection of jewelry and antiquities, all of which were intended to revive an imagined lost time of countless riches and rêveries.

In pondering this lost time, probably best symbolized by the very long life of the wealthy and hugely influential Henri Pharaoun, I remembered the 1999 reception hosted by Ingea's friend, the late owner of the Hotel Carlton, in his southern Kesserwān villa in Ajaltoun, high above the mountains of Antelias. There, in the midst of Orientalist paintings, Persian rugs, and bookshelves full of French symbolist poetry, I felt as if I were in a time capsule, far away from the realities I experienced in and around Beirut. To the sound of recited Arabic verses and the chanting courtyard fountain, our host reminded everyone present that "it was here, in the monasteries of the Christian mountains of Kesserwān, and nowhere else, that the *nahḍa* [Arab(ic) Renaissance] began." The reading of history being as it is, I could not resist thinking about the implications of the sheltered lives these privileged men led in pre-civil-war Lebanon and, manifestly, continued to live forty years later. It appeared to me that they staunchly avoided mixing socially with those they considered their inferiors—with the notable exception of sexual adventures, which enabled some of them to regularly transcend otherwise unwaveringly imposed boundaries.

In this context of past and present boundary crossings, I could not help but think about the *ḥammām* (bathhouse) that was located in Zoqāq al-Blāṭ, a mere stone's throw away from Charles Ingea's house. During my

Charles Ingea's dwarfed mansion, July 19, 2013.

visits over the years, I had never seen the old man there in person, nor did I meet any of his acolytes, for that matter. However, I occasionally saw Salim, although we did not know each other at the time. I thus wondered about the "zones of encounter" Ingea and his friends would contest and appropriate when they were the age of the young gay men I interacted with during my fieldwork in Beirut.

I saw Charles Ingea again in June 2011. He was eighty-two and had by then experienced a stroke and was marked by it. Salim was no more. "He was sick and died in Sudan, just a couple of days after having returned to his homeland," said Ingea. But it became clear that Salim had died of AIDS, a subject that was to remain taboo for his former employer who just uttered: "I did everything I could so that he gets good treatment. I even spent twenty thousand dollars on his behalf, to no avail, alas!" It transpired that Ingea had lost a close friend and was mourning deeply. Whether their relationship had been sexual at some point in their lives, I do not know, but their intimacy was to be reckoned with despite all class and racialized difference. Ingea's grief inside was complemented by the urban mayhem outside. While his idiosyncratic mansion still stood as some sort of testimony to a bygone era, the plots next to him had been dug out to make room for two gigantic nondescript apartment buildings that would dwarf—and eventually gobble up—Ingea's little world.

CHAPTER 8

"Seeing Oneself" and the Mirror Stage: The Ḥammām and the Gay Icon Fairuz

As we saw in the previous chapter, the "little world" of someone like Charles Ingea in and around the neighborhood of Zoqāq al-Blāṭ might be idiosyncratic on its own terms. However, it is part of a socio-historical reality that must be accounted for. Thus, I want to go back to another set of field notes and draw attention to different "little worlds" within the homosexual sphere in and around Beirut. They are zones of encounter of sorts that, theoretically, are shaped by what I understand to be a Lacanian maze of bodies and mirrors. To exemplify my theoretical assumptions, I begin by paying a brief but intense visit to the oldest of the few local bathhouses. The *ḥammām an-nuzha al-jadīd*—the New Amusement Bathhouse, as it were—functioned for several decades in the very heart of Zoqāq al-Blāṭ. It was a principal venue for gay men until its management was changed in 2011 in order to get rid of "sexual debauchery," a move that anticipated its closure shortly thereafter.[1]

The Mirror Stage and the Ḥammām an-Nuzha al-Jadīd

"Ḥammām an-nuzha al-jadīd: Bains turcs" (New Amusement Bathhouse: Turkish Baths): that's all the notice outside says. Next to it are green-framed posters picturing the "vanished" imam Moussa Sadr. Nureddine, the muscular Iraqi refugee from Kurdistan, who grew up in a Damascene shantytown, gives every customer a towel at the entrance to this voluptuous purgatory. There is a strong link in the minds of many between bathhouses and sensual pleasures. Despite its Orientalist resonance, this old idea contributes to the half-brothel/half-magic mystery of these public establishments. But, who knows? In the caldarium, the man who *khasso*

Resting room in *ḥammām an-nuzha*, May 23, 2011.

(is concerned) may, after all, only find the promised purifying waters, clear and warm. Or, perhaps not. In the steam room, Élie wears his towel loosely, covering his best parts. A golden cross hangs from a chain around his neck to formally demonstrate that he is from the "other side"—that is to say, from the east and beyond the former *khaṭṭ al-tamās* (Green Line).[2]

Personal interaction: *After making me reveal the location of my own residence, which, for a long time, had consistently been a western one (starting with Zoqāq al-Blāṭ, then Rās al-Nabaʿ, before moving to Qas Qas, and eventually Ḥamra and Clémenceau), Élie asks me how I could have possibly—in the case of Qas Qas—lived next to Sabra and Shatila, the Palestinian refugee camps, in Beirut's southwest. "Isn't it dangerous down there?" "Well, danger, you know . . ." I mumble, ". . . it's kind of relative." Raising his right eyebrow, he leaves the steam room and climbs up the ladder to the dry sauna.*

During this brief interaction, Hussein, a hairy guy, was quietly sitting on the marble in the corner of the room. We start chatting about the weather outside and the steam inside. Having discovered, from my intonation, my western Mediterranean origins, he asks me, referring to the intricacies of the "amusement" haven we are in, whether in our cities in the Maghrib "something like this—you know what I mean" exists. I guess my answer is once again a sheep-

ish one. "You know," I say to him, "I left Algeria, the island-less country of the islands, when I was barely sixteen, so I was too young to get introduced to the delights of high-rising temperatures." I discern another raised brow, and I wonder whether the reason for that is Hussein's disbelief in my story or whether he was mocking my rather late maturity. Luckily, it's getting too hot in the caldarium; I crave the cold shower.

For the moment, it remains contrary to its apparent character that this locale may only be in the service of bodily hygiene. There is always a great temptation in the unknown, and in the possibility of danger, an even greater one. The New Amusement Bathhouse gives rise to those dangerous dreams: a doubly mythical sentiment that almost nothing can articulate. First, the intimacy at heart of an assumed public—yet intimate—if not altogether secret, place; second, a forceful contrast, effective only for the person who has already experienced these kinds of hydrotherapeutic follies.

To undress, under any pretext, can be a symptomatic act, or a simple imprudence. The ostensible references to Orientalist rêveries may very well be attached to the experience of the *ḥammām*. However, within its undoubtedly limited frame, this experience has been an integral part in more than one gay life in Beirut. By facilitating the homoerotic encounter, regardless of whether in the form of one or more sexual timely diversions, the *ḥammām* in its few incarnations in Beirut played in the post-civil-war period a pivotal role in the production of local queer space, and this, despite all setbacks.

Back in the steam room, I meet both Élie and Hussein again. This time, Pierre who prefers to be called "Peter" joins them. "We are 'open-mind[ed],'[3] ma heyk? *[aren't we?]" How ephemeral the art of naming is! I think to myself. It is a mere deterministic categorization that society at large bestows upon you. And it goes both, if not more, ways: "Boutros" turns easily into "Pierre" and "Pierre" melts lightly down into "Peter." What comes next, one may ask? "Pete?" At any rate, for the moment, I avoid the headache that results from trying to digest what Lebanon appears to be all about.*

Sitting on the marble bench in the tepidarium, I adopt the appreciativeness of a child. Wandering through this steaming labyrinth of voluptuous pleasures seems now like the mixing of colors on an artist's palette. I start imagining the task of anthropology as mixing with a fragmentary fantasy the different locales and their people before applying them on a huge theoretical canvas, one that leaves no room for superfluous justifications. The game with the Other does not ex-

press life; through the gaze, it precisely makes it—even if in limited forms. And yet, life withstands gazes continuously: the spectacle will always go on.

In the infernal place of the ḥammām, to gaze at each other becomes also a play before the play, where the transcending of surfaces and the circumspect sexual intercourse with the bearers of orifices represent a challenge to all the participants. It is a mating meeting in which each one throws his performative weight onto the scales of mutual competition—seldom mild but often without pity.

While discovering the maze on the stage of "amusement," where the scale model of a bathhouse in Zoqāq al-Blāṭ meets the greater universe of Beirut, the initially merely gazing individual experiences a sexually inspired complex. This translates into an unusual congregation of bodies in which the protagonists may, at times and in almost a formal fashion, represent different sides of Lebanon's spatially segregated sectarian communities. For brief moments, while we are taken on a journey that shows how our perceptions of the abode shape our thoughts, memories, and dreams, the fixed spatialization of mental maps appears to crumble here and there by opening up—albeit, ultimately, in just as ephemeral a fashion—to an almost accidental "encounter."[4]

The interlacing polyphony of bodies meets the contrapuntal texture of communitarian loyalties and sometimes is even able to undo them in time and space—never mind the brevity of the Lefebvrian moment, an instant that privileges the spatial—physical and mental—over the temporal, but without discounting the latter. Subsequent to the experience of individual gratification, many return from their arousing journey not only reasserting the "right" links to a solidified chain of invented traditions, but also often as the incarnate guarantors for any form of social normativity, ranging from innocent repression to unruly self-denial. It is a guarantee that potentially harbors consequences that are even more berserk, especially when unachieved immediate sexual gratification gives way to deeply felt frustration.

In all the hazy politics of steam and virility taking place in a Beiruti *ḥammām*, the participant observer, in his relentless attempts at "participant objectification," cannot but be absorbed by profound and defiant thoughts—or, at least, so I felt at the time. Like food, drinking, sleeping, and bathing, a vapory intercourse can produce intense effects. They do not last, however. The search for gratification becomes a pattern and is repeated, here and elsewhere. Nonetheless, the search is finite. Life reveals itself as some near-death experience, and our latent, sometimes manifest, surreptitious minds will do anything to make it intriguing, and, if possible, repeatedly so. In the meantime, excrescences and orifices, places where borderlines between two bodies and between the body and the world as such are overcome, regularly manage to converge fleetingly with locations where exchanges and reciprocal orientations are, despite everything, carried out. Although the social mirror of assumed respectability might be hanging near the caldarium, transgressive bodily reflections are always covered in fog. Moreover, while such a social mirror is intended to reflect a *clear* image of the gazing individual, it might be on the floor, projecting in its bits and pieces an *indistinct* bursting body.

Yet, the relation between the body and the space it inhabits (as well as the mirror that projects such a relation) is necessarily a social one. Within the thoroughly contested setting of Beirut, this relation sustains an inherent immediacy, but it alters itself perpetually. The urban space in and around the Lebanese capital presents the queer individual with a living image and, therefore, with a mirror in which his body can be seen, or gazed at. In anthropology, the classical fieldwork situation is a "stage" in point. When the anthropologist arrives in a foreign city or a distant country, s/he experiences the originally unknown space with the entire sensory apparatus of the body—hence the significance of activating the anthropologist's senses. Smells and tastes, legs and feet orient, or oftentimes disorient, the adapting anthropologist-cum-*flâneur*, whose daily practice of walking is essential in making sense of the environment such as the queer stroller lives in. With the sense of hearing, *he* perceives the contradictory qualities of voices, sounds, and noises as they may be felt, for example, on certain stretches of Beirut's Corniche. What happens spatially around *her*, regardless of whether in- or outside, becomes apparent through the intricacies of the relentlessly gazing eye. But, ultimately, in a city like Beirut, where the activity of gazing and looking prevails as an integral part of the encounter, the question remains: What kind of bodies is the eye gazing at?

As Friedrich Nietzsche declares in his *Philosophenbuch* (*The Philosopher's Book*), "every form [i.e., gestalt] belongs to the subject."[5] Within this tangled association between a ceaselessly molding form and an ultimately diachronic content, bodily interactions are being foreseen, where "the apprehension of the surface[s] [happens] by and *through* the mirror."[6] By perceiving surface(s) and, by extension, space in a transcendent way—that is to say, "through" and not "in" the mirror—reflection and, therefore, self-awareness transform the body into a contextualized and spatial entity. The body—or, for that matter, the subject—is the one who, through the mirror, sees and thus becomes aware of himself or herself. However, within the homosexual sphere in Beirut, many concerned homosexual individuals, instead of breaking the molds of society, end up being broken by the molds. In turn, to apply space to the body or, for instance, to coerce the anti-normative subject into calibrated social molds, shows that many subjects, as a consequence, "belong" very well to their respective forms, not the other way around.

The body can never be conceived of as a unified and autonomous entity. It is rather always already, and necessarily so, a fragmented one. Thus, it is only among the countless reflections of the social mirror that one can potentially localize the emergence of alternative discourses, which, as a result, may—or may not—defy in some meaningful way the numerous rigidities of social constraints. This social mirror may be hanging near the caldarium and covered in fog or it may be on the floor as the bits and pieces of a bursting body, which is slipping away from the claws of the dominant discourse.

In Jacques Lacan's seminal seven-page rendering of what he famously coined as "the mirror stage," the revealing reflection permits the subject who gazes to elude the fragmentations of the body through language, in a way making sense of that fragmentation by using words. However, instead of only "forming the function of the *I*"[7] and condemning the Ego to synchronic rigidity, the mirror stage also indicates a surpassing toward and within a space that is practical and, at the same time, symbolic—that is to say, imaginary. But if Lacan's mirror—after all, a socio-historical fixture of Parisian grand-bourgeois apartments—is conceived as the very place where identities are formulated, one has to point out that the function of the mirror is not limited to sending back to the *I* (i.e., the subject or the Ego) its own image. The mirror, as an evanescent and culturally ever-fascinating object, also points to the immanent spatial repetition of the body. The *I* and its other (i.e., the image seen and gazed at) face each other. They are seemingly similar, and even identical, yet differ utterly from each other, the image having no depth and no weight. Moreover, right and left are there, but they are reversed. And bodily reflections might be obstructed by fog or multiplied by the bits and pieces of a broken mirror.

Significantly, however, the Ego perceives not only its double, but also the very context within which its identity gets formulated. This mirror-context is, by definition and before all, a spatial one. Thus, concrete premises in and around Beirut, such as the *ḥammām*, become the arena for a spatially and temporarily privileged context. In it, the embodied gay Ego, in his relentless attempt to look into the Lebanese hall of mirrors, is always joined by other bodies, who indulge in the same activity, one that perpetually shapes individual, as well as particular group, identities. This process is necessarily contingent on a variety of complex interactions between an allegedly permissive world inside (for instance, the imagined intimacy of the bathhouse's caldarium) and the numerous normative worlds outside. At the same time, by jointly looking into that social hall of mirrors, the individual body and its many doubles forcibly engage in interactions that not only happen to create difference, but potentially also spaces of alternative identity formations that, down the rocky social road of Lebanese stringencies, may defy the diverse array of local normative constraints.

Thus, to analyze thoroughly the homosexual sphere in Beirut translates not only into the importance of emphasizing Lebanese group dynamics along with their individual crystallizations, but also into a close look at the spatial context of the capital city itself where, mediated by the many convolutions of a particular social world, geography ends up orchestrating desire. It is a context in which identities are perpetually formulated and appropriated in all kinds of ways. What these identities have in common is visual recognition. Before forming the function of the *I* (i.e., any subject in general or the gay body in particular), a mirror from the 16th arrondissement in Paris that is transplanted onto the micro-social stage of Beiruti narcissism always forms first and foremost the function of the "eye." Whether it is within the spatial confines of a bathhouse or within an open space like Beirut's Corniche, the complex practices of steady looks and gazes remain paramount. Any kind of encounter is always initiated by the integral activation of understated gawps and gapes that selectively screen the familiar faces of those who, for example, pass a specific stretch of the Corniche at a specific moment. The gaze, in short, evaluates the respective party according to his or her timely relevance to the gazing protagonist.

Such a timely relevance can be projected upon others, but it is also often projected upon oneself, whereby the individual assumes a position of what is suggestively called in Lebanese Arabic *shawfat al-ḥāl* (literally, the state of looking at oneself), a state of mind that roughly translates into "arrogance," and a strong feeling of self-importance, also referred to as "attitude" in English-speaking quarters. It is a state that distinguishes its practitioners from everybody else, but it also links them to a generalized performance of conceit and haughtiness, from which to separate oneself remains a difficult task due to peer pressure and the fear of exclusion.[8]

In an analogy with Lacan's mirror stage, I was haunted by the image in which *mafṣumīn* ("schizophrenic" gay men in Beirut) "looked at themselves," a visual fetish of sorts to compensate for a lack that intrigued me, especially given the context in which they were busy checking out some while ignoring others.[9] This applies to the goings-on in the *ḥammām* where prestige, respect, and status were momentarily acquired by the "right attitude," namely, one that was based on an elaborate performance of a distancing arrogance in which one "saw oneself" in the complex hall of mirrors of Lebanese vanities. The latent suggestive nature of gazes is thus usually coupled with evocative bodily postures that become manifest in those instances when the individuals involved mutually recognize, through the sharing of certain encoded performances, that they all *khassun* and *fāytīn bil-jaw* (are concerned and part of the [gay] atmosphere).

The performance of arrogance, and thus *infiṣām shakhsī* (schizophrenia), is always based on instances of a "gazing recognition" that only becomes apparent within a concrete spatial context. In being appropriated, this context facilitates the construction and contestation of individual and group identities that are based on the capacity of the body to fragment and reconstitute itself. This context forecloses and permits the fragmentation of the body along with the various identities attached to it. Yet, it does so not only by making sense of it through language and the use of actual words, but also through a whole set of complex bodily performances, of which the gaze is just one, albeit pivotal, component.

The image of Beirut as a buzzing, unsettling, and ever-thrilling playground of hyper-animated people and streaming automobiles is the context par excellence in which any number of cultures and "spheres" are produced, appropriated, and unremittingly contested. As a consequence, my space is, in a way, the context of which I would be the text. Both my body as well as my body's Other are intrinsically linked to the different reflections and shadows that their respective spaces project. The moving intersections in Beirut that touch, reach, threaten, or favor my body—as well as all the other bodies—form a common zone that can ultimately facilitate the encounter between myself and the Other. This common zone is undoubtedly shaped by the inherent fragmented nature of the body and allows for gaps and tensions, contacts, and cuts. It repeats and yet creates a difference that, down the road, may constitute an altogether alternative space where encounters between different individuals become possible. Through this opening up, "disidentifications" are formed by allowing the negotiation and potential transformation of dominant culture.[10] This space comes to be lived in its profundities that are themselves composed of repetitions, echoes, and repercussions.

Queering the Male Body Between Mountain and Sea

Queer Beirut is an urban ethnography that attempts to come to grips with the multiple dimensions of lived space that shape the Lebanese capital in its various profundities. Yet, to write about Beirut while leaving out spaces that are not exclusively urban is impossible. If one tried such a thing, it would defeat the purposes of an urban ethnography meant to pay close attention to the countless human dynamics that run the spatial gamut of what the country extends to its various urban dwellers. It is for this very reason that I highlight the importance of Paradise Beach for the local homosexual sphere. *Al-baradays* remains a point of reference, even though its very existence is under perpetual threat of becoming one more nondescript "family-friendly" resort. It is a reference that remains a fixture on a queer mental map. And, who knows which sandy stretches between Tripoli and Ṣūr will gain a similar momentum at some point in the future?

A totally different "non-urban" space—in a way, more difficult to circumscribe than Paradise Beach—has managed over the years to attract, for a variety of reasons, large numbers of gay men from and around Beirut. The space in question is *al-jabal* (the Mountain), as opposed to *al-baḥr* (the Sea). However, as emblematic as the Mountain is with respect to Lebanese collective identity politics, I do not want to enter a lengthy discussion on the fundamental importance of the *dayʿa* (the [arche]typical mountain village), but rather take the reader on a swift ethnographic journey to Beiteddine, the palatial premises of the yearly summer festival that carries the same name. Here are some of my edited field notes:

Friday, August 9, 2002, shortly after sunset. The road that leads from the coastal highway south of Beirut into the Shūf Mountains was filled with vehicles driving up to the village of Beiteddine where the aged singer Fairuz was scheduled at 9:00 p.m. to give the first of her two concert installments during the summer music festival organized on the premises of the local palace. Of course, le tout Beyrouth *had to be part of this unique social extravaganza, even if that summer evening attracted much more than just black Mercedes cars that had embarked on the forty-five-kilometer trip (twenty-eight miles), carrying passengers laden with hairspray and jewelry from the hot and humid sea level up to the moderately temperate heights of the Shūf.*

Private automobiles and buses with Syrian and Jordanian license plates were among those vehicles on their slow, albeit tenacious, journey through the scenic gateway into the mountainous area marked by the village of Kfar Ḥīm. Pass-

ing and honking at each other in a relentless and unswerving fashion, drivers proceeded on a relatively narrow road toward the village of Deir al-Qamar, or through the alternative route via the town of Baaqlīn, before eventually reaching the plateau that forms the large makeshift parking lot behind the Beiteddine Palace. To the east, the flat lot overlooked the darkened, yet still very much visible, Barūk Mountain chain that, at this advanced hour, hauntingly dominated the awesome panorama.

Driving his mother's metallic gold Honda Accord and eager to park as close as possible to the performance stage, Jad tried to pull into one of the few empty spots along the village's main street, in front of the private houses built in the traditional sandstone architecture of the region. However, the ubiquitous presence of the stringent darak *(Lebanese police/gendarmerie) forced him to abandon this plan, making it instead necessary for us to leave the Honda some three hundred meters behind the palatial concert venue. On that large open area of rubble-covered ground, all kinds of people, with the more or less skilled help of ever-excited, waving attendants, were in the tumultuous process of parking their cars. The otherwise virtually empty ground had been suddenly transformed into a bustling scene reminiscent of a beehive. It seemed as if half the registered automobiles in and around Mount Lebanon were converging in the area at that particular hour. Their occupants, wearing the season's full range of expensive dress shirts and other glossy evening garments, slammed doors and, while chatting with each other as well as on their ubiquitous cell phones in an informal yet perceptibly tense manner, went on walking on the broken stones in their high heels and polished moccasins.*

The parking attendants, recruits from a local Maronite scout regiment, escorted the visitors toward the exit of the makeshift parking lot, where a minibus stood ready to shuttle them to the Palace. In groups of five or six, the passengers entered those vehicles, which in Lebanon are called "vans." Under normal circumstances, the vans would have been used exclusively by those less affluent classes who, in their daily lives on the coast and in the rural hinterland, depended on the arguably modest facilities of the country's public transport system—in other words, a micro with all the sociocultural baggage attached to it.

Jad, Marwan, and I boarded the next available van, as did another group, three men in their fifties accompanied by an equal number of opulently dressed fake blondes, merrily swinging their handbags. The women were all at least twenty years younger than their companions. Instantly, the minibus was filled with a too-intense scent: Christian Dior's J'adore mixed with the dominant tang of Chanel's Allure for men.

—"Yī! Shū hall karkabeh!" (Gee! What a mess!) exclaimed one of the three

women. She was in the humbling process of squeezing her body into one of the foldable chairs that connected the seats on each aisle of the minibus.

—"Anwar, why didn't you let us out in front of the palace entrance so that we wouldn't have to go through this ordeal?" asked the same young lady who was admonishing her male companion while at the same time moving her small Longchamp leather bag nervously from one shoulder to the other. By making a disgruntled face, she not only revealed the layers of Givenchy makeup that totally coated her features, but also the plastic nature of her aquiline nose, most probably a product of the surgical offices of AUH's[11] *widely known Dr. Nabil Fuleihan.*

Sporting a light blue designer summer suit, Anwar was wearing an eye-catching gold watch on his hairy wrist. And almost every single one of his fingers was adorned with at least one ring that featured the same ostentatious richness of the yellow metal. Caught in the midst of a situation that required him to assume a position located halfway between compassion and patriarchal authority, he did not have a chance to properly respond to his whining female partner. Rather, his potential reactions were preempted when the driver of the minibus, an unassuming mountain dweller in his late forties, shifted the gears of his vehicle in such a hazardous way that all the passengers were praying to make the few hundred meters separating the parking lot from the Beiteddine Palace without major casualties.

—"Ṭawwil bālak ya mʿallim!" (Take it easy, maestro!) was the only phrase Anwar was able to shout angrily, thus shifting his growing annoyance away from the young lady and toward the middle-aged driver. As the minibus came to a final halt, after two or three minutes of a highly bumpy ride, the three women sulked their way through the aisles, clearly showing to all present their resentment for the deeply felt grievances they were experiencing. In an explicit demonstration of controlling virility, one of the other two men pulled his ranting friend away from the potential victim, but not before Anwar shouted some extraordinary insults in the direction of the otherwise stoic driver. After the door was deafeningly slammed, the only thing I was able to overhear, and that came from inside the van, was a somewhat discreet yet decisive "kiss ukhtak yā ʿarss!" (your sister's cunt, you pimp!)

Walking toward the small piazza that faces the main entrance into the Beiteddine Palace, Marwan decided that he needed a Bacardi Breezer before the start of the concert. To calm his nerves, he said. The minibus incident had clearly left us with an intensified adrenaline rush that needed to be tamed with some alcohol. In summer 2002, the intoxicating agent of choice for the hip and trendy, as well as for anybody else intent on having their own share of the faddish rainbow, was provided by the well-known international and family-owned liquor conglomerate. With its fancy multicolored rum mixes, the San Juan, Puerto Rico–based Bacardi Corporation had successfully launched a major campaign to conquer the ever-conquerable Lebanese market of consuming sensations and appearances.

At around 8:30 p.m., we were in the midst of that very market in a rectangular concrete space situated at the bottom of a large staircase below the village's main street. By now, it was full of people who clustered around the many rough-and-ready stands, trying to buy anything from drafts of the locally brewed Laziza Beer to different varieties of manaʾīsh, the celebrated versions of a Lebanese mountain snack, half herb bread, half pizza.

Holding onto our bright tinted bottles, the three of us argued about whose flavor was the tastiest as we paraded gregariously among the crowds of the festively dressed bourgeoisie. Was it Jad's pinkish mixture of cranberries and rum or Marwan's orange taste of fruity peach? At least, both agreed that my supposedly refreshing lime, perhaps due to its all-too-artificial-looking green pigmentation, was not really worth its inflated price. Through an overt display of homoerotic insinuations, Jad made sure that his enunciations about the superiority of his particular Breezer transcended the conversational confines of our little circle. His deliberations became largely more magnificent in his unhampered interactions with other groups of young men, some of whom were apparently known to him from previous encounters in queer-identified places in and around Beirut. Even if kept understated in part, these interactions remained strategically studied, leaving their keen recipients with no doubt about the specific intentions. In this lighthearted moment of playful flirtation, Marwan could not resist chastising Jad in one of the fake annoyed tones that only he was able to perform. By using the grammatical feminine, he exclaimed theatrically: "Uff! Baʿdik mheyyajeh? Khlasna ba'a bi hal-ʾissas tabaʿik!" (roughly translated: Oh my God! Are you still horny? Let's get over with these stories of yours!). "Uffayn!" responded Jad, but not without winking at one of the young men he was flirting with.[12]

The concert was about to start while the elegant crowds were still entering the vast outer courtyard of the Beiteddine Palace. It was during the long reign of the very resourceful Emir Bachir that Italian architects designed the entire compound in the early nineteenth century as a space originally intended for princely public gatherings. In accordance with the local socio-religious circumstances, which historically have tended to result in a dire politics of various sorts of sectarian affiliations, the builders of the imposing mountain palace had bestowed on their distinctive architectural creation the suggestive name "House of the Faith," Beiteddine in Arabic. For the occasion of the 2002 summer festival, however, faith as such did not play much of a role, at least not overtly. Like every year since the launching of the festival in the mid-1980s, the whole salamlik[13] was

Salamlik and *ḥaramlik* of the Beiteddine Palace, April 2003.

converted into a huge open-air theater. On its makeshift stands and benches were placed thousands of those uncomfortable white plastic chairs that were the perching symbol of more than one social congregation in and around the Middle East.

Having purchased mid-range tickets costing the equivalent of US$60 each, Jad and Marwan immediately proceeded to the middle of Zone C, toward two of those white plastic chairs that were covered with thin camping cushions. My heart sank when I looked down the rows and spotted Rachid, the previous year's object of my unrequited desire, and Khalil, his conceited companion. At this late hour, preoccupied by the thought of whether Rachid had seen me as well, I kept thinking about those shoddy pillows that were totally dampened by the evening humidity that had gathered high above the Mediterranean.

In locating the tiny spot on the horizon where the sea—couched between the coastal hills of south Lebanon—was disappearing bit by bit within the darkness of the late evening, I realized that the high amount of moisture in the air seemed to have also affected the tightness of the stylish white-and-red silk shirt that Rachid had put on that night. He was consciously displaying his upper body when I fleetingly caught his eye. Along with the short, chubby Khalil and an entourage of bejeweled Beiruti bourgeoises, young and old—probably their colleagues at the TV station—the ever-attractive Rachid was walking down the stands toward Zone A, which by now was full of self-declared local VVIPs exchanging the latest gossip.[14]

In contrast to the continuously confident theater of the privileged that was in full action before me, I had to content myself with a seat in Zone E, squarely *numbered D42. By paying a bargain price amounting to US$20—more than seven times cheaper than its counterparts in the front rows—I had earned my very own white plastic chair, along with a clammy cushion. Its pattern of alternating small blue and white squares reminded me of the niggling nature of the entire setup in which I had found myself trapped. Being forced into the back line of seats in the converted* salamlik *felt like a defeat. Whereas Khalil sat with Rachid in the front rows, I was sitting alone, a clear sign both of failed love and of the seemingly never-ending budget economy of a graduate student conducting fieldwork in Lebanon.*

As a result, I had to passively comply with the spatial inconvenience caused by the hundred meters or so that separated me from the main stage near which the over-excited audience—at the forefront of which was Rachid—was awaiting Fairuz. The moon, along with all the stars of the firmament, was rising above the Shūf. To accentuate the effect of designed majesty, the platform, decorated with a sea of trumpet-shaped white lilies, had been put up against the magnificent background of the great staircase leading to the ḥaramlik, *the private quarters of the Beiteddine Palace. Meanwhile, however, sitting in Zone E on the damp pad of seat D42 had not only cost me a great view, but it also resulted in a wet butt. Thus, along the stratified lines of the Lebanese bourgeoisie, to be placed in one of the back rows turned out to be a much worse social bargain than the bottle-green lime Breezer I had purchased shortly before.*

Notwithstanding the relative physical discomfort of some patrons like myself, the general excitement among the crowds sitting in the Palace's outer courtyard made itself clearly felt when a full orchestra of mostly Armenian-Lebanese musicians filled the stage, followed by the youthful-looking conductor, Karen Durgarian. Mr. Durgarian was somewhat on the short and skinny side, his long and curly black hair deliberately disheveled. The small suit looked almost as if it were at least two sizes larger than necessary to fit the maestro's scrawny body. The little man stood in stark contrast to some of the conventionally dressed matriarchal violinists he was there to conduct.

However, in their anticipatory effervescence, only comparable to the imagined arrival of some redeeming messiah, the nervous men and women who surrounded me in Zone E did not seem to notice the almost comical disparity in bodily proportions onstage. With the first notes of "Misraḥiyyat lūlū" ("Lulu's Play"), written by the Rahbani brothers, the initial cheering applause emanating from all zones across the salamlik *transformed into an overall exhilaration before giving way to a relatively nervous silence in expectation of Fairuz's imminent appearance.*

The introductory part of the concert ended slowly but surely when the Diva finally took the platform, walking imperiously—if not to say imperially—on a crimson carpet toward the center of the stage. All of a sudden, there she stood, stoic and unapproachable as always, "enframed" like Mexico's Virgen de Guadalupe, not by an all-encompassing body halo, but by trumpet-shaped white lilies that provided Fairuz at this particular moment with an aura that could not have been more divine. She was wearing a long and glitzy evening gown designed by the local gay fashion icon Élie Saab. The colored touches of the classic two-piece garment married a pasty pink with a soft orange that became almost transparent along its lengthy sleeves. It looked like the wings of a bird of paradise, one of the rarest kinds.

Initially, the concert had been advertised as a collaboration between the Diva and her son, Ziad Rahbani, the domesticated enfant terrible of the Lebanese music scene since the turbulent days of the civil war. Hence, the print on the ticket that prominently featured both names. Meanwhile, however, rumors spread that mother and son had quarreled for one reason or another. In turn, the disagreement had led to a change in the concert program that, instead of giving prominence to the son's more contemporary work, ended up reflecting the considerably older songs written by her husband and brother-in-law.

It was Assy, the Diva's late husband, whose mythical artistic partnership with his brother, Mansour, formed the basis of the celebrated musical theater in and around pre-civil-war Lebanon in which Fairuz generally took the pivotal part of the "pure and singing" Lebanese mountain girl.[15] *Meanwhile, the alleged filial dispute that night resulted, during the first part of the concert, in a rendering, almost exclusively, of the famous tunes written by the Rahbani brothers. Nonetheless, the second part did not come up short in ultimately paying tribute to the "terrible Ziad." The aging Diva—born in Beirut's neighborhood of Zoqāq al-Blāṭ in 1935—was in the process of captivating her devout listeners. Despite initial difficulties in finding the accurate pitch of her voice, Fairuz managed to shine after the second stanza of "fi ahweh ʿall mafra'" ("In a Café at the Crossroads"). It was one of the many songs written by Assy and Mansour Rahbani that virtually all of the audience knew by heart. Without making much noise, but still visibly mesmerized, most of the people around and on the benches below me sang quietly in unison. At times, I could hear the occasional oddball who, by raising his voice above the muttering rest, would attract equally loud but disapproving reactions.*

With no complaining spectators behind him, a young man, most probably in his early twenties, stood up in the very last row of the converted salamlik. *He was accompanied by a group of five other male youths whom I had seen earlier in conspicuous interaction with my friend Jad. Wearing tight pants made from a reversible white fabric with an undistinguishable pattern woven into it, the young man was dressed in a pinkish silk dress shirt, as if he had anticipated matching the shades of the Diva's very own wardrobe. In the relative darkness of Zone E, I was able to distinguish a well-groomed goatee along with impeccable carbon-colored eyebrows, plucked recently and enhanced by some easily discernible black eyeliner.*

The young man looked even more ecstatic than the others. Almost as a simulacrum of the original—i.e., the Diva who was busy delivering the panoply of those melodious sounds onstage, all of which were cheered by her audience—the immaculately dressed young man stood there as if by design. Not totally unaware of the effects his bodily performance was having on his immediate surroundings, he held a white tissue, spreading both arms as if in the midst of some religious ceremony of entreaty. Coming close to portraying the unmistakable figure of the late Egyptian female singer 'Umm Kulthūm (minus the impenetrable sunglasses, that is), the young man mimicked Fairuz's demeanor in all its stoic, yet stately, detail.

As far as he and his peers were concerned, it was readily clear that the Lebanese singer had to be much more than what I initially anticipated. In fact, she transcended the mere symbolism in relation to which she bore the marks of an immaculate national representation created passionately by an imagined community called Lebanon. Her history had to reach much deeper than the purported innocence of a young woman who was above any suspicion and merrily singing on the embattled slopes of Mount Lebanon.

In fact, it was during the fifteen years of the civil war (1975–1990), when Fairuz categorically refused to perform inside her country, that the admired vocalist started to publicly exclaim "Ana lubnān!" (I am Lebanon!) Despite the singer's politically motivated boycott, she never moved abroad, and her inimitable voice continued to be heard all over the country's media outlets, running the ideological gamut of continuously mushrooming radio stations associated with the various militias fighting against each other at the time. However, apart from heralding imagined ideals that emphasized a pristine rural Lebanon, far away from the daily cruelties of the war, the overtly patriotic tone of many of the new songs, written for the most part in the 1980s by her son Ziad Rahbani, shifted its focus away from the original idyllic scenery of the *dayʿa*.[16] In contrast to Assy and Mansour Rahbani's *misraḥiyyāt* ([musical] plays) twenty years earlier, the son's lyrics embraced the country as a whole, notably the bustling urbanity of its emblematic capital.

This significant shift is best illustrated by the album *Māʿariftī fīk*,[17] which came out a couple of years after the bloody Israeli invasion of

Lebanon in 1982. Artistically, the traumatic experience of *al-ijtiyyāḥ* (the Invasion), as the Israeli military Operation Freedom for Galilee is referred to in Arabic, gave momentum to Joseph Harb's adaptation of Joaquín Rodrigo's intensely emotional *Leitmotiv* in the second movement of the *Concierto de Aranjuez*. Under the title "Lī bayrūt" ("For Beirut"), the adaptation of the musical piece, marked in the original as *adagio*, eventually became part of *Māʿariftī fīk*. It captured not only all the fast and, at times, slowing sentiments attached to the mitigated love the city of "fire and smoke" inspired in its war-torn dwellers, it also became some kind of intimately shared hymn that testified to the common will of survival in and around Lebanon's capital.

As a powerful symbol of the city—and, moreover, the nation—Fairuz experienced not only the general confirmation of her unchallenged position during the fifteen-year Lebanese civil war, she also embraced its social ramifications willingly herself. In part, the studied means by which she displayed her own body, ranging from her legendary stoicism onstage to the corporeal concealment in a private life that has always been kept secret from the outside world, gave way to a general treatment of undue reverence sometimes bordering on hagiography. The iconic image of the impervious *ʿadrāʾ* (virgin) started early on, without much conscious awareness on the part of her awestruck fans. Meanwhile, the production, followed by the monumental representation, of her virginal aura coincided with two intrinsically logical—albeit contradictory—circumstances that cemented the central place that Fairuz, a Greek Orthodox Christian, came to occupy over six decades within the larger pan-religious Lebanese national imaginary.

On the one hand, the projected image of the singer, similar to that of the Virgin Mary, turned into an image around which many Lebanese, regardless of their sectarian affiliation, congregated in search of a common ground. On such common ground, an identification, reconciliatory in tone, was supposed to take place despite all the ephemeral aspects implicit in its realization. On the other hand, the intention of some of her fans to look for socio-cultural cohesion never discounted a parochial sense of exclusive ownership by others. To a certain extent, this paradox explains why, during the civil war, one would hear the same tunes over and over on a multiplicity of radio stations diametrically opposed to each other in respective ideologies.

Based on religious attributes of redemption and atonement, the symbolism attached to the image of the singer Fairuz was formed, by both Christians and Muslims, to fulfill discrete aspirations for social reconciliation and collective improvement within a heavily divided citizenry, notwithstanding the exclusive character of some of its agendas. The consequences of that symbolism were many. For one, repeated reminders of the pre-civil-war past—a period representing to many the country's golden age, where the innocence of a singing mountain girl often amounted to the virtuousness of a whole nation—planted the seeds for a better future. This selective process of constructing and sustaining collective memory privileged a doctored image of the past by eclipsing many complexities of the present. Within this confined context, the construction of a common icon such as Fairuz and its projection, in the form of an immaculate image, onto the ever-embattled national stage allowed for the hardships of the present to be repressed and for a future to be imagined as a space in which the Lebanese would be saved from seemingly irreversible decline.

Moreover, if the aloof image of Fairuz stood intentionally for the impervious *ʿadrāʾ*, while being simultaneously appropriated in various and, at times, opposing ways as a symbol of the eternal homeland, the immaculate attributes and aura of the former had necessarily to be part of the latter's configuration. This sentiment had become all the more reinforced with the singer's emphatic declaration "Ana lubnān!" (I am Lebanon!) Since Fairuz was the "pure Virgin" who proclaimed herself as being one with Lebanon, then Lebanon must at least share some aspects with the clean and untarnished state of the singer's commonly asserted image. Consequently, the popular translation of the gestalt of the innocent and honorable Virgin into a symbol representing the nation as a whole indicates the yearning expressed by many Lebanese for a fusion of elements and experiences amounting to more than just the sum of its historically conflicting parts. Having continuously exposed the contradictions of the country's social realm, these factors eventually contributed to filling a void, the lack of something whose existence had always haunted the lived experience in Lebanon, even if it has never really been part of it.

The disparity between reality and its multiple interpretations notwithstanding, this marked lack remains relevant, and even essential, in keeping up with the local imagination. Over the years, the will to fill this lack has led to the appropriation of the safe and sound image of an unblemished icon as a symbol of national virginity, utterly removed from the realities of daily life. At the same time, in an oblique yet palpable sense, the attribution of virginal qualities to an abstract notion, such as the idea of the country or the nation, pays direct tribute to those who indulge in it in the first place. In a nearly Durkheimian fashion, and despite all intrinsic complexities of the matter at hand, it is safe to say that the socio-cultural phenomenon Fairuz is Lebanon worshipping itself, and this on more than just one level. Akin to a set of strongly held positions that generate and determine a variety of identification processes, Fairuz represents, along with all her social and national significance, some fundamental characteristics of Lebanese society. Ultimately, the image of either the innocent singing mountain girl or of the all-embracing and all-transcending Diva, whose legendary detached demeanor persists in enthralling the masses, becomes that very society. And, in that society, the selective construction of memory translates into a subliminal urge to celebrate itself without much further thinking on every possible occasion. Under these circumstances, Lebanese society keeps indulging ad infinitum in the perpetuation of its self-generated hagiography. It is an auto-description virtually removed from reality where one "looks at oneself" perpetually in a distorted mirror of deceit and arrogance and in a concerted effort to generate and maintain one's own fictitious and false feeling of confidence and security.

Despite local abilities to form, as well as sustain, symbolic images and ideas reminiscent of a national virginity that sublimates many earthly difficulties and problems encountered in daily life, the socio-cultural phenomenon Fairuz and its various appropriations on the ground go well beyond the narrow slopes that link the various peaks of Mount Lebanon to the Mediterranean sea. Limiting Fairuz's effect to Lebanon would not only be an all-too-restricted reading that is highly Lebano-centric in character and thus false, but it would also disregard completely the importance that the singer holds for much of the rest of the socio-political entity known as the Arab world, including large parts of its Diaspora. To use Timothy Mitchell's notion again, Fairuz was and continues to be "enframed" by domestic and regional politics.[18]

The aftermath of the Six Day War of 1967 witnessed not only a renewed military defeat of the Arab armies, but also the loss of substantial chunks of the national territories of Egypt, Jordan, and Syria. Next to the Sinai Peninsula and the Golan Heights, the remaining parts of what had been nominally still Palestine, even if under either Jordanian or Egyptian political control (i.e., the West Bank, East Jerusalem, and the Gaza Strip), came under direct Israeli occupation. The Sinai Peninsula was returned to Egypt after an official peace treaty between the two countries in the late 1970s, but the Syrian Golan and East Jerusalem were unilaterally annexed by Israel in the early 1980s. The West Bank and Gaza, however, became a ruthless Israeli playing field in which military occupation, various Jewish settlement policies, and half-baked Palestinian autonomy programs, over the decades, have been at the forefront of modern-day colonial practices and experimentations heralding the contemptuous modus operandi of divide and rule.

In 1967, the renewed loss of territory was followed by a total moral collapse that went well beyond the regional borders of the Nile Valley, on the one hand, and the *bilād al-shām* (the Levant), on the other. After all, Palestine "had gone" in its entirety without anybody actually doing anything. Yet, having become a formal part of official scripts written in more than one capital between Marrakech and Muscat, the *(q)'adiyya al-filistīniyya* ("The Question of Palestine") degenerated into a painful repetition of empty pledges. Apart from growing into a mantra, this hollow and politically motivated speech making betrayed itself over time while disintegrating into all kinds of governmental lip services that routinely spanned the whole of the Arab world. The tangible plight of the Palestinians themselves, however, remained continuously overlooked by virtually every one of the self-proclaimed presidents, kings, and princes struggling with the uncertain legitimacy of their respective power.[19]

Moreover, while an overwhelming majority of Palestinians had been turned into eternal refugees, official Arab rhetoric never managed to obliterate the underlying resentment the regimes behind it kept covertly cultivating against that involuntarily dispersed people. This resentment, fostered by all of the various regional authorities in charge, became a notorious tenet among the political elites in Lebanon. Ever since the Palestinian *naqba* ("Catastrophe") of 1948, these elites have excelled in bringing aggrieved feelings into play in the most ruthless and premeditated ways. Whether on the basis of class indignation or on the constructed image of a "foreign" Muslim (i.e., Sunni) wave threatening the sectarian balance within the country, successive Lebanese administrations made sure that the refugees, who had been overwhelmingly excluded from the jealously protected inner echelons of their host society, could never change their socio-legal status were they to stay in Lebanon permanently. Meanwhile, however, in and around Beirut, the general deprivation inside the refugee camps, on the one hand, and the utter lack of social access for their occupants outside them, on the other, would result in a social predicament with a political mixture that became increasingly explosive.[20] This highly volatile concoction would soon enough transform the nationally instrumentalized resentment into but one foreseeable factor leading ultimately to the various smaller wars that made up the first half of the larger civil strife in Lebanon (1975–1990).

Moreover, the active cultivation of the particular indignation felt toward the Palestinian refugee population did not cease with the Israeli invasion during the summer of 1982. Neither did it stop with the evacuation of the PLO cadres surrounding Yasser Arafat that followed nor with the bloody massacres of Sabra and Shatila shortly thereafter. Even the closing stages of the civil war in 1990 did not lead to the end of these resentments.

Similarly, in the new millennium, many Lebanese would readily persist in arguing that the Palestinian refugee problem had been at the root of the Lebanese civil war. This obdurate contention is not to be encountered on the right of the political spectrum alone, but is much more encompassing in its capacity to bring together an array of otherwise divergent views that converge in agreement on this particular issue. It is a contention that betrays an intentionally selective reading of history, where the culpability of the civil war is exclusively bestowed upon one group whose legal refugee status has in part permitted its host society to turn it into some kind of perpetual internal Other.

Yet, within the context of such selective historical appropriations, the importance that Fairuz holds for much of the Arab world is noteworthy on more than one account. In the 1960s and 1970s, "The Question of Palestine" was taken up by many songwriters to whose work the Diva lent her distinctive voice. Tunes like "Zahrat al-madā'in" ("Flower of all Cities") were sung in praise of Jerusalem, the city that "embraces the old churches and wipes away the sorrow from the mosques," and as a political gesture of Arab nationalism that made sure references to Christianity and Islam were represented equally along a conspicuous absence of anything Jewish and—by implication—Israeli. Among a number of other songs, "Zahrat al-madā'in" could be seen as forming part of the official rhetoric current at the time, but without the underlying resentment against the Palestinian refugees that remained prevalent in other places. This lack notwithstanding, "Zahrat al-madā'in" and other songs were listened to across the ideological board. Whether for their Arab nationalist content, conveyed through explicit lyrics and marching melodies, or for the bits and pieces of Christian—and generally—Muslim citations, there was something in the songs that compelled everybody to keep tuning to the various radio stations that played them.

Furthermore, shortly after the 1967 Arab military defeat by Israel, Fairuz started engaging with a selection of songs with a lyrical content that went not only far beyond her previous eulogies surrounding the Lebanese *day'a*, but also transcended the geopolitical boundaries of Lebanon and Palestine. Apart from the timely tributes to the "The Holy City" of Jerusalem—*al-Quds* in Arabic—the Diva addressed a repertoire of songs that ran the gamut of almost all the Arab world's major cities. Baghdad, Cairo, Damascus, even Tunis—these Arab capitals became the subject of something akin to an encyclopedic urban songbook intended in part to celebrate the idea of an Arab unity at a point in time in which the reality on the ground could not have been further removed from such an idea.

My attempt here is to show how, over the decades, Fairuz, the emblematic and pervasive Lebanese diva, has been able to capture effectively the attention of a large number of different audiences around the Arab world and beyond. No doubt, some of them have been motivated by individual artistic affinities. Others, however, were inspired and enthralled by the ideological potential found in Fairuz's singing, a potential they gladly put to work according to their respective political agendas. Given the stature of the Grande Dame as a pan-national and pan-religious icon, akin to a Reina del Líbano y Emperatriz del Mundo Árabe (to return to the image of the Virgen de Guadalupe[21]), larger than life and widely and uncritically admired by seemingly everybody, Fairuz embraced a multiplicity of identities—not only political and religious, but also in terms of gender and sexuality.

Returning to the palatial compound of Beiteddine and to some of the mesmerized, if not to say ecstatic, listeners sitting on the white plastic chairs, I remind the reader of the young man who had come with a group of his friends with whom Jad had been flirting before the beginning of the concert. The young man mimicked Fairuz's demeanor in detail. He was part of a larger contingent of gay men who had come from all corners of Lebanon and beyond. When I write "contingent," I certainly do not have a unified group in mind. Rather, I am suggesting that the homosexual sphere in Lebanon functioned as a substantial pillar of Fairuz's fan base, even more so since the Diva assumed the undisputed identity of a national icon during the country's civil war.

Moreover, Fairuz had everything many of the gay men I knew admired in terms of an ideal(ized) figure of the perfect—and quite androgynous—woman onto which one could easily project countless dreams and yearnings. With androgyny came an ambiguous sexuality, which formed the content of many conversations I had with men like Rachid, who devoted his free time to the development of websites dedicated to the singer's music and personal history. Was Fairuz a lesbian? Many of my friends asked this question. Some had a definite answer to it. Others preferred the suspense of an uncertain response. As was to be expected, the rapprochement that was often made between the Egyptian 'Umm Kulthūm and the

Lebanese Fairuz always included the rumors, pertinent or not, about the older, sunglasses-wearing diva's own homosexuality.

It would be a mistake to limit the worship by numerous gay men in Beirut of distinguished women singers, like Fairuz or 'Umm Kulthūm, to their real or alleged homosexuality. There are examples that could easily contradict such a theory, namely the eternally bridal Sabah or the Egypto-Italian French *vedette* Dalida mentioned at the beginning of this book. Throughout, both women have captured the passionate attention of young gay men, even though one (Sabah) was born in 1927 and the other (Dalida) committed suicide in 1987. What I argue for is something a little bit different from what I have stated so far. Rather my reasoning is to focus on a crucial characteristic common to queer diva worship, but also to the stars—like Fairuz, Dalida, and Sabah—themselves. This crucial characteristic has to do with the power of camp and its ability to counter and defy heteronormativity within a context that would otherwise have difficulties tolerating anything potentially dissident.

Moreover, given Fairuz's national status as some sort of virgin goddess, it becomes easy for anybody to "love" and thus actively—i.e., performatively—"worship" her. Therefore, if such a love happened to include the minute mimicry of the entirety of what is perceived to be her very own state of existence, so be it! Especially, on an occasion like the Beiteddine Festival, where Durkheim's definition of religion could not be a more tangible one, it slowly but surely becomes "safe" for a young gay man to show up wearing a pinkish silk dress shirt and tight pants made from a reversible white fabric and move his body in sheer ecstatic momentum.

My attempt in this chapter has been to show how the fragmented nature of the queer body creates a difference that has the potential—albeit without the necessary teleology attached to it—to constitute alternative spaces. Such spaces can be a *ḥammām* or a particular concert at the Beiteddine Festival, in which encounters between individuals from different backgrounds become possible. My various examples have been intended to provide ethnographic evidence for that possibility. Yet, these spaces in and around Beirut orchestrate desire in more than just one way. Importantly, they enable individual bodies and their performances to move from what is primarily invisible, as far as the ordinary social eye is concerned, toward a spatial assertion of a queer presence. It is this complex move—or rather intricate process—toward a mounting visibility that enables the invisible to become irrevocably visible. However, as we will see next, it is a progression of sorts that can take on a regressive character as well.

CHAPTER 9

Phenomenology and the Spatial Assertion of Queerness: Spatial Alienation, Anthropology, and Urban Studies

By way of active appropriation and contestation, various spaces in and around Beirut have the capacity to orchestrate the desire of those who inhabit them. In some cases, they allow queer bodies and their respective performances to move from what is primarily invisible toward a spatial assertion of a presence that has to be socially reckoned with. At the same time, in orchestrating desire, space ends up embodying a double nature. It is this general double existence that helps queer individuals in Beirut proceed with their various bodily performances from what is ostensibly invisible to the ordinarily visible.

Making the Invisible Visible and Vice Versa

The process of thinking about the double nature of space certainly does not stop with the image of a young Beiruti gay man looking into the social mirror of Lebanese serendipities. Theoretically, the principles surrounding the very concept of the double are concomitant with Merleau-Pontyan phenomenology, where the study of essences, including the essence of perception and consciousness, forms the core of the French philosopher's concerns.[1] This philosophical approach, however, is intended to provide an immediate description of human experience, namely as a direct mode of access to reality, in which the very background is perception. For that matter, the peculiar urban amalgamations of Beirut—a self-declared metropolis, albeit crushingly provincial, that, according to most appearances, invites the invisible to become visible—urge the participant objectifier to push his or her understanding of phenomenology a little further in order to understand why, despite efforts to assert difference, many social and spatial manifestations in and around Beirut still manage to actively suppress visibilities that are judged as being too conspicuous by rendering them invisible again.

On the one hand, the inherent fragmentation of the body, as manifest in Lacan's "mirror stage," not only contradicts the existence of essences, it also actually provides the very site for difference to emerge. In recovering some of the bits and pieces of a fragmented body, be it through language or bodily performance, many of the young gay men in Beirut appropriate and contest spaces in and around the city that pose a challenging alternative to the otherwise overbearing social normativities in Lebanon. After having been coerced into social invisibility—for instance, through the closure of a particular social venue (e.g., the Café Sheikh Manoush, Paradise Beach, or the *ḥammām an-nuzha*)—the individual who *khasso* (is concerned) becomes visible once more, and, this time, in a different place firmly anchored within the larger urban geography.

On the other hand, contrary to the direct understanding of experience in Merleau-Ponty's phenomenology, in Beirut, the actual spaces of regained (queer) visibility are circuitous ones. While sharing a double nature, these spaces are, for the most part, fluctuating, and yet, they remain pivotal. Generally, they amount to double spaces that allow for "(re)orient-ations" and non-normative individual performances.[2] The resulting "performative spaces" do not only display real doubles that facilitate alternative and challenging openings, they also, often enough, make the regaining of visibility obsolete. As a consequence, these performative spaces reveal fictive doubles where the individual becomes the prisoner of a false self, revolting against the artifice of conventional discourse. Moreover, these fictive doubles provide an extensive stage for a widespread neurosis that defines, but is in no way limited to, the homosexual sphere in Beirut. It is a neurosis of sorts that is itself motivated by an overwhelming frustration, one that ranges from the vicissitudes of the potential sexual encounter to the larger ramifications of social life in Lebanon.

Despite recurrent claims that "naḥna open-mind, ma heyk?" (we are open-minded, aren't we?), the common self-denial among gay men, which in a country like Lebanon usually translates further into the widely uttered phrase "Ana mesh heyk" (I'm not like that), is often coupled with a generalized rejection of what is perceived as difference. Regardless of whether it is idiosyncratic, this difference, or what is identified as such, always points to a stigma that is immutably attached to the Other. This Other is often perceived by a man who, for whatever reason, "looks at himself" (i.e., is arrogant) as some anachronistic and paradoxical representation that does not need to be engaged with as a coeval counterpart. Thus, as the likely preliminary result of a neurotic and therefore exceedingly frustrated performance, many gay individuals, perceived by others as different, give up the initial quest for visibility and self-assertion. Instead, these individuals often wind up opting for an "invisible comeback." As opposed to recognizing—let alone accepting—difference, many men indulge in the deceptive politics of normative mimicry, which leads to the undisputed and definitive outcome of a paramount flight toward the anticipated safety of social invisibility. Furthermore, in a country like Lebanon, such mimicry always takes place in conjunction with the overall social pressure imposed on many to conform to certain fixed social ideals and behaviors. Discouragingly enough, the resulting anxiety often pushes the most genuine characters into the deceitful trap of social normativity, where the pitfalls tend to materialize in projected arrogance and, sometimes, psychological as well as physical aggression.

This complex deployment of aggression and violence fosters relations of identity formations that are frontal and every so often overbearing to the single individual. Thus, it is important to stress the significance of a resulting "zone of encounter" that in itself is oppositional and contradictory in character. For that matter, the very word *encounter* presupposes a confrontation that indicates a conflict between two or more parties. Accordingly, following the prefix *en*, the meaning of the linguistic element *counter* is based on the preposition *against* that generally denotes antagonism. Linguistically, this becomes manifest in the Romance languages; for instance, in the French translation *rencontre*, the element *contre* also translates back into the English preposition *against*. In Arabic, the word *muṣādafa*, which I privilege over its synonym *liqāʾ* (meeting), does not just translate into *encounter* or *unexpected concurrence*. The verb *ṣadafa*, from which the feminine noun is derived, denotes primarily an action that emphasizes the movement of turning away from, avoiding, or even shunning the very person the encounter has produced in the first place.

In stressing the importance of these linguistic connotations, I do not intend to argue that the various zones of encounter within the Lebanese male homosexual sphere are reduced to aggression, hostility, and resentment. After all, informed by chance, prospect, and opportunity, the related term *ṣidfa* (coincidence) points to the possibilities that always form an integral share of the larger equation. Nonetheless, the complex elements of tension, anxiety, and pressure remain part of an overall picture that illustrates the frontal and overpowering relations of alternative identity formations in Lebanon. The production of queer space there is equally connected to an orchestration of desire, which is based on individual and collective bodily performances and which continuously highlights the transformative potential of the very notion of encounter.

Thus, morality in the context of the ever-so-changeable homosexual sphere in Beirut remains an ambiguous—albeit unremittingly pivotal—matter. The formulation of certain experiences and their spatial interpretations and appropriations is, for the most part, prompted by groups of individuals who urgently need to perpetually find—if not imagine—zones where the "encounter," unexpected but full of expectations, takes place. As either an open or closed matrix that frames the homosexual encounter, the various spaces in and around Beirut often function as not just zones of encounter, but also of "alienation." It is a template against which material, psychological, and spatio-temporal fixities converge in a multiplicity of ways. The concept of alienation as such is a notion that Karl Marx first introduced as *Entfremdung* in the original German in his early *Grundrisse* (*Outlines*).[3] In this general theory of capitalism, Marx accounted for the transformation of human relations into things through the action of money, commodity, and capital.

In terms of the context of my present research, I want to extend this notion of alienation to aspects of individual, as well as social, identity formation as they relate to the social formation of queer identities and locate it spatially within the urban fabric of post-civil-war Beirut. In so doing, I further point to the ways in which, within the homosexual sphere in Beirut, this particular understanding of alienation not only renders commodity fetishism possible, but also how it eventually gives way to psychoanalytic associations concerning spatial identification that range from outright repression to more complicated practices of disavowal. In the meantime, these transformed human relations exert their coercive and lasting power over individuals and lead to an understanding of the production of space as being a culturally, as well as socio-politically, overdetermined product, where the individual identity is perpetually shaped by the spatial production and reproduction of social relations.

One of the most striking aspects of a spatially conceived formation of "queerness" in Beirut is that it actually prompts its practitioners to look for places that could become signs—"spatial signs" of sorts—that are convenient references capable of displaying their difference as identity. Thus, what ends up becoming a place of identification (for instance, the Café Sheikh Manoush or the Corniche) is neither the actual material "thing" (i.e., the premises of the café or the particular stretch of the promenade) nor its sign (i.e., closed or open space for the homosexual encounter), but the idea of the relation between the two. Although I in no way intend to overemphasize the distancing notion of an "idea" that may overly—and thus falsely—separate the particular individual from any given place, I nonetheless wish to underscore the importance of the relational aspect regarding the production and reproduction of space. I therefore dismiss an absolute (i.e., unyielding) understanding of such an idea.

In fact, my effort here has been to show that the site of the absolute does not exist. Or, if at all, it subsists only as some sort of emptiness, one that evokes an esoteric mystery. With this relational aspect of space in mind, the spatial production of queerness in Beirut transforms without major difficulty into a para-referential discourse, one that ultimately becomes associated with the lived idea of a social "lack." This is an important idea that is inseparable from the Lacanian definition of human desire—namely, a desire that is based on the inevitability of having to accommodate such an idea. As a consequence, the existence of that social lack, and the need to accept and deal with it as a concrete and "visible" reality, points ultimately to what I refer to as the myth and "invisibility" of queer subjectivity in Lebanon.

Anthropology and Urban Studies

During the years I spent slowly strolling along the various streets and avenues of Beirut and across the city's conspicuously small number of public squares, a multiplicity of questions haunted my mind and continue to do so to an extent that cannot be overestimated. I asked myself how I, as a queer-thinking anthropologist, was to conduct proper ethnographic fieldwork within the physical and mental framework of an urban setting such as the Lebanese capital. For instance, how could such a *Querdenker* contribute meaningfully to the broad field of urban studies, especially given the field's primary concern with the practical planning—rather than the theoretical assessment—of cities? In the case of Lebanon, I asked myself how an anthropologist was to respond to professionalized—i.e., applied—approaches that focus on a certain history of planning where the colonial heritage of ruling and erecting met with the obliviousness and amnesia of so-called independent local potentates and their various subjects. Moreover, I wondered about how such a person, trained in sociocultural theory, could tackle the subject of urban regulations, even if they were found to be socially counterproductive. Admittedly, these were all questions that challenged me, the queer-strolling anthropologist, tremendously—and they continue to do so today.

As to the explicitly rich and conflicting example of Lebanon, I asked myself one other question: Was the anthropological interest in urban studies destined to be a mere intellectual footnote in a long-lasting debate that, for the most part, has involved politicians, urban planners, and architects? Or might the discipline of anthropology actually contribute in some constructive way to a larger agenda capable of transcending academic parochialism?[4] As far as the latter is concerned, I dared—and still dare—to be optimistic. An anthropology invested in urban studies offers a number of perspectives that do not necessarily provide grand narratives about how political decision makers proceed in drawing lines of power on the maps of officialdom. In fact, the discipline looks back on a long and multifaceted tradition, one that is not just based on the political intricacies of spatial planning, but rather on the multiple social ramifications of what may potentially come out of such a development. These ramifications immerse any practitioner who is ready to activate his or her senses in the city's assailed consciousness. Such an immersion is rather like navigating through a Dalí landscape of baffling clues, memory lapses, and visual hallucinations in an attempted reconstruction of urban personality that is simultaneously a perpetual search for missing—if not to say, "lacking"—elements.[5]

In the case of Beirut, it is *after*—and not only *before*—the plans have been set and the actual buildings have been erected that the anthropologist is professionally most implicated. S/he assesses the many ways in which the newly produced space can be appropriated and contested by its very dwellers, those originally *intended* to dwell, but also by others moving up stealthily from the margins. Subsequently, the countless spatial appropriations and successive contestations occur despite initial political determination on which the original plans may—or may not—have been predicated. To say the least, Beirut is a complex urban entity that has been determined historically by the politics of setting and sustaining all sorts of boundaries according to various scales of class and ethno-sectarian segregation. As such, Lebanon's capital compels any anthropologist working the fields of this city's complicated urban fabric to find out how particular places within it are first perceived and later appropriated by certain groups and how these places become a larger social theater of perpetual contestation among its numerous dwellers.

However, this specific order of things is anything but rigid, especially since unpredictable negotiations on the ground are almost always part of a picture that comprises a range of social interactions. These interactions vary from seemingly random and unintended individual human encounters to the willfully anticipated collective contestation of particular street blocks that happens across all social boundaries, their particular configurations notwithstanding. The resulting lines of spatial contestation are all-encompassing and run throughout the entirety of the city, regardless of whether one deals with central or peripheral locations. Thus, the contingency of both center and periphery (as well as everything in between) is far from translating into a socially hierarchical model. Yet, given the historical significance of many urban sites in and around Beirut, one's attention as an anthropologist is almost always automatically drawn toward areas that appear to be key to the convoluted mental geography of the city and consequently, the nation at large. Along with its various spaces, *ḍownṭown* has been such a key area of primary political and socio-historical importance for the country. It also, however, has undergone repeated construction, destruction, and reconstruction over the many years of its tortuous history. In such an exceptionally convoluted place, many of the lines of spatial contestation come together and form a zone of individual possibilities, but also, sometimes, of unequivocal social limitations.

While *ḍownṭown* has been far from unique in representing a key site for a majority of gay men, it is nonetheless a prime example of a zone of encounter. That is to say, despite all policing activities on the ground, it is a tangible meeting place within the city for people who would not have otherwise come together had it not been for this particular location. Certainly, there are other sites—the Corniche or, as a matter of fact, the beach or a particular concert setting—that can be of similar momentousness. My necessarily selective discussion confronts the imagined idea of a center with that of a periphery, even if it is in no way intended to discount the importance inherent in neighborhoods tendentiously marginalized by commending perspectives I am reluctant to emulate. As I have shown, in Beirut, such perspectives are often driven by a social élitism that perpetually gains its "indiscreet" bourgeois bearings by compelling those who ostensibly do not fit to indulge in a conformist frame of mind. It is an élitism that is intended to solidify the projected vision of a domineering social order where precedence tends to be given to a collective performance amounting to a cultural masquerade that unfolds precisely in such exposed places as *ḍownṭown*. As a result, the countless daily lives that are experienced differently in the various neighborhoods of the city remain easily overlooked, even by individuals whose initial intentions were those of greater inclusion.

Thus, when approaching the subject of rampant and often unacknowledged social differences in Beirut, I do not want to fail to notice the significance of localized experiences. These experiences are often—but certainly not always—limited spatially to the relatively small area of the home or, for that matter, to an individual's respective neighborhood, a familiar place that frequently lacks diversity, which is then sought elsewhere. Therefore, the largest part of what constitutes the formation of queer identities is contingent on the production—i.e., contestation and appropriation—of queer spaces in and around the city. In Beirut, it is "open" spaces like the city center or the Corniche that people from different walks of life can patronize—for the most part—equally, even if such appropriation remains always predicated on the distinctions brought about by shifting socio-economic and political capital.

The initial opening in 2001 of *ḍownṭown*, with its glitzy façades featuring extravagant restaurants and expensive shops, culminated almost ten years later in Beirut Souqs, where the intricate maze of the completely destroyed Levantine marketplace was replaced by the sterile symmetry of a neoliberal mall. Many social critics voiced their concerns about the project, initiated by Rafik Hariri and his acolytes at the time.[6] Yet, for the anthropologist, it remains important to assess the individual and collective appropriation and contestation of a place, regardless of its political origins. This is why my focus is on the intricate bodily techniques that make such a "tournament of value" within the contested space of *ḍownṭown* possible in the first place.[7] This especially applies to the vicissitudes of gay identity formations, along with their recurrent disavowal.

As we will see through the following ethnographic vignette, part of the vicissitudes of gay identity formation in Beirut has to do with particular patterns of post-civil-war consumerism and the ways in which certain spaces become contested and appropriated as "queer" by different individuals, but never without the usually defiant character of their respective social environments.

Queer Assertions and "Homosexual Homophobia"

"Ḥa shūfak bi'l Dunkin!" (I'll see you at Dunkin'!) This exclamation had become commonplace in Beirut ever since the donut-selling franchise transformed, almost overnight, into the aspired public stage for large numbers of queer Lebanese, especially young boys wearing tank tops, tight jeans, and, very often, circumspect makeup. The great attraction of the otherwise bland Dunkin' Donuts chain, and specifically its *ḍownṭown* division after its opening in the early 2000s, for young Lebanese queers may in some aspects be trivial, but it is still worth examining within the larger context of gendered consumption practices in post-civil-war Lebanon. On the one hand, during the late 1990s, the chain's older branches in the northern suburb of Zalqā and on East Beirut's Sassine Square (both discussed at the beginning of this book) had a history of drawing relatively large queer-identified crowds. On the other hand, the fact of sipping cheap, tasteless coffee in a country with a coffee tradition that otherwise privileges the strong and dark nature of the stimulating beverage, and, at the same time, being voluntarily exposed to the gaze of others is all the more relevant when it comes to understanding the unbroken popularity of the locale at that particular time juncture. Yet, the question remains, how is it possible that Dunkin' Donuts had remained popular among queer-identified individuals in Lebanon despite the widely disclosed homophobic incidents that have perpetually occurred on its premises?

The local management repeatedly justified the donut shop's policies of ejecting certain kinds of customers by claiming that those who were asked to leave displayed a "conspicuous behavior" not in tune with the intended "family atmosphere" of the café. In every instance, those ejected were young men characterized by the management as "overtly feminine" and thus incompatible with the officially aspired character of the venue. However, even though its various locations around the capital city had repeatedly banned queer-identified customers, Dunkin' Donuts had remained throughout a popular hangout for Lebanese gays and lesbians. Everything changed in 2005 with the beginning of the stalemate between the Siniora government and its opposition at the time, a highly volatile political situation that transformed previously bustling *ḍownṭown* into a ghost town where many venues, such as Dunkin' Donuts, had to close their doors.

Yet, what was behind these directed practices in the early 2000s of removing undesired customers according to their gendered behavior? More importantly, why did other gay men, seemingly undisturbed, continue to frequent the place, as if nothing had happened to their fellow customers? The perceived lack of any sense of "solidarity" among the people who remained seated at Dunkin' Donuts resulted in part from the fear of becoming socially ostracized. This prevalent disengagement has to do with the consequences of resisting self-identification. "Ana mesh heyk" (I'm not like that), say many gay men in Beirut, ambiguously, as they reject an "overtly feminine" customer, resulting in the frequent disavowal of the possibility of a gay identity on their own part. In contrast, lesbians, being less invested in the dire politics of constantly maintaining a defendable public persona, are often sanctioned socially as mere "fag hags." In the early days, however, many lesbians empathized with the attacked young homosexual men, but rarely stood up to defend them publicly.

While this book is based, for the most part, on research I conducted among young gay men, most of whom self-identified as such, I occasionally interviewed homosexual men in their forties, fifties, and older, as was Charles Ingea. Many of these older men would have been reluctant, for a number of reasons, to equate sexual orientation and practice with any kind of gender identity politics. My research mostly excluded lesbians, regardless of age, due to the difficulty—if not the impossibility—of accessing the specifically "female" homosexual sphere. This does not mean, of course, that I did not interact with lesbians in Beirut. I most certainly did. The major difference is a qualitative one and based on my own identity as a man who could not have taken part in many social events that exclusively catered to women.

Despite my lack of direct access to the explicitly female homosexual sphere in Beirut, I not only knew that it existed but also that it was quite a thriving one. Yet, apart from a variety of social venues, like particular cafés and bars that drew composite crowds, it was more difficult for me to locate that sphere within the larger public realm in Beirut partially because of the numerous places within the urban fabric that, according to time and space, transformed unmistakably into zones of male homoerotic encounters, but not into their female equivalents. A further and crucial qualitative difference between the social ramifications of male and female homosexuality in Lebanon is the complicated politics of visibility and the spatial contestation of power on which it is based. A lesbian might often be exposed to similar social and family pressures about getting married as would a young gay man, but her perceived threats to a socially sanctioned masculinity are often different from the threats embodied by a male "effeminate" person.

However, to locate female homoerotic desire within the wider public realm in and around Beirut, one must look at a certain number of social venues that have for a long time attracted an exclusively female clientele. To be sure, this attraction does not always translate necessarily into homoeroticism, let alone homosexuality, but, from what I know, sexual connotations are rarely far away. Take, for instance, so-called women's baths, whereby I do not mean the equivalent of the men's *ḥammām*, but rather "seaside baths" that can be accessed only by women. For a long time, the most notable was Beirut's *masbaḥ ʿajram*, located at the eastern end of the Corniche in ʿAyn al-Mraisseh. While it was in operation, I never went there, of course, but according to what I was told, the general atmosphere of the bath was, to a great extent, homoerotic, yet without being necessarily lesbian in implication. The same thing applied to a relatively large compound near the airport that was closed off to the outside world and where a publicly displayed notice bore the prominent inscription *masbaḥ lil-sayyidāt* (bath for ladies).

It must be said that both these examples are somewhat limiting because of their socio-cultural specificity and the simple fact that they failed to attract most of the younger women who considered themselves hip and trendy. In addition, given their location, these baths tended to cater to an almost exclusive West Beiruti, or Muslim, clientele, thus leaving out large segments of the general female population in Lebanon. Lesbian public visibility became more and more salient at the turn of the millennium, however. Initially, such presence manifested itself in conjunction with the attendance of gay men. Later, a good number of bars and cafés opened. There, the customers were almost exclusively women and the overall female homoerotic character could hardly be ignored, let alone dismissed as being socio-culturally irrelevant. Bars like Ḥamra's Madame Om, with its suggestive homonymic gender-bending name, or Gemmeyzeh's Life Bar had been identified by the hip scene as clearly "lesbian" venues. Needless to say, there is a wealth of research to be done when it comes to the subject of lesbian social venues in Beirut.[8] Despite their various activist rivalries, lesbian-run groups such as Meem and Nasawiya have been vocal, notably through magazines like *Bekhsoos* and other online newsletters mostly written in Arabic and English. In 2009, with the support of the German Green Party's Heinrich-Böll-Foundation, Meem published an English-language collection of women's testimonies *Bareed Mista3jil* [*Mail in a Hurry*]*: True Stories* that focuses on female homosexuality. Although many of the stories border on a clichéd representation of a reality that is a multifaceted one, to say the least, the book constitutes an important beginning.[9]

The politics of homophobia and masculinity in Lebanon ultimately include men *and* women, and thus intersect with the larger dynamics of gender writ large. Yet, in their peculiar individual convolutions, homophobia and masculinity push many queer men and women into a dire performance of frequently having to maintain a defendable public persona. Consequently, the struggle over one's sexual identity in Beirut translates not only into explicit bodily practices and performances that vary according to space and circumstance, but also into the recurrent reproduction—by gay men as well as by lesbian women—of a heteronormative social makeup that results in the rejection of those individuals who, for one reason or another, do not fit the larger frame. Very often, it is precisely the set of attitudes, displayed by those who on the face of it do not fit, that reminds some gay men, for instance, of all the expressions of their own identity that do not conform to the widespread ideal of masculinity and that society tells them to repudiate.

Part of the answer as to why some queer-identified customers had been banned from certain places, and this without experiencing any sort of substantial support from other homosexuals—male or female—present at the scene, can be traced to a prevalent and socially generalized difficulty in accepting radical difference in Lebanon. Confronted with "conspicuous"—that is to say, "inappropriate"—behavior by young men who are far from embodying the traditional power attributes in a society dominated by the ideal of strong and virile males, the management of a coffee shop such as Dunkin' Donuts, in its stated straightforward argumentation, actually did nothing more than reconfirm this very ideal. In fact, this reconfirmation is a good example of how homophobia gets enacted and, therefore, internalized in Beirut, where "conspicuous" behavior often tends to be understood as some kind of threat to the larger social principle.

Accusations from within the male homosexual sphere in Lebanon that target the "effeminate" (i.e., "inappropriate") behavior of those who do not fit the social norm focus on men who are viewed as a source of gendered embarrassment and who manage to endanger the social image of an uncontested masculinity that generally fails to be questioned, let alone refuted, by large parts of that sphere. In the end, these recurring complaints develop into an internalized homophobia that reenacts all the biases and mechanisms of rejection entertained by the rest of Lebanese society. It is further an indignation that silently sanctions the various means of state suppression legitimized by Article 534 of the country's Penal Code that outlaws all "sexual activity that is contrary to nature."[10]

This generalized atmosphere of hostility often leads to a sweeping tendency to *shawfat al-ḥāl* (arrogance) by being some sort of a dandy, adept at charming or humiliating others while remaining opaquely cool. Namely, it is a collective display of arrogance, indifference, and pretense toward those who are not in tune with the exigencies of social conformity. It is a collective display of haughtiness, which has as its most pliant proponents those "dandied" homosexuals who have internalized a heightened sense of disavowal that is built on the larger repudiation of sexual difference. Ironically, however, before repudiating the "inappropriate behavior" of others through a composite process of projection of one's own repressed desires and fantasies, the homosexual individual has to first register the others' bodily performative expressions. This registration, in turn, never happens without the enticement caused by the "inappropriate" demeanor in question. This particular kind of registration, often followed by attraction before it transmutes into overt repudiation, is frequently linked to specific spaces in Beirut. Oddly enough, this particular dynamic becomes manifest, for instance, in relation to such social venues as Dunkin' Donuts because they facilitate in a variety of ways the peculiar convolutions of the local queer encounter.

Although not exclusively, the queer encounter is to be found within the larger context of conspicuous consumption and global consumerism. For those Beirutis who have some money to spend, there is never a better place from where to indulge in the elaborate local practice of seeing and being seen than a social venue like the outdoor café. Certain streets and promenades—such as the Corniche, Sassine Square, or Ḥamra Street—may fulfill similar purposes for the parading protagonist, but they lack in structural rigor and thus are rather unsuitable for anybody who is interested in celebrating wholeheartedly the city's distinctive politics of status and prestige. In the early 2000s, queer celebrations that tended toward the direction of a greatly elaborate bodily enactment of social distinction were to be found in places like Dunkin' Donuts, as well as in some other international franchises. Many of these social venues captured the integrality of a universe in which the diverse logics were only revealed by a close look at both their individual as well as collective performative manifestations.

In early summer 2001, on the centrally located Maarad Street in *ḍownṭown*, two establishments began to attract a particular clientele. Whereas Dunkin' Donuts tended, immediately after its launching, to bring in customers mostly in their teens and twenties, a café directly next to it, gingerly called "Scoozi," had become the playground for slightly more mature patrons who sported presumably heavier wallets. To be sure, there were some similarities between Scoozi and the earlier mentioned social hotspot Caspar and Gambini's. Yet, the latter distinguished itself clearly from the former by catering to customers whose heteronormativity could not have been easily ignored, even if some of them were self-identified gay men. The general ambience at a place like Scoozi was undeniably different, despite the ways in which it advertised itself. Whether the management had intended it or not, the Italian-sounding café was clearly a hangout for *tantāt*.

Both Scoozi and Dunkin' Donuts were closely connected places that functioned as focal points for thorough visual checkups within the homosexual sphere in Beirut. Nevertheless, there were many differences. At Dunkin' Donuts, a younger crowd took advantage of the locale's relatively affordable prices, while enjoying the full vista of the main promenade in *ḍownṭown*. Scoozi, in contrast, was not a fast food café. It had hired waiters to cater to its customers and was, therefore, more expensive than its showy pink-and-orange neighbor. Being more exclusive, Scoozi had become by early fall 2001 a magnet for those who could afford it and who were generally senior in age to the coffee drinkers next door at Dunkin' Donuts. Moreover, it was a place where, almost per definition, ejection policies were less likely to be enforced. This crucial qualitative difference pointed to another structural conundrum when it came to understanding the intricate social ramifications of spatially located queer identity formations in Lebanon at the time.

Over the years during which I observed the various individual and collective bodily performances on *ḍownṭown*'s Maarad Street, I realized that what made it treacherously "safe" for a male homosexual customer in post-civil-war Lebanon to sit at a social venue like Scoozi was the probability he would not exhibit a behavior that was deemed "inappropriate" by those sitting immediately around him. Or, at least, his demeanor would not be understood directly as such—that is to say, inappropriate and non-normative. It occurred to me that regardless of what he genuinely does, the older and financially potent male is more likely to embody the larger social ideal of masculinity than his younger counterparts at Dunkin' Donuts. From all I saw on that main artery, the older customer at Scoozi actually ended up fitting the overall social norm perfectly. Even if he publicly indulged in so-called effeminate behavior or was considered by some a "total queen," his potential critics, regardless of their own identity, would not necessarily label it as such. The alleged "inappropriate" character of his behavior would instead be gladly overlooked by those individuals who, under different circumstances, would have manifested undoubtedly the strongest homophobic biases.

I encountered the same rationale—or logic—throughout the period of my research in Lebanon. It operated on different levels, including the specific level of sexuality and sexual practice. For instance, while the all-pervading ideal regarding anal penetration and the convoluted politics of "top" versus "bottom" (two English terms that are widely used in all spoken vernaculars) verbally hailed the innate supremacy of the penetrator, as opposed to the penetrated, the non-verbal reality of the sexual act was generally different: the self-declared alpha male top (*dakkar*) revealed himself as an unquestionable bottom within the intimate sphere of a private bedroom. Therefore, regardless of the actual sexual position, the man who publicly managed to embody the social ideal of masculinity, and thus "topness," fit a norm that found itself reproduced again and again, even though the reality of the sexual practice could not be further removed from that very norm. In resisting the coyest self-identification as queer individuals, some Lebanese gay men projected an image, if not of self-hatred, then of poignant dislike onto the registered "conspicuous" Other. It was an "Other" who first might have enticed some attraction, but who eventually was repudiated altogether in a long and convoluted process.

Over the years, I gave much thought to the intricacies of this process. While I consulted many explicatory models, I found one of the earliest psychoanalytic interpretations of the complexity at hand to be the most compelling. I maintain this, even if I am willing to gladly acknowledge that the psychoanalytic interpretation I advance here only covers one part of reality, for this reality exhibits a complexity that always needs to be further contextualized within the particularities of the larger historical and socio-cultural frame of the ethnographic place in question. Therefore, in trying to come to grips with the repudiation of difference within the homosexual sphere in Beirut, I understood that it actually functioned to a good extent as the foundation of basic defense. Moreover, this repudiation was part of an individual protection mechanism that Freudian psychoanalysis refers to as "disavowal of difference."[11]

Sigmund Freud, in his later work on fetishism, interpreted this type of contradiction, one that is based on enticing attraction and a following repudiation of the object under scrutiny, as "disavowal" or *Verleumdung*. As a basic defense mechanism, disavowal fosters a split in the ego, leading it to first acknowledge—or be enticed by—and second reject outright what it perceives to be reality. Following this particular line of interpretation, I found many gay men in Lebanon (some of them self-identified as such, others not) confronting a conflict between the registration of the reality of their own sexual orientation (as well as that of others around them) on the one hand, and the social objection to that reality, on the other. By emphatically proclaiming, "Ana mesh heyk" (I'm not like that)—an utterance I heard almost daily from gay men who, on an individual basis, considered themselves *dakkar* (virile/masculine man)—many queer men in Beirut verbally repudiate the "inappropriate" behavior of other men and, by the same token, allow for the disavowal of their own sexual and, sometimes, "feminine" behavioral inclinations.

In other words, these men register—and not necessarily in negative terms, at first—the particularities of their own, as well as others', non-normative sexual orientation. They never do so, however, without also opting for the possibility of peering through the normative and exceedingly judgmental lenses of their immediate peer group. These lenses tend to be shared, if not reinforced, by a society whose overall hostility toward dissident sexualities remains all too often unbridled. In this peculiar case of homophobia within the homosexual sphere in and around Beirut, the vindictiveness of the former (i.e., the registration of something that needs to be repudiated) becomes the defensive substitute that actively reacts to the general "disturbance" of the latter (i.e., a largely hostile society). Therefore, the initial objection turns not only into *rejection*, but also into *abjection*, a state that inherently disturbs conventional identities and their cultural perceptions.[12] Accordingly, the social reality of sexual difference in Lebanon often translates into an actuality that is disavowed by the one *khasso* (who is concerned) because its unconditional acknowledgment is believed to provoke traumatic levels of anxiety that are bolstered by the dominant social forces.

To actively engage in the appropriation of space—be it in the rather loose form of particular social venues, like Dunkin' Donuts or Scoozi—can further the emergence of a platform for what I call, with reference to Judith Butler, the "performative iteration," where the reiterative power of discourse produces the phenomena that it regulates and constrains.[13] With a slight distinction from the original, I want to think of that platform as the very space where the Butlerian iterative formation of identities occurs not only through complex citational processes, but also through multifaceted performative bodily techniques that are spatially enacted. In both cases, however, to challenge the discursive, and oftentimes physical, affirmation of the paramount powers of society, of which arrogance and its vicissitudes are but the tip of the iceberg, remains a difficult task, to say the least.

In terms of the prevalent practice in and around Beirut of indulging in *shawfat al-ḥāl* (the state of looking at oneself) and thus displaying arrogance in the face of anything potentially unsettling, the most subtle and trenchant form of this affirmation is usually one of symbolic violence projected through collective cockiness and disregard for those perceived as

Other(s). It is a violence that Pierre Bourdieu describes as "gentle . . . imperceptible and invisible even to its victims, exerted for the most part through the purely symbolic channels of communication and cognition (more precisely, misrecognition), recognition, or even feeling."[14] Although it generally remains of symbolic nature—with the occasional outburst of physical aggression—this social violence is often enough appropriated by the state in the form of raids and other means of suppression, be they physical or bureaucratic.

In other words, the consequence of what I would like to call "homosexual homophobia" in Lebanon is part of the complicated performative struggles for "visibility." These struggles become most evident around the complex dynamics accompanying the appropriation and contestation of particular spaces around the country and, specifically, its capital city. Being always at the same time physical, social, and mental in nature, these spaces form the stage of context—or the wider field—against which the subject's individual performance becomes visible. While an indefatigably drawn-out city like Beirut provides the stage for all sorts of performative acts, their relentless visibility is always threatened with becoming invisible again.

In the specific case of Dunkin' Donuts, the situation was compartmentalized and involved a clear *internal* differentiation among the queer-identified clientele that culminated in homosexual homophobia. Although the "effeminate gay boys" returned to the café after the heteronormative discourse of the day declined, to a certain extent, in importance the following year, I would argue that homosexual homophobia is constantly being redefined, along with other social realities, in the country—be it through the social castigation of "devil worship," as we will see in the next and final chapter, or through other "scapegoating" practices.

CHAPTER 10

Raising the Rainbow Flag between City and Country: Dancing, Protesting, and the Mimetics of Everyday Life

I have given many examples of how certain places in and around the Lebanese capital are appropriated and contested by the homosexual sphere. Here I want to turn my attention to a social venue mentioned earlier, yet without further commentary. The place in question is the indelible Acid, a dance club that operated for about ten years in East Beirut's Horsh Tabet neighborhood. I want to add another close reading of a theoretically rich "closed space" because such a look permits me once more to assess the multifaceted dynamics of the queer encounter in Beirut, as well as the crucial role played by the state whenever it forcefully enters spaces it otherwise avoids.

Acid and the State

As compared to the old B018 club from the mid-1990s, which was located on a former wasteland, where the Orange Mécanique lounge bar was later built, Acid was a much less intimate place. The gay men I had met at the old B018 during the Israeli Operation Grapes of Wrath in spring 1996 had all but vanished when I returned to Beirut a couple of years later. Many had reportedly left the country in search of a better life abroad, be it in the Arab Gulf region, the global West, or any possible combination of the two. In contrast to the cozy atmosphere of the old B018, Acid was a raging flying saucer of a dance club. Perched on a hill overlooking the very area where post-civil-war Beiruti gay clubbing began (i.e., high above the site of the old B018), Acid shared a large parking lot with the nearby Futuroscope, an exhibition hall that catered to a limited number of annual fairs.

Given the club's huge success story, the management of Acid limited the opening of its venue to Friday and Saturday nights, charging every male patron an exorbitant entrance fee of LL 30,000 (US$20) and allowing female customers free admittance before midnight. Considering the overall bad economic situation and the fact that Acid was nothing less than a "gay club" (even if not formally advertised as such), the rationale behind the price and the differentiating gender policy was not clear. Yet, the policy did not seem to disturb anybody with whom I spoke. Mostly, I was told, it had to do with the management's paranoia regarding dealing with an exclusively male house. Even though the club's owners gladly took in plenty of "gay dollars," their concern was to "even things out" with the occasional woman who, despite the admission policy, often contributed money by sharing the entrance fee with a male companion in order to enjoy dancing to the hot rhythms of the season with or without her entry partner.

Acid was a semi-circular white construction that featured, on one end, two doors separated by a wall of blue ceramics. When illuminated at night, the club almost looked like an alien machine about to leave Earth for some foreign galaxy. "Cool" people began to stand in line at around 11:00 p.m. and the even "cooler" people (those who looked like "real men," were accompanied by "sexy female fake-blondes," or were just lucky to be on good terms with one of the hunky bouncers) were ushered in almost immediately. Inside, one entered a dark foyer used as a big walk-in box office where one paid the entry fee and received a coupon in return. The coupon was handed to a big man, dressed all in black. He attached neon plastic bracelets—the kind used for the same purpose at clubs all around the world—to wrists, and this was the formal entry procedure.

Acid could hold several hundred people on a good night, and it was rare to find it empty in the early 2000s, even though Friday nights were a bit slower than Saturdays. There was a huge dance floor in the middle of the club. The side of the entrance was flanked by a big stage, two half-columns on each side that functioned as individual mini-dance floors, and above it all, the omnipotent DJ mixing his spine-tingling tunes for the masses. Facing the entrance was one of the longest counters I had ever seen, fully stocked with cheap booze that would flow *à gogo* even before the evening had formally started. Most interesting to me was the design of that side of the club. High above the counter stood a dancing Shiva, the unrelenting Nataraja with his multiple arms and legs, as if to show to the crowds below what it took to have fun. While the statue of Nataraja in its peculiar Orientalist presence was one fixture that always attracted my attention, other points of interest—a bit livelier, but not much—were the three or four giant bouncers, who would totter on the dance floor, separating any male dancing couple whose bodies were perceived as being too closely intertwined. If caught in too "compromising" a dancing position, a couple quickly landed on the parking lot outside, unless the magic of *wāsṭa* provided them with some kind of moral, and practical, immunity.

It was impossible to mistake a dance floor bouncer for somebody else. All were dressed in black pants and t-shirts. They tended to be on the heavy side, and they all worked out to an unmistakable extreme. At some point, they even had blinking red lights, like those on the backs of bicycles, attached to their chests. At moments, it was quite a silly scene to follow: The clearly queer-identified crowds moving their feet and bodies as rhythmically as they could to the DJ's various sound arrangements, and, in the midst of everything, oversized, blinking gorillas trying to make sure that general amusement did not spill over into some immoral debauchery.

For some reason, the largest of the dance floor bouncers always recognized me. As far as I recall, we did not know each other from any other context, but he never failed to greet me by fervently shaking my hand. At the beginning, I always thought he might be mistaking me for somebody else, but with years passing, I got so used to this little ritual that I started looking forward to it. Some of my friends, who would pretty much always accompany me to Acid, even began teasing me, asking: "How's your cute gorilla doing tonight? *Ṣār already shī baynātkum*?" (Did something already happen between the two of you?) The answer to the second question was, of course, a clear *no*, for Acid's deafening loudspeakers made it impossible for the "gorilla" and me to even talk to each other, let alone move beyond the ritual of the handshake.

Around the time of my regular visits to Acid, between its opening in 1999 and 2004, I had heard on various occasions that the club experienced regular raids by security units of the Lebanese *darak* (police/gendarmerie). I was lucky that I was never present when such a forced entry by the local law and order happened. However, I distinctively remember one instance on a Saturday night in winter 2003 when some of my friends went to the club without me and returned in a state of shock. From what I was told, shortly after midnight, a unit of the Lebanese *darak* forcefully entered Acid, coercing the management to shut off all the lights before turning them on again.

However, instead of the usual dim, multicolored club lights, bright white spotlights were turned on. These intense lights were intended to blind those who had been, just moments ago, in the process of enjoying themselves. Oddly enough, when the *darak* arrived, all the dance floor bouncers suddenly vanished. It was then left to the police officers to move through the dance venue and inspect the, by now, terrified customers, who had evidently stopped moving and shaking, but rather stood there totally humiliated and in petrified anticipation. Shortly thereafter, all the female patrons were given permission to leave the premises. The men, however, were ordered to take off their shirts to permit a close and scrutinizing look at their upper bodies. Apparently, everybody complied without noticeable complaints.

As it turned out, the police were supposedly looking for tattoos, ostensibly a clear indication of "devil worship" on the part of those partygoers who had indelible dye markings somewhere visible on their skin. A few men were arrested at Acid that night and charged, not with devil worship as such, but with possession of drugs. (At the time, I was not able to find out what kind of "drugs" were involved and whether the individuals in question actually had "illegal substances" with them.) The rest were let go, but not without a 2:00 a.m. lecture on the positive influences of virtue versus debauchery.

It must be noted that winter 2003 witnessed one of the recurrent paranoid waves Lebanon experienced whenever the economic and sociopolitical situation fell into dire straits. To be sure, the very subject of devil worship was no national Lebanese invention and had its disturbing regional incarnations, notoriously in places like Egypt. What is important is that it provided some sort of rallying memento to parties, mostly conservative religious ones—Christian *and* Muslim—that would have otherwise never agreed on anything else. Within that logic, devil worship only seemed to afflict (male) youth culture, for its adepts were understood to be corrupted and thrown into the claws of further unrestrained self-indulgent behavior, like, for example, homosexuality.

Yet, what struck me as being highly noteworthy was the crucial fact that neither *mithlīyya* (homosexuality) nor, for that matter, *shudhūdh jinsī* (sexual deviance) became the official objections leveled against the "corrupted youth" at Acid. Instead, the authorities capitalized on the general devil worship paranoia of the moment and linked the young men's "abject behavior" with criminal activity—namely, the possession of illegal drugs. To complete this picture, I must include one more piece of information that shows the cunning absurdity of the entire issue, as well as the multiple, and, at times, competing agendas at work within it. As we have seen, innocent people get caught repeatedly within the same logic and must suffer the consequences of imagined negative identities that are deliberately projected on and ascribed to them. For instance, the discourse about "moral corruption" in early 2003 might have favored the intentions of some key players at the time, but it was not sufficient to unleash actual power politics.

Only a couple of days after the *darak* raid on Acid, what had initially been a timid rumor asserted itself. It appeared that the owner of the dance club had been in some financial disagreement with a competitor. As it happened, the competitor had important "contacts." Soon enough, those contacts metamorphosed into timely "help" in the form of official law enforcement. In trying to hurt his opponent, the competitor ended up hurting many others. Yet, his moral dilemma was a minor one since those he victimized were branded by many as not quite up to the overall normative moral standard.

What I am trying to suggest here is the peculiarity of the Lefebvrian "moment," which is based on a particular congruence, which is almost always necessary, of individual intentions, on the one hand, and general social perceptions, on the other, their respective problematic content notwithstanding. In other words, repressive actions, be they performed by the state or other authoritative agents, always need some form of validation. Such justification comes either in the shape of a discourse about "moral corruption" and the threat of "devil worship," as in the example from early 2003, or, as in the previous chapter, of a general perception that "conspicuous" and thus "inappropriate" behavior might endanger the supposedly intended "family atmosphere" of a cheap franchise café like Dunkin' Donuts. Thus, any given discourse virtually lubricates the intentions of those who have the power to use it for their own ends.

This being said, to be ejected from Dunkin' Donuts or to be humiliated at Acid does not mean, of course, that concerned "effeminate" young men or men, who happen to have tattoos, simply vanish from the contested surface of Beiruti social visibilities. They merely appropriate alternative places and persist in negotiating their way through the normative labyrinth. In the case of Acid, the same crowd that was humiliated on a Saturday night in winter 2003 returned to the dance club just about a week after the police raid. The place was packed—probably because of the free entrance—and the crowds danced rapturously to "It's Raining Men" by American R&B singer Martha Wash. All this points to perpetual changes in—if not to say challenges to—local hierarchies where official authority and the panoply of idealized masculinities are occasionally put into question, as shown by Michael Gilsenan's *Lords of the Lebanese Marches*, where ironic commentary, subversive laughter, and humor have the potential to "counterpoint" powers that otherwise are irreducible.[1]

As I have tried to show through the above example, homophobia, regardless of whether it is the homosexual version of it, is often based on its perpetrators' perception of "scandalous behavior" on the part of their victims. Fittingly, the word *scandal* (*faḍīḥa*) derives from the Greek *skándalon*, which originally meant "trap," but in the New Testament came to mean "cause of offense." Moreover, the word is translated in the King James Bible as "stumbling block." Furthermore, the relational framework of the Arabic *faḍīḥa* in mind, where scandal translates into exposure and possible mortification of the targeted subject, homophobia develops into the socio-cultural product of registration and repudiation of sexual difference mentioned in the previous chapter. Turning from politics to affect, homophobia grows ultimately into a shared trauma fostered by social exclusion—one that is iterative *as well as* spatial, where the small misery of the queer subject's position conflates with the larger misery of general social circumstances in Lebanon.[2]

Protesting under the Colors of the Rainbow: Another Story of Hadi

Within the homosexual sphere in Beirut, people obviously engage in homosexual practices where sex itself becomes an elicited desire existing in various social relationships. Generally, however, what is actually practiced sexually is located behind complex exercises of disavowal, where the talk oftentimes drifts away dramatically from the walk. At the same time, some people persist in their adamant reluctance to accept the ramifications of the slightest possibility of an equivalent social identity. As a consequence, instead of hunting down the all-too-often ephemeral emergence of a social identity, the queer-thinking anthropologist needs to look out for the various spaces that manage to accommodate homoerotic desire as well as the necessary conditions for a larger queer-identified encounter to happen. This is again the reason why I privilege the contingent notion of an "encounter," a spatial iteration of sorts, where, in dialogue with Judith Butler, social norms can be produced and reproduced in particular spaces, but also equally "undone," and where the fluidity of socially motivated individual characteristics makes itself palpable over the idea of a fixed social identity.[3]

What characterizes the spatial iteration of a queer encounter in Beirut? This undoubtedly depends on exactly what one is looking for. If it is instantaneous sexual gratification then many places could be the site of departure toward possible fulfillment. Suggestive gazes and evocative bodily postures may confront the informed observer strolling on certain stretches of Beirut's seashore promenade—the habitually celebrated Corniche—at certain times of the day or night, making it indirectly clear to him that the ostensibly nonchalant person sitting on the railing *khasso* (is concerned). The visual registration of the one *fāyit bil-jaw* (who is part of the atmosphere) is often followed by an apparently innocent—but heavily encoded—verbal and gestural interaction intended to make clear in performative terms the specific motivations of the individuals involved. At any rate, casual open spaces like the Corniche, the beach, or particular street corners within certain quarters of Lebanon's capital Beirut are by no means the only sites that provide the setting for either a contemplated male homosexual *jouissance* or, for that matter, the possibility of a sociopolitically meaningful queer identity formation.

As we have seen, Beirut is a city where the complex realities of its urban space cannot be understood without paying close attention to the local politics of sectarian segregation. In turn, it becomes significant to focus closely on particular streets, squares, or monuments, as symbolic markers associated with, among other things, the horrors of the 1975–1990 civil war. These markers are symbols invested with collective meaning and may be appropriated in different ways in the post-civil-war period by a group of people who assign to them new significance.[4]

The beginning of the U.S.-led invasion of Iraq in spring 2003, for instance, triggered dissent worldwide, culminating in giant demonstrations in, for example, New York, Buenos Aires, and London. Although Iraq is part of the Arab world, the region itself witnessed comparatively little public protest, a fact readily explained by the politics of local regimes fearing the hijacking of demonstrations by domestic opposition. This being said, a couple of thousand protesters gathered on March 15, 2003, in front of Beirut's National Museum. Located on the former *khaṭṭ al-tamās* (Green Line), which divided the city during the civil war between a largely Christian East and a predominantly Muslim West, the monument that locals simply call *maṭḥaf* (Museum) is itself a concrete symbol of the city's violent history. It was one of the major, and very bloody, crossing points where one could go from one sector of the city to the other, providing the political situation of the day permitted it. Back in 2003, the march against the war in Iraq was organized by various politically leftist associations and included activists from diverse NGOs (for example,

Antiwar protest in front of the National Museum, March 15, 2003.

Greenpeace). Also ubiquitous was the Syro-Lebanese secret service, the notorious *mukhabarāt*.

Raising flags of various political persuasions, especially in relation to parties organized along sectarian lines, is nothing new in Lebanon. What was distinctive on that spring day, however, was the waving of the national flags of those countries that had prominently opposed any military intervention in Iraq, namely France, Russia, and Germany. At the same time, a fourth banner appeared on the steps of *maṭḥaf*: the rainbow flag. Many protesters wondered what this flag was all about. Some even asked, “What country is this?” Other, more informed, protestors knew about the flag’s symbolism. Yet, they remained at a loss as to how it managed to become part of the larger antiwar protest, especially since it did not carry the Italian word *pace* in it, reminiscent of Italy’s pacifist party whose flags, at the very same time, had appeared on European and some American streets.

A small, semi-organized group of local gays and lesbians had formally gathered near the National Museum carrying a couple of rainbow flags and wearing T-shirts with the English inscription “exist.” What was even more striking was the fact that they were not alone in voicing their opposition. On the one hand, the protesters started their antiwar march toward Martyrs’ Square in the city center, walking on Damascus Street, the notorious thoroughfare that only twelve years earlier had been made infamous by snipers "protecting" their respective sides of the *khaṭṭ al-tamās*. On the other, a small number of unrelated individuals, mostly young men, took out "Out Against the War" posters that featured the colors of the rainbow. The message, albeit totally uncoordinated, was clear to some. For many bystanders whose language skills were not as sophisticated, the English words "Out Against the War" simply stood for the general sentiment "We are Against the War." They thought that the statement merely denoted the protestors' antagonism to what was, at the time, unfolding politically in neighboring Iraq.

To capitalize on this specific double entendre that characterized in part this particular period of protests, all of which coincided with the appearance of "queer symbols" within the public realm in and around Beirut, I interject one brief ethnographic example focusing on one of my interlocutors at the time that will further clarify my point. The reader will most certainly remember Hadi from earlier in this book. This young, self-identified gay man had been living away from his family and trying to make ends meet by navigating the high waves of local LGBT activism, leftist politics, and the art of belly dance—not to mention the personal dimension that linked him to individuals whose emotional commitment was rarely a given. In spring 2003, it seemed that Hadi was part of virtually every antiwar protest, regardless of the organizers or where it was staged. He was obviously integral to the March 15th demonstration, proudly holding up his sign that featured in colorful rainbow letters the words: "Out Against the War."

It was the very same sign that Hadi took only a short time later to a

"Out Against the War," March 15, 2003.

The anthropologist (right) and one of his friends, March 15, 2003.

different manifestation of organized antiwar sentiments, a demonstration held near the American embassy in ʿAwkar, a mountain village roughly half an hour northeast of Beirut. In Lebanon, the word ʿAwkar was—and continues to be—synonymous with the completely isolated and heavily fortified compound that the U.S. embassy became after it left West Beirut in the wake of the bombings on April 18, 1983, that had destroyed its premises in the capital. All this meant that, unless one had a valid reason and, therefore, an explicit invitation to venture into the compound, the closest one could get to the embassy was a Lebanese army and security checkpoint about a mile away from the fortified area's main entrance. The spring of 2003 witnessed a few peaceful demonstrations that took place in relative close proximity to that very Lebanese army and security checkpoint. The protests were intended to catch the attention of embassy officials, most of them bunkered in their compound a mile away, even though the distance might have been much greater as regards to their political and social convictions.

Also present on the day Hadi joined the protests at ʿAwkar was a contingent of men whose affiliation with Ḥizballah could have hardly been disputed. Their trimmed "Iranian" signature beards and the presence of yellow and green banners easily identified them. Hadi was in quite a jolly mood that day, according to a friend of ours who had also gone to ʿAwkar for the protests. (Since I was not present, my description is fully based on what I was told by my friend, as well as by Hadi.) Obviously not much concerned by the possible prospect of running into one of his brother's friends, Hadi held high his rainbow-colored sign and shouted, in English, at the top of his voice: "OUT AGAINST THE WAR!" As luck—or bitter irony—would have it, it did not take Hadi more than a couple of minutes before he rallied oratory support from within the Ḥizballah contingent. This resulted in a paradoxical stage setup on which a bearded chorus roared in unison, uttering unknowingly the same words that many LGBT activists around the world might have uttered during a period in which there was still hope that the U.S. military would not invade Iraq.

Save the funny and tragic character of the double entendre in relation to LGBT activism and Ḥizballah antiwar protestors, what my brief descriptions attempt to insinuate is the way in which a particular protest march condoned by most demonstrators, as well as by large parts of society, can be appropriated by different social groups. Regardless of whether one talks about the March 15, 2003, Beirut demonstration or the protests near the American embassy in ʿAwkar, the individuals involved take the opportunity not only to descend on the street, but also to make their specific concern visible to others. Mere "visibility," of course, does not guarantee a favorable response, let alone broad social understanding. The appropriation of certain urban spaces and sites that are invested with such deep symbolism—such as the National Museum, the former demarcating Green Line, and Martyrs' Square—points to the possibility of spatially locating the emergence of alternative discourses that are based on what I would like to call, in a renewed reference to Judith Butler, a "performative iteration" that has the capacity to assert itself within the larger sociopolitical debate.[5]

Again, to assert an agenda through visibility is certainly not an end in itself. Numerous repercussions are often part of the challenge. This became clear to me after a photograph (depicting myself as well as three other men carrying the rainbow flag), which had been taken by a journalist during the March 15, 2003, demonstration and printed a day later in one of the local daily newspapers with surprisingly positive comments, was reprinted a year after the event on the cover of a short-lived sensationalist magazine denouncing the "Nation of Lot" (i.e., Sodom and Gomorrah) taking over Lebanon.

Much can be said about why the magazine *Al-muḥāyed* (*The Neutral* [*sic*]) decided to reprint the picture (without mentioning the context in which it was taken) with an inflammatory condemnation of homosexuality and its alleged corrupting influence on Lebanese society.[6] Speculations at the time included such traded "facts" as marginalized journalists and their corrupt managers tried to carve out a professional niche only a "controversial" and "scandalous" topic could give them. Yet, despite all rumors, what I am most interested in showing is how, despite the probability that raising the rainbow flag for the first time in the heart of Beirut may prompt a vicious and violent counter-reaction, a globally inspired antiwar protest can provide the platform, or the general atmosphere, for a locally perceived—albeit often apprehensive—emancipatory understanding to emerge.

Moreover, in the case of Beirut, it is important to note again that such emergence, regardless of its momentary character, has been, for the most part, closely tied to key urban spaces, all of which are associated with past struggles within the city. Places like Martyrs' Square, *maṭḥaf* (National Museum), and the former *khaṭṭ al-tamās* (Green Line) are all spheres of previous, if not to say continuous, contestation among individuals and groups of a variety of persuasions. Oddly enough, such urban spaces have been providing the very setting, or stage, for the possibility of a politically meaningful queer identity formation to emerge.

Instances of perceived freedom can soon transform into a choking experience, however. As I tried to demonstrate, the organized re-imagination of queer identities in Lebanon happened, to a large extent, in the wake of the March 2005 Cedar Revolution and the withdrawal of Syrian troops, even if the 2003 spring antiwar demonstrations should not be underestimated. Despite the relentless violence that followed the military retreat of Lebanon's "big brother," many Lebanese understood the relatively short moment of lived liberation to be an opportunity to finally shake off some previously internalized fears. For the local LGBT group HELEM, this moment became the occasion on which to celebrate a joint "coming out," with all the accompanying international media coverage that one would have anticipated under such circumstances.

Further, it was the war unleashed by the Israeli army in July and August 2006 that permitted, at first, the increasingly visible community activism of this LGBT group. The summer 2006 war gave "queer" advocates the opportunity to put themselves at the forefront of some of the ad-hoc rescue efforts. It was an event that fomented ostensible inclusion, albeit a selective and temporary one.[7] However, the following political instability forced many of those gays and lesbians, who had already been in the process of becoming institutionalized over a period of four years, to momentarily retreat backstage. The argument intended to justify the retreat was that, given the politically delicate situation, the social visibility of any further activism could potentially lead to an increase in homophobic violence and to further hostile repercussions, thus bringing HELEM's efforts to a temporary dead end. Yet, possibilities remain open-ended. Despite recurrent momentary retreats by some activists, many reemerge in other guises, working on elections, for example, and engaging broad public discussions of queer and related issues.

Interior Experience, Social Space, and the Mimetics of Everyday Life

I want to conclude this chapter with a theoretical discussion by returning to one of my earlier points. I want to capture once more the reality of what I have called the "homosexual encounter" in Beirut and look again at the spaces or "zones" around the city that make it possible in the first place. This is only possible, I would argue, if one keeps highlighting the importance of different methodological angles that help make sense of the intricate social politics of appropriating and contesting urban space in post-civil-war Lebanon. Therefore, a disciplinary transversality that manages to integrate philosophical, sociological, historical, and literary, as well as linguistic, concepts into corresponding theoretical intersections becomes increasingly central in delineating the venturesome interplay between socio-cultural normativities, on the one hand, and the various tendencies that, within a spatial context, may potentially defy them, on the other. As regards the Continental European intellectual tradition, there have been numerous historical attempts to demarcate and explain this interplay, not all of which have accomplished their objective in accounting for its importance.

For instance, during the second decade of the twentieth century, the surrealists deciphered what they called in French *espace intérieur* and made an effort to extrapolate the passages and correspondences from this particular kind of (intimate) experience to social life as a whole.[8] Yet, in rejecting the very notion of the "everyday" (i.e., the actually lived experience of the *quotidien*) as a "bourgeois excrement of the mind," as André Breton disparagingly put it, the identification of the correspondences between an intimate subjectivity and the larger world, as well as the ways in which the latter was to be challenged by the former, increasingly became a task bordering on the impossible. In response to an always threatening failure to grasp how intimate subjectivity affected—and was affected by—the larger world, the surrealists claimed to subscribe to what Walter

Benjamin, within his own conjectural cogitations, had termed "profane illumination."[9] In so doing, they opted for a mellow evasion they called the "marvelous" (*le merveilleux*).[10]

In an altogether different—yet, to a certain degree, related—vein, the French eclectic thinker Georges Bataille wanted to link the surrealists' space of "interior experience" not only to the space of physical nature—let alone to the evasive shores of a hypothetical "marvelous"—but also to what he, in the most compelling fashion, understood as being "social space." For Bataille, social space featured a much higher complexity than the concept I have been using that is based on what Henri Lefebvre advanced, years after Bataille, in his own writings on urbanism. As some kind of ultimate foundation, Bataille's social space disclosed what he called the "forbidden" or "prohibited" (*l'interdit*), a category that he associated in his later magisterial work on eroticism with the *non-dit* (the "un-said"), itself a key notion that demanded what he termed "transgression."[11]

Over the years, I have found Bataille's theoretical writings highly illuminative as I considered the sensitive subject of socially marginalized identities in a place like Beirut. What attracted me most was not only the fact that Bataille's writings have as their focal point the multifarious production and reproduction of all sorts of social relations, but also that they attempt to make sense of these relations without discounting what Pierre Bourdieu, in a completely different context, would much later call "participant objectification." In other words, to navigate on a daily basis through the normative waters of Lebanese prohibitions and taboos—a large number of which are socially condemned in an almost Althusserian fashion by "interpellating" exclamations ranging from *ʿayb!* (shame!) over *ḥarām!* (forbidden!), to the disavowing *ana mesh heyk!* (I'm not like that!)[12]—is a strenuous enterprise for almost anybody careful enough not to fall prey to the many drowning undercurrents.[13] Yet, within the composite context of an embattled "social space," where, according to the most marvelous paradox, the kernel of what is forbidden is made clear to everybody, while, at the same time, prohibitions are asserted by avoiding talking about their very inceptions, transgressions of any sort become very often difficult to articulate. Instead, what tends to prevail within the homosexual sphere in and around Beirut is a reproduction of social relations where the multitudes of half-baked individual compromises—or sometimes the intermittent acquiescence—triumph over transgression and, for that matter, possible change.

Yet, it is also an act of "topophilia" in which I am engaged, where, as Gaston Bachelard put it, "[s]pace that has been seized upon by the imagination cannot remain indifferent space subject to the measures and estimates of the purveyor. It has been *lived in*, not in its positivity, but with all the partiality of the imagination."[14] It is that partiality to which I, as a queer-thinking and strolling anthropologist, want to be partial, for it also points to the tenuous process of producing queer space and asserting a queer presence in Beirut and the ways in which it is intertwined with a complex category of time, where nothing is static but prone to an unpredictable dynamism on the border of a spatial appropriation of sex that itself goes beyond a seemingly ready distinction, separating a dissident (i.e., queer) from a normative sexual orientation. For that reason, the differentiation and close analysis of the normative reproductive function and the greater spaces of homosocial *jouissance* are pivotal. As I have tried to show with my various ethnographic examples in this book, the individual and collective attempts at spatializing and asserting what I wish to call the "space of the *jouisseur*" point to a potentially transgressive and excessive kind of pleasure that is linked to the multifaceted nature of the individual involved. However, these attempts also carry the capacity to consume—if not devour—the living being through all sorts of social sacrifices and, sometimes, even individual suffering.

This being said, if the libido forms the organizing forces of all activities leading to *jouissance*, these activities have to be considered as the productive images of the ever-copious death drives that make a spatial appropriation of sex and gender in Lebanon's capital possible in the first place. Within a socially over-determined homosexual sphere like that in Beirut, the casual and disengaged pursuit of homosexual gratification and the continuous—albeit challenging—search for times and spaces of constructive creations are two sides of the same medal. This highly amalgamated medal is a working example and, in some ways, a paradoxical one. On its surface, the bodily drive to return to the state of quiescence that preceded our socio-cultural birth explains why so many individuals "look at themselves" and are drawn to embrace casualty and disengagement, and thus repeat painful or sometimes traumatic events (even though such repetition appears at first glance to contradict the drive to seek pleasure). Moreover, through such a compulsion to repeat and indulge in supposed comfort, many gay men in Beirut attempt to "bind" the experienced trauma. In this way, they allow themselves to return to this state of undisturbed quiescence—never mind its illusory character.

Yet, it is helpful to paraphrase Henri Lefebvre once more in order to discern the continuous and difficult search for times and spaces of constructive creations. For him, time, with all its socio-cultural constraints and limitations, inscribes itself continually onto space. As a result, the relation that space entertains with the lived reality of nature is but the "lyrical and tragic writing" of what links time to nature.[15] Contestation is, therefore, not a mere prerequisite for appropriation. Thus, in order to produce a particular social space in and around the Lebanese capital, the "concerned" individual has always to confront the phallic dimensions—not necessarily visible immediately to the uninitiated eye—of local spaces already in place.

Like many other cities that placidly experience the constancy of proclaimed transitions, Beirut translates into an urban realm that overtly privileges the treacherous assurances of built verticality. I have shown this in the context of *ḍownṭown*, but also as regards the new *manāra* (lighthouse). Within such a framework of architectural phallocracy, violence in its multiple manifestations—mental and physical—is not just latent and hidden, but very much on display in physical form as well as in the "discursive shape" of numerous "prohibitions" that come perpetually into play. Such social violence also becomes manifest in suppressing individual contestations to which gets opposed—or rather added—in an almost necessary social overtaking, the failure of their own potential transgressions.

The spatial existence of phallic—if not to say "phallocratic"—verticality, expressed in architecture and urban design in all but the exposed parts of Beirut, which are always prone to imminent physical destruction at any given time, originates within the various, and hierarchically very self-conscious, local socio-cultural pedigrees. The social as well as architectural manifestations of these pedigrees, which take up the form of arrogance and ostentation, point ultimately to the inherently compulsive and segregated nature of social space in Lebanon. Such compulsion demands, of course, a detailed social interpretation, especially since its manifestations are not always to be distinguished by merely looking at them from afar.

In general, social space is primarily a *lived* space and an architecture of concepts, forms, and laws with an abstract reality that always imposes itself upon the individually experienced reality of meanings, bodies, intentions, and desires. As the Lebanese historian Samir Kassir, who was savagely assassinated in the aftermath of the Cedar Revolution, argued in his stately *Histoire de Beyrouth*, the tension that has been characterizing the compulsions of social space in Lebanon since the local inception of modernity in the later part of the nineteenth century is played out unmistakably between "individual affirmation," on the one hand, and self-imposing "collective dynamics," on the other.[16] However, both currents and their various strained points of intersection cannot be understood without their respective and mutual spatial references.

Kassir used the revealing notion of "mimetic space" in order to delineate the practiced mimicry of a society that obstinately indulges in advertising an illusory diversity, but nevertheless chokes on the compulsive prescriptions of social conformity. To pressure anyone to adhere to fixed types of ideals and categories is the most potent compulsion that collective dynamics carry in coercing individual affirmation. It is a compulsion that may be strictly abstract. Or, with reference to Lacan's mirror stage and its important influence on the Althusserian repertoire of its perpetually "interpellating" exclamations of which *ʿayb!* and *ḥarām*! are but trivial, yet telling, examples, the compulsion may be very much manifest within the social fabric at large. Moreover, beyond the boundaries of such a fabric, social compulsion always has a concrete and shaping impact on the spatial—and, more particularly, architectural—configuration of the society of which it is a product.

Therefore, any kind of normative aspect always emerges from a specific space as well as from the ways in which this specific space gets indiscriminately destroyed by the various architectural phallocracies that rage in Beirut. In turn, the impact of social compulsion, reinforced by mostly devastating urban renewals in the post-civil-war period, directly constrains any sort of alternative affirmation that may be perceived as bearing some potential in defying society as a whole. Furthermore, as Kassir explained, all along the modern history of Beirut, the "phenomenon of mimicry . . . . went hand in glove with the [spatial] development of the city."[17] If one looks at the unabashed Disneyesque makeup of a decidedly commodified urban enclave that proclaims itself the "downtown" of a city the general character of which could not be further removed from the celebrated glitzy arcades on the centrally located Maarad street, imitation seems to always win over adaptation.

The compulsive presence of the seemingly most ordinary places in a city like Beirut, whether a particular building complex or even an entire neighborhood such as *ḍownṭown*, conveys the drama of an urban "scene" that, along with its stage and actors, is visually "seen" by everybody who feels pressured enough to be a part of it. However, while a multiplicity of bodies nonchalantly parade on the exhibition grounds of a city where normative excess is perpetually staged on its various catwalks of local vanities, there is certainly always a part that resists the constraints of a social framing and that remains necessarily an "obscene" component, one that, according to the inherent logics of Lebanese society, cannot and should not materialize in this space, but which is, nonetheless, perpetually in relation to it. The element of what I call "obscenity" demonstrates how collective fixities of any sort are not just surmounted by mere excess, but are also often circumscribed performatively in the most inventive ways. This also shows that the often-reproduced system of social rigidities is a matter of much more complicated consequence, namely one that puts the queer-thinking anthropologist in an almost impossible position to write about.

It is the fragmentation of the body that is precisely the material that feeds obscenity. For it is, as I have written earlier, in the bits and pieces of an alternative individual affirmation that collective dynamics, along with their resourceful compulsions, can be challenged. However, the Lebanese queer subject, who is per definition marginalized in a variety of ways by local politics and widely circulating understandings of ideals and commendabilities, has a difficult time manipulating the risky, though potentially enabling, techniques of obscenity. Therefore, to confront either the intricacies of Beiruti social space or its distinctive exhibition of signs and symbols tends to result in a large-scale sublimation that involves a perpetually compromising social mimicry rather than an overt revolt.

Further, having partly to recognize, on the one hand, the natural, sensual, and sexual differences imbued in male homosexual *jouissance*, but experiencing at the same time a sustained social adversity, on the other, literally freezes the homosexual sphere in Beirut and all the individuals that form it. In consequence, the sphere becomes particularly vulnerable to various kinds of external and internal aggressions, as well as to a rampant politics of internalized homophobia in Lebanon. To a great extent, skillful spatial practice, with its numerous techniques of contestation and appropriation, helps in producing spaces that come closest in providing the homosexual sphere in Beirut with the possibility of finding suitable niches and apposite avenues. Together with the resulting representations of space that are expressed through particular signs and symbols, social space in and around Beirut reflects the morphology of a society with a multifold nature that includes a multiplicity of zones of intersecting encounters and correspondences.

Both encounters and correspondences are, in turn, assigned to specific places through individual or collective forms of representation. As Lefebvre advances, "space is social morphology; it is to any 'lived' experience what the form is to any living organism, i.e., [it is] intimately linked to its functions and structures."[18] Yet, it is even more than that. To fully comprehend the social process of producing a space deemed as queer in

Beirut, one cannot emphasize enough the centrality of the body and its "morphological" capabilities of fragmentation. Any given subject's relation to urban space implies also the basic relation to his or her own (fragmented) body. To be sure, social spaces are anything but inert things: they are continuously used in a variety of ways and for a variety of purposes. As sites of dynamic lived experiences, they interpenetrate and overlap each other constantly.

In Beirut, the fractious conflation of what is being perceived, conceived, and lived, is never a simple—let alone a stable—one. It is not an abstract model. Rather, in their coexisting but immanent contingency, the moments of perception, conception, and lived experience must be linked together in order for the subject, as an intricate and dramatic member of any sort of social group, to pass from one to the other without getting lost, and therefore marginalized, in the process.

CONCLUSION

Struggling for Difference

That the right to be different makes sense only through the actual struggles to differ is an obvious statement. Similarly undoubted is the assertion that the differences created during these practical and, for that matter, theoretical struggles differ themselves from the socio-cultural particularities and distinctions that are induced within an existing and unremittingly lived everyday space like, for instance, the one experienced by queer individuals in Beirut.

The differences that merit being kept within the field of the queer-thinking anthropologist's attention, and upon whose reinforcement theory as well as practice can rely, can only be disclosed through a conscientious analysis of socio-cultural space and the numerous ways and techniques that enable many individuals and groups to continuously contest, appropriate, and adapt to it. As an integral condition of sorts, such an analysis must draw from disparate—and sometimes competing—methodological angles. Further, its idiosyncratic "line of attack" can only be conveyed convincingly by using different stylistic writing genres, which enable the *Querdenker* to engage in ethnographic montage and thus to assemble anew dissociated, yet very much related, elements in an effort to cover the whole panoply of the metonymies that define the complexities entailed in the practice of inhabiting socio-cultural space.

In other words, it is impossible to understand the production of a particular space, like the one contested by the homosexual sphere in Beirut, along with its conditions and ongoing intricate processes, without putting it in a critical perspective that highlights the importance of its specific socio-historical location. Queer space, like all spaces in and outside Lebanon, is socially constructed. It comes and goes and usually calls forth certain social relations within the homosexual sphere as well as between that sphere and the larger normative worlds that perpetually affect it. For many of those individuals in Beirut who appropriate it on a daily basis, queer space is both freeing and ensnaring. With the homosexual encounter, such space offers an opportunity for persons separated in other respects to come together in a particular place at a particular moment in time. Yet, by being a potential motivator, queer space and its production also function as a frustration device, namely in the shape of a catalyst that every so often reinforces the very social normativities it wants to defy.

All local particularities notwithstanding, a distinctive location like the ever-enterprising—yet greatly supercilious—Lebanese capital is far from forming some sort of cultural bubble, removed from its general environs and enjoying the fruits of some splendid isolation. Despite all self-declarations that function as advertisements to the contrary, Beirut is and remains an integral part of a larger world, one that is regional and global, where the circulation and translation of ideas are always shaped by local specificities. With that larger world, the city and the country entertain continuous and stern relations of perpetual appropriation and contestation. For that matter, any cogent anthropological approach trying to assess such an urban space must confront the countless ways and techniques in which any number of different individuals inhabit space while, at the same time, dynamically transforming it into the highest complexity of human dimensions. In so doing, this kind of anthropologically motivated urban study will ultimately have to deal with specific socially appropriated places and their larger context. More concretely, it will need to examine the socio-cultural distribution of bodies within these places. Apart from being continuously in relation to one another, these bodies also hold in their hands the capacity of fragmentation and, therefore, the latent ability to engender difference and, potentially, change.

The difficult and inveterate process of asserting a queer presence in Beirut has to be understood along these sensible lines. It is a process that operates by generating practices—sometimes astute and sometimes contradictory ones—from which a queer affirmation is incapable of separating itself due to the simple fact that it is also one of the delicate products generated by this process. At the end, after having expounded the intricacies of its own formation, the spatial production of just any sphere or, for that matter, culture (where the theoretical concepts are intrinsically linked to practical reality) will necessarily disclose itself as a challenging social process. This social process underscores the crucial elements of an everyday life that is constantly subjected to socio-cultural metamorphosis, making assertions (in)visible. It is, moreover, a process that must go *beyond* any assumed normative discourses that uphold the treacherous politics of dichotomies and naturalized hierarchies, as well as one which embraces the multiplicity of human possibilities within a city like Beirut.

On the very last page of Calvino's magnificent *Invisible Cities*, the Great Khan grumbles about Marco Polo's stories. The Emperor says: "It is all useless, if the last landing place can only be the infernal city, and it is there that, in ever-narrowing circles, the current is drawing us." To which the Venetian traveler lucidly responds:

> The inferno of the living is something that will be; if there is one, it is what is already there, the inferno where we live every day, that we form by being together. There are two ways to escape suffering it. The first is easy for many: accept the inferno and become such a part of it that you can no longer see it. The second is risky and demands constant vigilance and apprehension: seek and learn to recognize who and what, in the midst of the inferno, are not inferno, then make them endure, *give them space*.[1]

While it has no claim to make anything endure, *Queer Beirut* is intended as a small contribution toward showing how certain individuals deal with their respective everyday "inferno" and how they "give space" to expressions that do not always conform with what is socially expected from them. These can be expressions of "madness" and "love" that try to make sense of what I have called *junūn bayrūt* (the madness/love of Beirut) and the ever-shifting borderlines of a historically compound and disparate place such as Lebanon.

Notes

Prologue

1. Hugh Roberts, *The Battlefield: Algeria 1988–2002: Studies in a Broken Polity* (London: Verso, 2003).

2. Cf. Alice Kaplan, *French Lessons: A Memoir* (Chicago: University of Chicago Press, 1993).

3. For invaluable historical overviews of the Lebanese civil war, one journalistic and two scholarly, see Robert Fisk, *Pity the Nation: Lebanon at War* (Oxford: Oxford University Press, 2001); Samir Kassir, *La guerre du Liban: De la dissension nationale au conflit regional* (Paris: Karthala-CERMOC, 1994); and Theodor Hanf, *Co-Existence in Wartime Lebanon: Decline of a State and Rise of a Nation* (London: I. B. Tauris, 1994).

4. William Foote Whyte, *Street Corner Society: The Social Structure of an Italian Slum* (Chicago: University of Chicago Press, 1943), xxii.

5. Ibid., 358.

Introduction

1. For a classic ethnography on Tripoli written in the 1960s, see John Gulick, *Tripoli: A Modern Arab City* (Cambridge, MA: Harvard University Press, 1967).

2. For the similar concept of "self-making," see Jafari S. Allen, *¡Venceremos? The Erotics of Black Self-Making in Cuba* (Durham, NC: Duke University Press, 2011).

3. See Jasbir Puar's idea that citizenship is also a cultural process of subject-making. Jasbir Puar, *Terrorist Assemblages: Homonationalism in Queer Times* (Durham, NC: Duke University Press, 2007).

4. Pierre Bourdieu, *The Logic of Practice* (Stanford: Stanford University Press, 1992), and Michel de Certeau, *The Practice of Everyday Life* (Berkeley: University of California Press, 1984).

5. Rabih Alameddine, *The Hakawati* (New York: Knopf, 2008), 338.

6. Although overly quantitative in approach, Bruno Proth's study on French gay cruising sites is methodologically instructive. Bruno Proth, *Lieux de drague: scènes et coulisses d'une sexualité masculine* (Toulouse: Octarès, 2002).

7. Henri Lefebvre, *The Production of Space* (Oxford UK: Blackwell Publishing, 1991), 40.

8. Malek Chebel, *Le corps en islam* (Paris: Presses Universitaires de France, 1984).

9. Lefebvre, 40.

10. Judith Butler, "Critically Queer" in *Bodies that Matter: On the Discursive Limits of "Sex"* (New York: Routledge, 1993), 228.

11. See Jean Genet, *Un captif amoureux* (*Prisoner of Love*) (Paris: Gallimard, 1986).

12. de Certeau, 108.

13. Judith Butler, *Gender Trouble: Feminism and the Subversion of Identity* (New York: Routledge, 1989), and Eve Kosofsky Sedgwick, *Epistemologies of the Closet* (Berkeley: University of California Press, 1990).

Chapter 1

1. The Arabic expression *khasso* (pl. *khassun*) translates into English as "is/are concerned" and is used by self-identified gay men in Lebanon to refer to other gay men. Loosely, it could also stand for: "he/they is/are family." The same thing applies to *fāytīn bil-jaw*, the plural of *fāyit bil-jaw*, which roughly translates into "they/he are/is part of the [gay] atmosphere." Needless to say, the *jaw* (atmosphere or ambiance) can also refer to something entirely different (and not gay-related), depending on the very context in which the term is used.

2. Before the abolishment of the military draft in 2007, Lebanese law decreed that the national army could conscript only one male in a family of two or more brothers. A young man who was an only child, or who had one or several sisters, was exempt from military service altogether.

3. Cf. Lauren Berlant, "Intimacy: A Special Issue," *Critical Inquiry* 24 (1998): 281–288.

4. Since the closure of Acid in 2010, many other social venues in Beirut have attracted an explicitly queer following, including a dance club in the port area below Gemmeyzeh. This club, first called Milk and later Posh, was known for its weekend parties. On April 20, 2013, the club Ghost, in the East Beirut suburb of Dekwaneh, was raided and closed after the mayor, Antoine Chakhtoura, decided to get rid of what he called *noss rjāl* (half-men) and *liwāṭ* (faggots). See, for instance, Rania Massoud, "Arrestation de « travestis » à Dékouané: le chef de la municipalité se défend d'être homophobe," *L'Orient-Le Jour* (April 24, 2013): 1.

5. For a short exercise in linguistics that unravels the strands of imagery in the words *maqha* and *ahweh* (both translated as café) in literary and colloquial Arabic, see Muhammad Abi Samra (2012), "Maqha, Ahweh: An Etude in Café," *Portal 9*, issue 1 (Autumn 2012), Solidère Management Services, SAL.

6. Pierre Bourdieu, *Language & Symbolic Power* (Cambridge, MA: Harvard

University Press, 1991), 72–76. On the topic of cultural capital, see also his *Distinction: A Social Critique of the Judgment of Taste* (Cambridge, MA: Harvard University Press, 1991).

7. Pierre Bourdieu, *Outline of a Theory of Practice* (Cambridge, UK: Cambridge University Press, 1977), 78.

8. Ibid.

9. This is not unlike the "affective experience of radical emergence, in which lives and worlds play to great consequence between potential and closure," as elaborated in Naisargi N. Dave, *Queer Activism in India: A Story in the Anthropology of Ethics* (Durham, NC: Duke University Press, 2012).

10. Samir Khalaf, *The Burj* (London: Saqi Books, 2005).

11. Nawaf Salam, *'Itifāq al-ṭāef: 'Isti'āda naqdiyya/L'accord de Taef: Un réexamen critique* (Beirut: Éditions Dār An-Nahār, 2003).

12. For a thorough ethnographic discussion of early postwar reconstruction, see Aseel Sawalha, *Reconstructing Beirut: Memory and Space in a Postwar Arab City* (Austin: University of Texas Press, 2010).

13. Guy Debord, *La société du spectacle* (Paris: Gallimard, 1992), 15.

14. Cf. Walid Charara and Frédéric Domont, *Le Hezbollah: un mouvement islamo-nationaliste* (Paris: Fayard, 2004), and Mona Harb, *Le Hezbollah à Beyrouth (1985–2005): De la banlieue à la ville* (Paris: IFPO-Karthala, 2010).

15. See John Chalcraft, *The Invisible Cage: Syrian Migrant Workers in Lebanon* (Stanford: Stanford University Press, 2008).

16. Lebanese plural of the French word *tante* ("auntie"). Within the context of queer-identified crowds in Lebanon, *tante* defines any male homosexual declared to be effeminate and thus a "queen," although that perceived effeminacy is no requirement for the identification. Otherwise, the word is used—mostly among Christians—to formally address the sister of one's mother or father or the wife of one's uncle. It is also used as a term of respect for any older woman.

17. This is the very reason why I prefer to refer to Georgette as "he" rather than "she."

18. At the time of my fieldwork, fifteen hundred Lebanese liras represented roughly the equivalent of one U.S. dollar, a rate fixed and agreed upon at the end of the civil war at the beginning of the 1990s. In part due to this fixed exchange rate, it was customary to use the bills of both currencies, L.L. and US$, interchangeably. This has not changed at the time of the publication of this book.

19. Valérie Clerc-Huybrechts, *Les quartiers irréguliers de Beyrouth: Une histoire des enjeux fonciers et urbanistiques dans la banlieue sud* (Paris: IFPO, 2008).

20. For a linguistic analysis of gender within the context of the French language, see Natacha Chetcuti and Luca Greco, eds., *La face cachée du genre: Langage et pouvoir des normes* (Paris: Presses Sorbonne Nouvelle, 2012).

21. Plural of *ṭobjī*, which is a local derogatory term used to describe a male homosexual. The closest English equivalent would probably be the word "faggot."

22. While Article 534 of the Lebanese Penal Code outlaws all "sexual activity that is contrary to nature," nothing to date specifically addresses homosexuality in legal terms, despite attempts by some Lebanese parliamentarians to pass motions that would explicitly criminalize homosexuality.

Chapter 2

1. For a book that emphasizes the importance of narrative in capturing affect, representation, and resistance, see Dina Georgis, *The Better Story: Queer Affects from the Middle East* (Albany: SUNY Press, 2013).

2. Steven Seidman, "The Politics of Cosmopolitan Beirut: From the Stranger to the Other," *Theory, Culture & Society* 29, no. 2 (2012): 3–36, and Diane Singerman and Paul Amar, *Cairo Cosmopolitan: Politics, Culture, and Urban Space in the New Globalized Middle East* (Cairo: American University in Cairo Press, 2009).

3. See Éric Verdeil, *Beyrouth et ses urbanistes: Une ville en plans (1946–1975)* (Beirut: Presses de l'IFPO, 2009).

4. This challenge spatially juxtaposed Riād al-Ṣolḥ Square with Martyrs' Square. The former was occupied by the "March 8th Coalition"; the latter, by the "March 14th Alliance." Both refer to huge political rallies that took place in 2005 in the wake of the assassination of Rafik Hariri.

5. Timothy Mitchell, *Colonising Egypt* (Berkeley: University of California Press, 1991), 34 ff.

6. See Mathew Gagné, "Queer Beirut Online: The Participation of Men in Gayromeo.com," *Journal of Middle East Women's Studies* 8, no. 3, Queering Middle Eastern Cyberscapes (Fall 2012): 113–137.

7. The term *douwara69* refers to a person (female) who "gets around" and enjoys the 69 position of mutual oral sexual gratification. A widely used phrase in Lebanon, *t2borni* literally translates into "you bury me," but here has the context-dependent connotation "you're too much for me," "you turn me on so much."

8. Jens Hanssen, *Fin de Siècle Beirut: The Making of an Ottoman Provincial Capital* (Oxford: Clarendon Press, 2005), 13.

9. For an ethnographic study that has convincingly captured the very context in which an individual and collective commitment is inspired by a social consciousness that is undoubtedly channeled through a sectarian logic, but never without failing to acknowledge and address the country's broader socio-political picture, see Lara Deeb, *An Enchanted Modern: Gender and Public Piety in Shi'i Lebanon* (Princeton: Princeton University Press, 2006).

Chapter 3

1. See Éric Verdeil, Ghaleb Faour, and Sébastien Velut, *Atlas du Liban: Territoires et Société* (Beirut: IFPO/CNRS, 2007).

2. See Waddah Chararah, "From the Walled Town of Eight Gates to the Architecture of the City," *Portal 9*, issue 1 (Autumn 2012).

3. Samir Kassir, *Histoire de Beyrouth* (Paris: Librairie Arthème Fayard, 2003).

4. Nada Sehnaoui, *L'occidentalisation de la vie quotidienne à Beyrouth, 1860–1914* (Beirut: Éditions Dār An-Nahār, 2002).

5. Jens Hanssen, *Fin de Siècle Beirut: The Making of an Ottoman Provincial Capital* (Oxford: Clarendon Press, 2005), 55. See also Carla Eddé, *Beyrouth: Naissance d'une capitale (1918–1924)* (Paris: Sindbad, 2009).

6. See also Fawwaz Traboulsi, *A History of Modern Lebanon* (London: Pluto

Press, 2007), and Carol Hakim, *The Origins of the Lebanese National Idea: 1840–1920* (Berkeley: University of California Press, 2013).

7. Fuad I. Khuri, *From Village to Suburb: Order and Change in Greater Beirut* (Chicago: University of Chicago Press, 1975).

8. Kamal Salibi, *A House of Many Mansions: The History of Lebanon Reconsidered* (Berkeley: University of California Press, 1988).

9. Samir Kassir, *Considérations sur le malheur arabe* (Paris: Actes Sud, 2004), 31.

10. See Kristin Monroe, "Being Mobile in Beirut," *City & Society* 23, no. 1 (2011): 91–111.

11. William B. Helmreich, *The New York Nobody Knows: Walking 6,000 Miles in the City* (Princeton: Princeton University Press, 2013), 10.

12. Michel de Certeau, *The Practice of Everyday Life* (Berkeley: University of California Press, 1984), 93.

13. Cf. French *faire marcher quelque chose* (to make something work/walk) vs. *faire marcher quelqu'un* (to play a joke on somebody).

14. Walter Benjamin, "M [der Flaneur]," *Das Passagen-Werk*, vol. 1 (Frankfurt: Edition Suhrkamp, 1983), 524–569.

15. Susan Buck-Morss, *The Dialectics of Seeing: Walter Benjamin and the Arcades Project* (Cambridge, MA: MIT Press, 1989).

16. Louis Aragon, *Le paysan de Paris* (Paris: Éditions Gallimar, 1998).

17. Henri Lefebvre, *Rhythmanalysis: Space, Time and Everyday Life* (London: Continuum, 2004).

18. Pierre Bourdieu, *In Algerien: Zeugnisse der Entwurzelung*, ed. Franz Schultheis and Christine Frisinghelli (Graz: Camera Austria, 2003), 16, and, even more so, Pierre Bourdieu and Abdelmalek Sayad, *Le déracinement: La crise de l'agriculture traditionnelle en Algérie* (Paris: Les Éditions de Minuit, 1964).

19. Samir Khalaf and Per Kongstad, *Hamra of Beirut: A Case of Rapid Urbanization* (Leiden: Brill, 1973), 3. For an earlier contribution on Beirut's "Western-influenced identity," see Helmut Ruppert, *Beirut: Eine westlich geprägte Stadt des Orients* (Erlangen: Mitteilungen der Fränkischen Geographischen Gesellschaft, Band 15/16 für 1968 und 1969).

20. Carleton Coon, *Caravan: The Story of the Middle East* (New York: Holt, Rinehart, and Winston, 1958).

21. For a classic study on heterosexual (female) prostitution, see Samir Khalaf, *Prostitution in a Changing Society: A Sociological Survey of Legal Prostitution in Beirut* (Beirut: Khayats, 1965).

22. To "make someone" miss calls (i.e., to make missed calls; *missedcallāt* in Lebanese Arabic) was a way for the caller to avoid spending any valuable units (only the caller was charged), but it forced the called party to call back.

23. *Ashrafieh* is the Arabic equivalent of *Bellevue* (beautiful view).

24. Elias Khoury, *Al-jabal al-saghīr* (Beirut: Muassassat al-abhāth al-arabiyya), 1977.

25. The Greek Orthodox Sursock family constituted the first generation of modern Beiruti wealth (for the most part based on absentee landownership in the late nineteenth and early twentieth centuries Palestine). Shortly after World War II, Yvonne Sursock married Desmond Cochrane, an Irishman of lower nobil-

ity. Over the decades, "Lady Cochrane" became a prominent public figure in Lebanon.

Chapter 4

1. On the subject of camp, see Susan Sontag, "Notes on Camp," *Partisan Review* 31 (Fall 1964): 515–530.

2. While the syncretization of St. Barbara and Chango, the god of thunder, as celebrated by followers of Santería in Cuba was not known by my interlocutors in Lebanon, it remains important to note that part of the Catholic saint's appeal for many Caribbean voodoo celebrants is her ability to embody different characters.

3. Mikhail Bakhtin, *Rabelais and His World*, trans. Hélène Iswolsky (Bloomington: Indiana University Press, 1984).

4. Since 1948, UNRWA has been serving Palestinian refugees in historical Palestine as well as in neighboring Arab countries, notably Lebanon, Jordan, and Syria.

5. See Betty S. Anderson, *The American University of Beirut: Arab Nationalism and Liberal Education* (Austin: University of Texas Press, 2011).

6. Alain Ménargues, *Les secrets de la guerre du Liban: Du coup d'État de Bachir Gémayel aux massacres des camps palestiniens* (Paris: Albin Michel, 2004).

7. See, for instance, Lara Deeb, *An Enchanted Modern: Gender and Public Piety in Shi'i Lebanon* (Princeton: Princeton University Press, 2006), and Roxanne Varzi, *Warring Souls: Youth, Media, and Martydom in Post-Revolution Iran* (Durham, NC: Duke University Press, 2006) for Iran.

8. One of the most compelling accounts of the Sabra and Shatila massacres is Jean Genet's "Quatre heures à Chatila" ("Four Hours in Shatila"). An initially censored version was published in *Revue d'études palestiniennes*, January 1, 1983.

9. Julie M. Peteet, *Gender in Crisis: Women and the Palestinian Resistance Movement* (New York: Columbia University Press, 1991), 212.

10. Fernand Braudel, *Écrits sur l'histoire* (Paris: Flammarion, 1969).

11. See Zeina Maasri, *Off the Wall: Political Posters of the Lebanese Civil War* (London: I. B. Tauris, 2009).

12. Ahmad Beydoun, "A Note on Confessionalism," *Lebanon in Limbo: Postwar Society and State in an Uncertain Regional Environment*, ed. Theodor Hanf and Nawaf Salam (Baden-Baden: Nomos Verlagsgesellschaft 2003), 75–86, and Ussama Makdisi, *The Culture of Sectarianism: Community, History, and Violence in Nineteenth-Century Ottoman Lebanon* (Berkeley: University of California Press, 2000).

Chapter 5

1. The place is named for Zicco, an eccentric character of Beirut's politico-artistic stage. His love and admiration for the Brazilian player Zico led him to adopt the name as his own.

2. Brian Whitaker, *Unspeakable Love: Gay and Lesbian Life in the Middle East* (London: Saqi Books, 2006), 41 ff.

3. See Ghassan Makarem, "The Story of HELEM," *Journal of Middle East Women's Studies* 7, no. 3 (Fall 2011): 98–112.

4. Noteworthy is HELEM's in-house magazine *Barra*, which has been appearing regularly since March 2005. The Arabic word *barra* translates as "out," but it has a double connotation within the Lebanese context, where it also refers to anything outside Lebanon. It thus becomes a general space of yearning, awe, and apprehension.

5. See Lara Deeb, *An Enchanted Modern: Gender and Public Piety in Shiʿi Lebanon* (Princeton: Princeton University Press, 2006).

6. For a forceful collection of positions and testimonies by intellectuals, writers, and activists regarding homosexuality in Lebanon, see *Ruhāb al-mithlīyya: mawāqif wa shahādāt*, the 2006 volume published by HELEM in conjunction with the now defunct *CD-Thèque*.

7. See Michael Gilsenan, "Lying, Honor, and Contradiction," *Transaction and Meaning*, ed. B. Kapferer (Philadelphia: Institute for the Study of Human Issues, 1976), 191–219.

Chapter 6

1. *Shabāb* is the Arabic plural of *shāb* and translates into English as "male youngster."

2. Local human rights, women's, and citizenship organizations made a concerted effort to change the law's wording and prevent it from becoming even more reactionary. See *Al-jamʿiyya al-lubnāniyya li-ḥuqūq al-insān*, et al., *Al-karāma al-insāniyya fi qānūn al-ʿuqūbāt* (Beirut: Sader/*Al-manshūrāt al-ḥuqūqiyya*, 2003).

Chapter 7

1. For a fictional taxi driver's rendering of Beirut as a collage of waking dreams, see Rasha Atrash, "The Wizard of Caracas," *Portal 9*, 1 (2012).

2. In Beirut, the word *manāra* refers to either the old or the new lighthouse, as well as to the neighborhood (here with a capital *M*) around it. In a way, the neighborhood is the western extension of the Ḥamra district, at the westernmost tip of the city.

3. Nabil Kaakoush, "Hey Handsome," *Transit Beirut: New Writing and Images*, ed. Roseanne Saad Khalaf and Malu Halasa (Beirut and London: Saqi Books, 2004), 166–173.

4. Samir Khalaf, *Prostitution in a Changing Society: A Sociological Survey of Legal Prostitution in Beirut* (Beirut: Khayats, 1965), especially 13–50.

5. See Nada Abdel-Samad, *Wādī abu-jmīl: Qisas ʿan yahūd bayrūt* (Beirut: dār al-nahār, 2010).

6. This consideration is partly informed by Pierre Nora's *lieux de mémoire* (i.e.,

"realms" or rather, "sites" of memory). Pierre Nora and David P. Jordan, eds., *Rethinking France: Les Lieux de mémoire, Volume 2: Space* (Chicago: University of Chicago Press, 2006).

7. On April 18, 1983, the old U.S. embassy building became the target of a suicide bomber. The attack killed sixty-three people and happened in the wake of the intervention of a multinational force that included military personnel from countries such as France, Italy, and the United States.

8. Maurice Halbwachs, *On Collective Memory* (Chicago: University of Chicago Press, 1992).

9. Jad Tabet, *Al-iʿmār wal-maslaḥa al-ʿāma fil-turāth wal-ḥadātha: Madīnat al-ḥarb wa dhākirat al-mustaqbal* (Beirut: dār al-jadīd, 1996). See also Ziyad Baroud, et al., *Dhākira lil-ghad/Mémoire pour l'avenir/Memory for the future: Actes du colloque tenu à Beyrouth les 30 et 31 mars 2001* (Beirut: Éditions Dār An-Nahār, 2002), and Saree Makdisi, "Beirut, a City without History?" *Memory and Violence in the Middle East and North Africa*, ed. Ussama Makdisi and Paul A. Silverstein (Bloomington: Indiana University Press, 2006), 201–214.

10. On December 27, 2013, the Starco Building became the site of a bomb blast that killed the former Lebanese finance minister, Mohammad Shatah, along with seven others. Shatah had been part of the March 14th Alliance. In ostensible retaliation, a car bomb went off in Ḥizballah-dominated Ḥāret-Ḥreik on January 2, 2014.

11. Nora and Jordan, eds. *Rethinking France*.

12. Italo Calvino, *Invisible Cities* (New York: Harcourt Brace & Company, 1974), 10.

13. Tabet, 225 ff.

14. Hans Gebhardt, et al., *History, Space and Social Conflict in Beirut: The Quarter of Zokak el-Blat* (Würzburg: Ergon, 2005).

15. See Hala Halim, *Alexandrian Cosmopolitanism: An Archive* (New York: Fordham University Press, 2013).

16. See Carlos Ulises Decena, *Tacit Subjects: Belonging and Same-Sex Desire among Dominican Immigrant Men* (Durham, NC: Duke University Press, 2011). The book was written from the perspectives of immigrant communities in New York City.

Chapter 8

1. In neighboring Syria, as well as in Turkey and the Maghrib, regular visits to the *ḥammām* have long been de rigueur for many men and women, regardless of their social background and sexual orientation. In contrast, since the end of the 1975–1990 civil war, the *ḥammām* experience in Lebanon has been limited to a few establishments that typically cater to a queer male clientele. This includes Shahrazade in Burj Ḥammūd, El Cheikh near the Cola Bridge (which, despite all apparent success, closed shortly after it opened in the mid-2000s), and the more recent Agha, located behind the Hotel Bristol, close to the Ḥamra district. There is also the *ḥammām al-ʿabd* in Tripoli's old market, as well as the lesser-known

bathhouse just below the Casino du Liban in Maameltain, which has always been more a male brothel than a bathhouse.

2. For a novelistic rendering of *ḥammām an-nuzha*, see the German novel by Marko Martin, *Der Prinz von Berlin* (Berlin: Ullstein, 2001).

3. As part of a constructed self-confidence that feeds on a latent inferiority complex toward an imagined "West" and converts it into one of superiority toward what is considered the "East," the English term *open-minded*, or its local adjectival corruption *open-mind*, has been widely used in recent years as a local self-description in Lebanese Arabic. "*Naḥna open-mind*" would therefore translate into "we are open-minded."

4. See Gaston Bachelard, *The Poetics of Space* (Boston: Beacon Press, 1994).

5. Quoted from Henri Lefebvre, *The Production of Space* (Oxford: Blackwell Publishers, 1991), 181. The original German in *Das Philosophenbuch* reads: "Alle Gestalt ist dem Subjekt zugehörig. Es ist das Erfassen der Oberflächen durch den Spiegel."

6. Ibid., emphasis added.

7. Jacques Lacan, "Le stade du miroir comme formateur de la fonction du Je," in *Écrits*, vol. 1 (Paris: Éditions du Seuil, 1999), 92–99.

8. One of the popular and widely circulating Arabic terms used within the homosexual sphere in Beirut to describe somebody who is befallen by such a state of mind is *mafṣūm* (loosely translated as "schizophrenic"). The *mafṣūm* suffers from *infiṣām shakhsī* (split personality) and is perpetually caught between the various challenges that compel him to conform to the normative ideal of "looking at himself."

9. Laura Mulvey, "Visual Pleasure and Narrative Cinema," *Screen* 16, no. 3 (1975): 6–18.

10. See José Esteban Muñoz, *Disidentifications: Queers of Color and the Performance of Politics* (Minneapolis: University of Minnesota Press, 1999).

11. AUH is American University Hospital, which is affiliated with the American University of Beirut (AUB).

12. The exclamation *uff!*, along with its dual form *uffayn!* and plural *uffūf!* (the last two are idiosyncratic inventions and rarely used), circulates widely in Lebanese daily verbal interactions. It expresses annoyance, but also momentary complaint about basically anything and everything. There are times when one can have a conversation in which the exclamation is used in virtually every sentence, much to the chagrin of my friend and fellow anthropologist, Sonali Pahwa. During a visit to Beirut from Cairo, where she did research on Egyptian experimental theater, she could not believe her ears and the sorry fact that her friend had taken up the "natives' bad habit."

13. This Ottoman Turkish term refers to the part of the house open to guests who do not have access to the *ḥaramlik*, which is the domain of the family.

14. To mark distinction and willful ostentation, the term *VVIP* (Very Very Important Person) is widely used in Lebanon and encountered at a range of, for example, social events or restaurants with valet parking.

15. Christopher Stone, (2007) *Popular Culture and Nationalism in Lebanon: the Fairouz and Rahbani Nation*, Routledge Studies in Middle Eastern Literatures

(Abingdon, UK: Routledge, 2007), and Fawwaz Traboulsi, "Crisis and Memory in the Theater of the Rahbāni-Brothers and Fayrūz," *Crisis and Memory in Islamic Societies*, ed. Angelika Neuwirth and Andreas Pflitsch (Beirut: Ergon Verlag Würzburg, 2001), 499–508.

16. The word for "village" in Lebanese Arabic, generally referring to the various rural communities in and around Mount Lebanon that distinguish themselves in character from the urbanity of the coastal capital, Beirut.

17. The vernacular phrase is loosely translated into English from Lebanese Arabic into either "what I know of you" or "the way I know you."

18. Timothy Mitchell, *Colonising Egypt* (Berkeley: University of California Press, 1991).

19. See Ziyad Clot, *Il n'y aura pas d'état palestinien: Journal d'un négotiateur en Palestine* (Paris: Max Milo., 2010).

20. See Julie Peteet, *Gender in Crisis: Women and the Palestinian Resistance Movement* (New York: Columbia University Press, 1991), and *Landscape of Hope and Despair: Palestinian Refugee Camps* (Philadelphia: University of Pennsylvania Press, 2005).

21. The Virgen de Guadalupe is generally referred to as "Reina de México y Emperatriz de América" (Queen of Mexico and Empress of the Americas). For the purpose of my analysis, I appropriate this concept to describe Fairuz as "The Queen of Lebanon and the Empress of the Arab World."

Chapter 9

1. Maurice Merleau-Ponty, *Phénoménologie de la perception* (Paris: Gallimard, 1963). English translation: *Phenomenology of Perception*, trans. Donald A. Landes (New York: Routledge, 2012).

2. Sara Ahmed, *Queer Phenomenology: Orientations, Objects, Others* (Durham: Duke University Press, 2006).

3. Karl Marx, *Grundrisse der Kritik der politischen Ökonomie* (Berlin: Dietz, 1953).

4. See, for instance, Nabil Beyhum, ed., *Reconstruire Beyrouth: Les paris sur le possible* (Lyons: Études sur le Monde Arabe, 1991); Samir Khalaf and Philip S. Khoury, eds., *Recovering Beirut: Urban Design and Post-War Reconstruction* (Leiden: Brill, 1993); Peter G. Rowe and Hashim Sarkis, eds., *Projecting Beirut: Episodes in the Construction and Reconstruction of a Modern City* (Munich: Prestel, 1998); Eric Huybrechts and Chawqi Douayhi, eds., *Reconstruction et réconciliation au Liban: négotiations, lieux publics, renouement du lien social* (Beirut: Les Cahiers du CERMOC, N°23, 1999); and Joe Nasr and Eric Verdeil, "The Reconstructions of Beirut," *The City in the Islamic World*, vol. 2, ed. Salma K. Jayyusi, et al. (Leiden: Brill, 2008), 1115–1142.

5. Mona Fawaz, "An Unusual Clique of City-Makers: Social Networks in the Production of a Neighborhood in Beirut (1950–75)," *International Journal of Urban and Regional Research* 32, no. 3 (2008): 565–585; Mona Fawaz, "Neoliberal Urbanity and the Right to the City: A View from Beirut's Periphery," *Develop-*

ment and Change 40, no. 5 (2009): 827–852; and Mona Fawaz, Mona Harb, and Ahmad Gharbieh, "Living Beirut's Security Zones: An Investigation of the Modalities and Practice of Urban Security," *City & Society* 24, no. 2 (2012): 173–195.

6. See Elias Khoury, "*Miroir brisé*," *Beyrouth: La brûlure des rêves* (Paris: Éditions Autrement, 2001), 58–64.

7. See Arjun Appadurai, ed., *The Social Life of Things: Commodities in Cultural Perspective* (Cambridge, UK: Cambridge University Press 1986), and Anne Meneley, *Tournaments of Value: Sociability and Hierarchy in a Yemeni Town* (Toronto: University of Toronto Press, 1996).

8. The same applies to transgender and transsexual identities in Lebanon. The notable exception has been the respected journalist Hazim Saghieh's study tracing the life of an Algerian transsexual who finds herself in Beirut. See Hazim Saghieh, *Mudhakkarāt randa al-trans* (*Memoirs of Randa the Trans*) (Beirut: dār al-sāqī, 2010).

9. *Meem, Bareed Mista3jil: True Stories* (Berlin: Heinrich-Böll–Stiftung, 2009).

10. It is important to note that in summer 2013, the Lebanese Psychiatric Society distanced itself officially from "reparative therapies" still practiced in Lebanon. This happened in the aftermath of the closure of the nightclub Ghost (note 4, chapter 1) and the ensuing controversy within the Lebanese media. See "La Société libanaise de psychiatrie, l'homosexualité et les thérapies réparatrices . . . ," *L'Orient-Le Jour* (July 12, 2013): 4.

11. Alan Bass, *Difference and Disavowal: The Trauma of Eros* (Stanford: Stanford University Press, 2000), 7.

12. See Julia Kristeva, *Powers of Horror: An Essay on Abjection*, trans. Leon S. Roudiez (New York: Columbia University Press, 1982).

13. Judith Butler, "Performative Acts and Gender Construction: An Essay in Phenomenology and Feminist Theory," *Theatre Journal* 40, no. 4 (December 1988): 519–531.

14. Pierre Bourdieu, *Masculine Domination* (Stanford: Stanford University Press, 2001), 1–2.

Chapter 10

1. Michael Gilsenan, *Lords of the Lebanese Marches: Violence & Narrative in an Arab Society* (Berkeley: University of California Press, 1996).

2. Pierre Bourdieu, ed., *La misère du monde* (Paris: Éditions du Seuil, 1993).

3. Judith Butler, *Undoing Gender* (New York: Routledge, 2004).

4. Lucia Volk, *Memorials and Martyrs in Modern Lebanon* (Bloomington: Indiana University Press, 2010).

5. Judith Butler, "Performative Acts and Gender Construction: An Essay in Phenomenology and Feminist Theory," *Theater Journal* 40, no. 4 (December 1988): 519–531.

6. Hānī al-Khatīb, "Qawm lūṭ ahyā' yurziqūn wa yuṭālibūn bi-huqūqihim!" *Al-muḥāyed* 2 (March 2004): 6–9.

7. This is reminiscent of how liberal politics incorporate certain queer subjects into a large heteronormative fold. See Jasbir K. Puar, *Terrorist Assemblages: Homonationalism in Queer Times* (Durham, NC: Duke University Press, 2007).

8. André Breton, *Manifestes du surréalisme* (Paris: Gallimard, 1999).

9. Walter Benjamin, *Illuminationen: Ausgewählte Schriften* (Frankfurt: Suhrkamp Taschenbuch, 1977).

10. Breton, 25.

11. Georges Bataille, *L'érotisme* (Paris: Les Éditions de Minuit, 1957).

12. The English translations are only approximate ones, for they do not render the complex moralizing connotations of these exclamations.

13. Louis Althusser, "Ideology and Ideological State Apparatuses (Notes towards an Investigation)," *Lenin and Philosophy and Other Essays* (New York: Monthly Review Press, 2001), 127–187, especially 170 ff.

14. Gaston Bachelard, *The Poetics of Space* (Boston: Beacon Press, 1994), xxxvi, emphasis added.

15. Henri Lefebvre, *La production de l'espace* (Paris: Anthropos, 2000), 114.

16. Samir Kassir, *Histoire de Beyrouth* (Paris: Librairie Arthème Fayard, 2003), 246 ff.

17. Ibid., 247, my translation from the French.

18. Lefebvre, *La production de l'espace*, 112. The English translation is slightly different from the one I provide here. It is to be found on page 94 of Donald Nicholson-Smith's version.

Conclusion

1. Italo Calvino, *Invisible Cities* (New York: Harcourt Brace & Company, 1974), 165, emphasis mine.

Glossary of Transliterated Arabic Terms

Transliterating Arabic words using the Latin alphabet is a plodding endeavor and can quickly turn into a vacillating enterprise. To better represent the code-switching practices of my interlocutors, I ideally would have used the Arabic original along with its own script. Since this was not possible, I felt compelled to draw on a modified version of transliteration principles established by the *International Journal of Middle East Studies* (*IJMES*). In so doing, I transliterated some of the Arabic words by using Modern Standard Arabic (MSA) and others by using the Arabic vernacular spoken in Lebanon. Some Arabic words commonly employed in English are spelled partly according to a different set of time-honored conventions—including the occasional use of Latin capital letters, which do not have their equivalent in Arabic.

Arabic consonant letters and their equivalent Latin letters in transliteration (*hijā'ī* order):

ا ب ت ث ج ح خ د ذ ر ز س ش ص ض ط ظ ع غ ف ق ك ل م ن ه و ي

y w h n m l k q/' f gh ʿ ẓ ṭ ḍ ṣ sh s z r dh d kh ḥ j th t b ā

'abaḍāyy big man
ahweh/maqha café/coffee shop
al-(q)'aḍiyya al-filisṭīniyya The Question of Palestine
al-baḥr the sea
al-baradays Paradise [Beach]
al-būr the port (in reference to the Beirut bus station located near the city's harbor)
al-ḍāḥiya the [southern] suburb [of Beirut]
al-dayʿa the village
adīra "strong queen" (or a queer-identified person who inspires others)
aḥbāsh "Abyssinians" (in reference to a Sunni Muslim group and their mosque in Zoqāq al-Blāṭ)
ajnabī/ajānib foreigner/foreigners (used mostly in reference to Westerners)

"ana mesh heyk!" "I'm not like that!"
'arabī Arab[ic] (used here in reference to Arab[ic] pop music)
arguīleh water-pipe
austostrade highway
"'ayb!" "Shame [on you]!"
ayyām bayrūt the days of Beirut (in reference to the PLO's presence until 1982)
azān al-maghrib the call for the Muslim prayer at sunset
barbāra [St.] Barbara (in reference to the saint's celebration on December 4)
bilād al-shām the Levant/"Greater Syria"
burj tower (in reference to Beirut's former historic center)
daftar al-jaysh army pad
dakkar virile/masculine man or perceived/self-declared "alpha male top"
darak police/gendarmerie
ḍownṭown vernacular term used to refer to Beirut's refurbished new center
fadīḥa scandal
fāyit bil-jaw/fāytīn bil jaw part of the [gay] atmosphere
gazdūra stroll
gharīb/ghurabā' strange[r]/strangers
ghazzal love poetry
gzāz fumées tinted windows
ḥammām bath[house]
"ḥarām!" "[this is] forbidden!"
ḥaramlik "private" quarters of an Ottoman palace
ḥārat al-sharamīṭ [female] whores' quarter
ḥarb tammūz July War (in reference to the Israeli onslaught in 2006)
ḥaṭṭa traditional headdress [mostly from the Gulf]
HELEM: ḥimāya lubnāniyya lil mithliyīn wal muzdawijīn wal mughayirīn "DREAM": Lebanese Protection for Lesbians, Gays, Bisexuals, and Transgenders
Ḥizballah Party of God (in reference to the Shī'ī political party/militia)
ibn 'ayleh son of a [respected] family
al-jabal the mountain
jaggal gigolo
jenaynat al-samāḥ Garden of Forgiveness
junūn/majnūn/majnūna/majanīn madness/madman/madwoman/mad(wo)men
ka'b [high] heel
Katāeb [the Lebanese] Phalange (right-wing Christian political party)
khalīji from the [Arab-Persian] Gulf
khamstalāf Five Thousand [Lebanese Lira]
khasso/khassun is concerned/are concerned (i.e., is/are queer-identified)
al-khaṭṭ al-mubāshar The Direct Line (activist group in Beirut)
khaṭṭ al-raīsī main artery (e.g., Ḥamra Street)
khaṭṭ al-tamās demarcation line (i.e., "Green Line")
kizib/tifnīs lying
liqā' meeting
lubnān Lebanon
liwāṭ/lūṭī sodomy/"son of Lot" ("faggot," pejorative term for a gay man)

ma'ānak small Armenian lamb sausages
maḍāfa formal reception area
madrasat al-ḥikmeh School of Wisdom
mafṣūm/mafṣumīn/infiṣām shakhsī schizophrenic (sing./pl.)/schizophrenia-split personality
maḥal/maṭraḥ place
majlis al-nuwāb Assembly of Deputies
manāra lighthouse
man'ūshat (sing.)/*mana'īsh* (pl.) *jibneh-jambon* Lebanese snack, half–herb bread/half-pizza, with cheese and ham
marad ghayr qābel lil-shifā' incurable illness
masīḥī Christian
matḥaf [The National] Museum
maẓāhir appearances
micro/van public bus
mithlī/mithlīyya homosexual/homosexuality
mukhabarāt Secret Service[s]
muṣādafa/ṣadafa encounter (n.)/encounter (v.)
musalsal (sing.)/musalsalāt (pl.) television series
mutaṣarrifiyya Ottoman Province [of Mount Lebanon]
"naḥna open-mind!" "We are open-minded!"
naqba [Palestinian 1948] Catastrophe
nejmeh star
noss r'jāl half-men
al-Quds Jerusalem
raqs sharqī Oriental dance
rayyes chief
sā'a clock
salamlik "public" quarters of an Ottoman palace
ṣān'a fake/artificial (f.)
service shared taxi
shāb/shabāb male youngsters
sha'bī popular
shādh/shudhūdh jinsī pervert/sexual perversion
shahīd/shuhadā' martyr/martyrs
shakhṣiyyāt personalities
shalehāt "chalets" (beach bungalows)
shamm al-hawwa "smell the air" (i.e., having a stroll)
sha'r shāyib gray hair
sharmūṭ/sharmūṭa/sharamīṭ prostitute (m./f., sing.)/prostitutes
shawfat al-ḥāl "the state of looking at oneself" (i.e., arrogance)
shish-ṭaouk marinated and grilled chicken sandwich
ṣidfa coincidence
siyāra car
souq market
ṭā'ifiyya sectarianism
tante/tantāt auntie/aunties (gay man/men identified as effeminate)

ṭobjī/ṭabājna faggot/faggots
traboulsi Tripolitanian (sometimes also used to refer to a gay man)
ulfat affinity
al-uwwāt The [Lebanese] Forces (Christian right-wing militia/political party)
waqf religious endowment
wāsṭa preferential treatment
al-yasūʿīyyeh The Jesuit [University]
zaʿīm/zuʿamāʾ leader/leaders
zajjal traditional musical poetry slams intended to sing the praises of newlyweds

Bibliography

Abdelhady, Dalia. *The Lebanese Diaspora: The Arab Immigrant Experience in Montreal, New York, and Paris*. New York: New York University Press, 2011.

Abdel-Samad, Nada. *Wādī abu-jmīl: qisas ʿan yahūd bayrūt*. Beirut: dār al-nahār, 2010.

Abela, Guy. *Caravanes*. Paris: La Pensée Universelle, 1983.

Abi Samra, Muhammad. "Maqha, Ahweh: An Etude in Café." *Portal 9*, 1 (Autumn 2012). Solidère Management Services, SAL.

Abu-Lughod, Lila. *Do Muslim Women Need Saving?* Cambridge, MA: Harvard University Press, 2013.

———. *Veiled Sentiments: Honor and Poetry in a Bedouin Society*. Berkeley: University of California Press, 1986.

———. "Writing Against Culture." In *Recapturing Anthropology: Working in the Present*, edited by Richard Fox, 137–162. Santa Fe, NM: School of American Research Press, 1991.

Ahmed, Sara. *Queer Phenomenology: Orientations, Objects, Others*. Durham, NC: Duke University Press, 2006.

Alameddine, Rabih. *The Hakawati*. New York: Knopf, 2008.

———. *Koolaids: The Art of War*. New York: Picador, 1998.

———. *The Perv*. New York: Picador, 1999.

———. *An Unnecessary Woman*. New York: Grove Press, 2013.

Al-jamʿiyya al-lubnāniyya li-ḥuqūq al-insān (Lebanese Human Rights Association). *Al-karāma al-insāniyya fī qānūn al-ʿuqūbāt*. Beirut: Sader/al-manshūrāt al-ḥuqūqiyya, 2003.

al-Khatīb, Hānī. "Qawm lūṭ aḥyā' yurziqūn wa yuṭālibūn bi-ḥuqūqihim!" *Al-muḥāyed* 2 (March 2004): 6–9.

Allen, Jafari S. *¡Venceremos? The Erotics of Black Self-Making in Cuba*. Durham, NC: Duke University Press, 2011.

Althusser, Louis. "Ideology and Ideological State Apparatuses (Notes towards an Investigation)." In *Lenin and Philosophy and Other Essays*, 127–187. New York: Monthly Review Press, 2001.

Al-Tifāshī, Shihābudīn Ahmad. *Nuzhat al-albāb fīmā lā yūjad fī kitāb*. Beirut: Riad El-Rayyes, 1992.

Anderson, Betty S. *The American University of Beirut: Arab Nationalism and Liberal Education*. Austin: University of Texas Press, 2011.

Appadurai, Arjun, ed. *The Social Life of Things: Commodities in Cultural Perspective*. Cambridge, UK: Cambridge University Press, 1996.

Aragon, Louis. *Le paysan de Paris*. Paris: Éditions Gallimar, 1998.

Arbid, George. *Karol Schayer, Architect (1900–1971): A Pole in Beirut*. Berlin: Birkhäuser Architecture, 2012.

Asad, Talal. "Secularism, Nation-State, Religion." In *Formations of the Secular: Christianity, Islam, Modernity*, 181–201. Stanford: Stanford University Press, 2003.

Atrash, Rasha. "The Wizard of Caracas." *Portal 9*, 1 (2012): 141–151. Solidère Management Services, SAL.

Bachelard, Gaston. *The Poetics of Space*. Boston: Beacon Press, 1994.

Bakhtin, Mikhail. *Rabelais and His World*, translated by Hélène Iswolsky. Bloomington: Indiana University Press, 1994.

Barakat, Huda. *Ḥajar al-ḍaḥak*. Beirut: dār anahār, 1990. (*The Stone of Laughter*. Northampton, MA: Interlink Books, 2006.)

Baroud, Ziyad, Ahmad Beydoun, Samir Kassir, Amal Makarem, Alexandre Najjar, and Nizar Saghieh. *Dhākira lil-ghad/mémoire pour l'avenir/Memory for the Future: Actes du colloque tenu à Beyrouth les 30 et 31 mars 2001*. Beirut: Éditions Dar An-Nahar, 2002.

Bass, Alan. *Difference and Disavowal: The Trauma of Eros*. Stanford: Stanford University Press, 2000.

Bataille, Georges. *L'érotisme*. Paris: Les Éditions de Minuit, 1957.

Benjamin, Walter. *Illuminationen: Ausgewählte Schriften*, vol. 1. Frankfurt: Suhrkamp Taschenbuch, 1977.

———. "M [der Flaneur]." In *Das Passagen-Werk*, vol. 1. Frankfurt: Edition Suhrkamp, 1983.

Benslama, Fethi, and Nadia Tazi, eds. *La Virilité en Islam*. Paris: Intersignes, 1998.

Berlant, Lauren. *Cruel Optimism*. Durham, NC: Duke University Press, 2011.

———. "Intimacy: A Special Issue." *Critical Inquiry* 24 (1998): 281–288.

Beydoun, Abbas. *Taḥlīl dam*. Beirut: Riyad el-Rayyes, 2002.

Beydoun, Ahmad. "A Note on Confessionalism." In *Lebanon in Limbo: Postwar Society and State in an Uncertain Regional Environment*, edited by Theodor Hanf and Nawaf Salam, 75–86. Baden-Baden: Nomos Verlagsgesellschaft, 2003.

Beyhum, Nabil, ed. *Reconstruire Beyrouth: Les paris sur le possible*. Lyons: Études sur le Monde Arabe, 1991.

Bouhdiba, Abdelwahab. *La sexualité en islam*. Paris: Presses Universitaires de France, 1975.

Bourdieu, Pierre. *Distinction: A Social Critique of the Judgment of Taste*. Cambridge, MA: Harvard University Press, 1991.

———. *In Algerien: Zeugnisse der Entwurzelung*, edited by Franz Schultheis and Christine Frisinghelli. Graz: Camera Austria, 2003.

———, ed. *La misère du monde* (Paris: Éditions du Seuil, 1993).

———. *Language & Symbolic Power*. Cambridge, MA: Harvard University Press, 1991.

———. *The Logic of Practice*. Stanford: Stanford University Press, 1992.

———. *Masculine Domination*. Stanford: Stanford University Press, 2001.
———. *Outline of a Theory of Practice*. Cambridge, UK: Cambridge University Press, 1977.
Bourdieu, Pierre, and Abdelmalek Sayad. *Le déracinement: La crise de l'agriculture traditionnelle en Algérie*. Paris: Les Éditions de Minuit, 1964.
Bousquet, Michel, and Iskander Habache. *Avoir 20 ans à Beyrouth*. Paris: Editions Alternatives, 2000.
Boustani, Carmen. *La guerre m'a surprise à Beyrouth: Récit*. Paris: Karthala, 2010.
Braudel, Fernand. *Écrits sur l'histoire*. Paris: Flammarion, 1969.
Breton, André. *Manifestes du surréalisme*. Paris: Gallimard, 1999.
Brown, Wendy. *Walled States, Waning Sovereignty*. Cambridge, MA: Zone Books, 2010.
Buck-Morss, Susan. *The Dialectics of Seeing: Walter Benjamin and the Arcades Project*. Cambridge, MA: MIT Press, 1989.
Butler, Judith. "Critically Queer." In *Bodies that Matter: On the Discursive Limits of "Sex."* New York: Routledge, 1993.
———. *Gender Trouble: Feminism and the Subversion of Identity*. New York: Routledge, 1989.
———. "Performative Acts and Gender Construction: An Essay in Phenomenology and Feminist Theory." *Theatre Journal* 40, no. 4 (December 1988): 519–531.
———. *Undoing Gender*. New York: Routledge, 2004.
Calvino, Italo. *Invisible Cities*. New York: Harcourt Brace & Company, 1974.
Chalcraft, John. *The Invisible Cage: Syrian Migrant Workers in Lebanon*. Stanford: Stanford University Press, 2008.
Charara, Walid, and Frédéric Domont. *Le Hezbollah: Un mouvement islamo-nationaliste*. Paris: Fayard, 2004.
Chararah, Waddah. "From the Walled Town of Eight Gates to the Architecture of the City." *Portal 9*, 1 (2012): 182. Solidère Management Services, SAL.
Chebel, Malek. *Le corps en islam*. Paris: Presses Universitaires de France, 1984.
———. *Dictionaire amoureux de l'islam*. Paris: Plon, 2004.
Chetcuti, Natacha, and Luca Greco, eds. *La face cachée du genre: Langage et pouvoir des normes*. Paris: Presses Sorbonne Nouvelle, 2012.
Clerc-Huybrechts, Valérie. *Les quartiers irréguliers de Beyrouth: Une histoire des enjeux fonciers et urbanistiques dans la banlieue sud*. Paris: IFPO, 2008.
Clot, Ziyad. *Il n'y aura pas d'état palestinien: Journal d'un Négociateur en Palestine*. Paris: Max Milo, 2010.
Coon, Carleton. *Caravan: The Story of the Middle East*. New York: Holt, Rinehart, and Winston, 1958.
Daoud, Hassan. *Bināyat matilde* (*Matilde's House*). Beirut: dār anahār, 1983.
Debord, Guy. *La société du spectacle*. Paris: Gallimard, 1992.
Decena, Carlos Ulises. *Tacit Subjects: Belonging and Same-Sex Desire among Dominican Immigrant Men*. Durham, NC: Duke University Press, 2011.
De Certeau, Michel. *The Practice of Everyday Life*. Berkeley: University of California Press, 1984.
De Genova, Nicholas. *Working the Boundaries: Race, Space, and "Illegality" in Mexican Chicago*. Durham, NC: Duke University Press, 2005.

———. "The Queer Politics of Migration: Reflections on 'Illegality' and Incorrigibility." *Studies in Social Justice* 4, no. 2 (2010).

Deeb, Lara. *An Enchanted Modern: Gender and Public Piety in Shi^ci Lebanon*. Princeton: Princeton University Press, 2006.

Deeb, Lara, and Harb, Mona. *Leisurely Islam: Negotiating Geography and Morality in Shi^cite South Beirut*. Princeton, NJ: Princeton University Press, 2013.

———. "Sanctioned Pleasures: Youth Negotiations of Leisure Sites and Morality in al-Dahiya." In *Arab Youth/Social Mobilisation in Times of Risk*, edited by Samir Khalaf and Roseanne Saad Khalaf, 303–318. London: Saqi Press, 2011.

Eddé, Carla. *Beyrouth: Naissance d'une capitale (1918–1924)*. Paris: Sindbad, 2009.

El Khalil, Zeina. *Beirut, I Love You: A Memoir*. London: Saqi Books.

El-Rouayheb, Khaled. *Before Homosexuality in the Arab-Islamic World, 1500–1800*. Chicago: University of Chicago Press, 2005.

Fawaz, Mona. "Neoliberal Urbanity and the Right to the City: A View from Beirut's Periphery." *Development and Change* 40, no. 5 (2009): 827–852.

———. "An Unusual Clique of City-Makers: Social Networks in the Production of a Neighborhood in Beirut (1950–75)." *International Journal of Urban and Regional Research* 32, no. 3 (2008): 565–585.

Fawaz, Mona, Mona Harb, and Ahmad Gharbieh. "Living Beirut's Security Zones: An Investigation of the Modalities and Practice of Urban Security." *City & Society* 24, no. 2 (2012): 173–195.

Féghali, Pascale. *Le quartier de Sanayeh à Beyrouth: Une exploration filmique*. Beirut: IFPO, 2009.

Fisk, Robert. *Pity the Nation: Lebanon at War*. Oxford: Oxford University Press, 2001.

Gagné, Mathew "Queer Beirut Online: The Participation of Men in Gayromeo .com." *Journal of Middle East Women's Studies* 8, no. 3 (2012): 113–137.

Gebhardt, Hans, Dorothée Sack, Ralph Bodenstein, Andreas Fritz, Jens Hanssen, Bernhard Hillenkamp, Oliver Kögler, Anne Mollenhauer, and Friederike Stolleis. *History, Space and Social Conflict in Beirut: The Quarter of Zokak el-Blat*. Würzburg: Ergon, 2005.

Genet, Jean. "Quatre heures à Chatila." *Revue d'études palestiniennes* (January 1, 1983).

———. *Un captif amoureux* (*Prisoner of Love*). Paris: Gallimard, 1986.

Georgis, Dina. *The Better Story: Queer Affects from the Middle East*. Albany: SUNY Press, 2013.

———. "Masculinities and the Aesthetics of Love: Reading Terrorism in *De Niro's Game* and *Paradise Now*." *Studies in Gender and Sexuality* 12 (2011): 134–148.

Ghoussoub, Mai. *Leaving Beirut: Women and the Wars Within*. London: Saqi Books, 1998.

Gilsenan, Michael. *Lords of the Lebanese Marches: Violence & Narrative in an Arab Society*. Berkeley: University of California Press, 1996.

———. "Lying, Honor, and Contradiction." In *Transaction and Meaning*, edited by B. Kapferer, 191–219. Philadelphia: Institute for the Study of Human Issues, 1976.

Gulick, John. *Tripoli: A Modern Arab City*. Cambridge, MA: Harvard University Press, 1967.

Hakim, Carol. *The Origins of the Lebanese National Idea: 1840–1920*. Berkeley: University of California Press, 2013.
Halbwachs, Maurice. *On Collective Memory*. Chicago: University of Chicago Press, 1992.
Halim, Hala. *Alexandrian Cosmopolitanism: An Archive*. New York: Fordham University Press, 2013.
Hanf, Theodor. *Co-Existence in Wartime Lebanon: Decline of a State and Rise of a Nation*. London: I. B. Tauris, 1994.
Hanssen, Jens. *Fin de Siècle Beirut: The Making of an Ottoman Provincial Capital*. Oxford: Clarendon Press, 2005.
Harb, Mona. *Le Hezbollah à Beyrouth (1985–2005): De la banlieue à la ville*. Paris: IFPO-Karthala, 2010.
HELEM. *Ruhāb al-mithliyya: mawāqif wa shahādāt*. Beirut: La CD-Thèque, 2006.
Helfer, Joachim, and Rashid Al-Daif. *Die Verschwulung der Welt: Rede gegen Rede, Beirut-Berlin*. Berlin: Edition Suhrkamp, 2006.
Helmreich, William B. *The New York Nobody Knows: Walking 6,000 Miles in the City*. Princeton: Princeton University Press, 2013.
Hourani, Albert, and Nadim Shehadi, eds. *The Lebanese in the World: A Century of Emigration*. London: Center for Lebanese Studies/I. B. Tauris & Co. Ltd. Publishers, 1992.
Humaydan, Iman. *Bā' mithl bayt mithl bayrūt*. Beirut: dār al-massār, 1997.
Huybrechts, Eric, and Chawqi Douayhi, eds. *Reconstruction et réconciliation au Liban: négotiations, lieux publics, renouement du lien social*. Beirut: Les Cahiers du CERMOC, No. 23, 1999.
Jaber, Rabih. *Bayrūt madīnat al-ʿālim*. Beirut: dār al-ādāb, 2003.
Joseph, Suad. "Civic Myths, Citizenship, and Gender in Lebanon." In *Gender and Citizenship in the Middle East*, edited by Suad Joseph, 107–136. Syracuse, NY: Syracuse University Press, 2000.
———. "Gendering Citizenship in the Middle East." In *Gender and Citizenship in the Middle East*, edited by Suad Joseph, 3–30. Syracuse, NY: Syracuse University Press, 2000.
———. "My Son/Myself, My Mother/Myself: Paradoxical Realities of Patriarchal Connectivity." In *Intimate Selving in Arab Families: Gender, Self, and Identity*, edited by Suad Joseph, 174–190. Syracuse, NY: Syracuse University Press, 2000.
Kaakoush, Nabil. "Hey Handsome." In *Transit Beirut: New Writing and Images*, edited by Roseanne Saad Khalaf and Malu Halasa, 166–173. Beirut and London: Saqi Books, 2004.
Kanna, Ahmed. *Dubai: The City as Corporation*. Minneapolis: University of Minnesota Press, 2011.
Kaplan, Alice. *French Lessons: A Memoir*. Chicago: University of Chicago Press, 1993.
Kassir, Samir. *Considérations sur le malheur arabe*. Paris: Actes Sud, 2004.
———. *Histoire de Beyrouth*. Paris: Librairie Arthème Fayard, 2003.
———. *La guerre du Liban: De la dissension nationale au conflit regional*. Paris: Karthala-CERMOC, 1994.
Khalaf, Samir. *The Burj*. London: Saqi Books, 2005.

———. *Lebanon Adrift: From Battleground to Playground*. London: Saqi Books, 2012.

———. *Prostitution in a Changing Society: A Sociological Survey of Legal Prostitution in Beirut*. Beirut: Khayats, 1965.

Khalaf, Samir, and Per Kongstad. *Hamra of Beirut: A Case of Rapid Urbanization*. Leiden: Brill, 1973.

Khalaf, Samir, and Philip S. Khoury, eds. *Recovering Beirut: Urban Design and Post-War Reconstruction*. Leiden: Brill, 1993.

Khater, Akram Fouad. *Inventing Home: Emigration, Gender, and the Middle Class in Lebanon, 1870–1920*. Berkeley: University of California Press, 2001.

Khoury, Elias. *Al-jabal al-saghīr*. Beirut: Muassassat al-abhāth al-arabiyya, 1977.

———. "Miroir brisé." In *Beyrouth: La brûlure des rêves*, 58–64. Paris: Éditions Autrement.

———. *Yalo*. Beirut: Dār al-ādāb, 2001.

Khuri, Fuad I. *From Village to Suburb: Order and Change in Greater Beirut*. Chicago: University of Chicago Press, 1975.

Klaes, Ulla. *"Und ich sitze hier ohne jede Angst . . ." Texte und Arbeitsnotizen aus dem Nachlaß von Ulla Klaes (1993–1998)*. Berlin, 2000.

Kristeva, Julia. *Powers of Horror: An Essay on Abjection*, translated by Leon S. Roudiez. New York: Columbia University Press, 1982.

Lacan, Jacques. "Le stade du miroir comme formateur de la fonction du Je." In *Écrits*, Vol. 1, 92–99. Paris: Éditions du Seuil, 1999.

Lefebvre, Henri. *The Production of Space*, translated by Donald Nicholson-Smith. Oxford, UK: Blackwell Publishing, 1991. Translation of *La production de l'espace* 4th ed. Paris: Anthropos, 2000 (originally published in 1974).

———. *Rhythmanalysis: Space, Time and Everyday Life*. London: Continuum International Publishing Group, 2004.

L'Orient-Le Jour. "La Société libanaise de psychiatrie, l'homosexualité et les thérapies réparatrices . . . ." *L'Orient-Le Jour* (July 12th, 2013): 4.

Maalouf, Amin. *Les désorientés*. Paris: Grasset, 2012.

———. *Les identités meurtières*. Paris: Grasset, 1998.

Maasri, Zeina. *Off the Wall: Political Posters of the Lebanese Civil War*. London: I. B. Tauris, 2009.

Makarem, Ghassan. "The Story of HELEM." *Journal of Middle East Women's Studies* 7, no. 3 (Fall 2011): 98–112.

Makdisi, Saree. "Beirut, a City without History?" In *Memory and Violence in the Middle East and North Africa*, edited by Ussama Makdisi and Paul A. Silverstein, 201–214. Bloomington: Indiana University Press, 2006.

Makdisi, Ussama. *The Culture of Sectarianism: Community, History, and Violence in Nineteenth-Century Ottoman Lebanon*. Berkeley: University of California Press, 2000.

Martin, Marko. *Der Prinz von Berlin*. Berlin: Ullstein, 2001.

Marx, Karl. *Grundrisse der Kritik der Politischen Ökonomie*. Berlin: Dietz, 1953.

Massoud, Rania. "Arrestation de travestis à Dékouané: le chef de la municipalité se défend d'être homophobe." *L'Orient-Le Jour* (April 2013): 1.

Meem. *Bareed Mista3jil: True Stories*. Berlin: Heinrich-Böll–Stiftung, 2009.

Ménargues, Alain. *Les secrets de la guerre du Liban: Du coup d'État de Bachir Gémayel aux massacres des camps palestiniens*. Paris: Albin Michel, 2004.

Meneley, Anne. *Tournaments of Value: Sociability and Hierarchy in a Yemeni Town*. Toronto: University of Toronto Press, 1996.

Merleau-Ponty, Maurice. *Phénoménologie de la perception*. Paris: Gallimard, 1963. English translation: *Phenomenology of Perception*, translated by Donald A. Landes. New York: Routledge, 2012.

Mermier, Franck, ed. *Liban: Espaces partagés et pratiques de rencontre*. Paris: IFPO, 2008.

Mermier, Franck, and Christophe Varin, eds. *Mémoires de guerres au Liban (1975–1990)*. Paris: Sindbad, 2010.

Messick, Brinkley. "Subordinate Discourse: Women, Weaving, and Gender Relations in North Africa." *American Ethnologist* 14, no. 2 (May 1987): 210–225.

Mitchell, Don. *The Right to the City: Social Justice and the Fight for Public Space*. New York: Guilford Press, 2003.

Mitchell, Timothy. *Colonising Egypt*. Berkeley: University of California Press, 1991.

Monroe, Kristin. "Being Mobile in Beirut." *City & Society* 23, no. 1 (2011): 91–111.

Morgensen, Scott Lauria. *Spaces Between Us: Queer Settler Colonialism and Indigenous Decolonization*. Minneapolis: University of Minnesota Press, 2011.

Mulvey, Laura. "Visual Pleasure and Narrative Cinema." *Screen* 16, no. 3 (1975): 6–18.

Muñoz, José Esteban. *Cruising Utopia: The Then and There of Queer Futurity*. New York: New York University Press, 2009.

———. *Disidentifications: Queers of Color and the Performance of Politics*. Minneapolis: University of Minnesota Press, 1999.

Najjar, Alexandre. *Pour la Francophonie*. Beyrouth: Dar An-Nahar, 2008.

Nasr, Joe, and Eric Verdeil. "The Reconstructions of Beirut." In *The City in the Islamic World*, Vol. 2, edited by Salma K. Jayyusi, Renata Holod, Attilio Petruccioli, and André Raymond, 1115–1142. Leiden: Brill, 2008.

Nietzsche, Friedrich. *The Will to Power*. New York: Random House, 1967.

Nora, Pierre, and David P. Jordan, eds. *Rethinking France: Les Lieux de mémoire, Volume 2: Space*. Chicago: University of Chicago Press, 2006.

Peteet, Julie M. *Gender in Crisis: Women and the Palestinian Resistance Movement*. New York: Columbia University Press, 1991.

———. *Landscape of Hope and Despair: Palestinian Refugee Camps*. Philadelphia: University of Pennsylvania Press, 2005.

———. "Male Gender and Rituals of Resistance in the Palestinian Intifada: A Cultural Politics of Violence." In *Imagined Masculinities: Male Identity and Culture in the Modern Middle East*, edited by Mai Ghoussoub and Emma Sinclair-Webb, 101–126. London: Saqi Books, 2000.

Proth, Bruno. *Lieux de drague: scènes et coulisses d'une sexualité masculine*. Toulouse: Octarès, 2002.

Proust, Marcel. *Du côté de chez Swann (À la recherche du temps perdu I)*. Paris: Gallimard, 1988.

Puar, Jasbir. *Terrorist Assemblages: Homonationalism in Queer Times*. Durham, NC: Duke University Press, 2007.

Roberts, Hugh. *The Battlefield: Algeria 1988–2002, Studies in a Broken Polity*. London: Verso, 2003.
Rowe, Peter G., and Hashim Sarkis, eds. *Projecting Beirut: Episodes in the Construction and Reconstruction of a Modern City*. Munich: Prestel, 1998.
Ruppert, Helmut. *Beirut: Eine westlich geprägte Stadt des Orients*. Erlangen: Mitteilungen der Fränkischen Geographischen Gesellschaft, 1969.
Saghieh, Hazim. *Mudhakkarāt randa al-trans* (*Memoirs of Randa the Trans*). Beirut: dār al-sāqī, 2010.
———, ed. *The Predicament of the Individual in the Middle East*. London: Saqi Books, 2001.
Salam, Nawaf. *'Itifāq al-ṭāef: 'Istiʿāda naqdiyya/L'accord de Taef: Un réexamen critique*. Beirut: Éditions Dar An-Nahār, 2003.
———. *La condition libanaise: Des communautés, du citoyen et de l'État; suivi de L'émergence de la notion de citoyenneté en pays d'islam*. Beirut: Éditions Dar An-Nahar, 1998.
Salibi, Kamal. *A House of Many Mansions: The History of Lebanon Reconsidered*. Berkeley: University of California Press, 1988.
Sawalha, Aseel. *Reconstructing Beirut: Memory and Space in a Postwar Arab City*. Austin: University of Texas Press, 2010.
Schmitz, Markus. *Kulturkritik ohne Zentrum: Edward W. Said und die Kontrapunkte kritischer Dekolonisation*. Bielefeld: transcript, 2008.
Scott, Joan W. "Gender: A Useful Category of Historical Analysis." *The American Historical Review* 91, no. 5 (December 1986): 1053–1075.
Sedgwick, Eve Kosofsky. *Epistemologies of the Closet*. Berkeley: University of California Press, 1990.
Sehnaoui, Nada. *L'occidentalisation de la vie quotidienne à Beyrouth, 1860–1914*. Beirut: Éditions Dar An-Nahar, 2002.
Seidman, Steven. "The Politics of Cosmopolitan Beirut: From the Stranger to the Other." *Theory, Culture & Society* 29, no. 2 (2012): 3–36.
Singerman, Diane, and Paul Amar. *Cairo Cosmopolitan: Politics, Culture, and Urban Space in the New Globalized Middle East*. Cairo: American University in Cairo Press, 2009.
Sontag, Susan. "Notes on Camp." *Partisan Review* 31 (Fall 1964): 515–530.
Stolleis, Friederike. "The Inhabitants of Zokak el-Blat: Demographic Shifts and Patterns of Interaction." In *History, Space and Social Conflict in Beirut: The Quarter of Zokak el-Blat*, edited by H. Gebhardt and S. Sack, 175–211. Beirut: Orient-Institut der DMG Beirut, 2005.
Stone, Christopher. *Popular Culture and Nationalism in Lebanon: the Fairouz and Rahbani Nation*, Routledge Studies in Middle Eastern Literatures. Abingdon, UK: Routledge, 2007.
Tabet, Jad. *Al-iʿmār wal-maslaḥa al-ʿāma fil-turāth wal-ḥadātha: Madīnat al-ḥarb wa dhākirat al-mustaqbal*. Beirut: dār al-jadīd, 1996.
Traboulsi, Fawwaz. "Crisis and Memory in the Theater of the Raḥbānī-Brothers and Fayrūz." In *Crisis and Memory in Islamic Societies*, edited by Angelika Neuwirth and Andreas Pflitsch, 499–508. Beirut: Ergon Verlag Würzburg, 2001.
———. *A History of Modern Lebanon*, London: Pluto Press, 2007.

Varzi, Roxanne. *Warring Souls: Youth, Media, and Martyrdom in Post-Revolution Iran*. Durham, NC: Duke University Press, 2006.

Verdeil, Éric. *Beyrouth et ses urbanistes: Une ville en plans (1946–1975)*. Beirut: Presses de l'IFPO, 2009.

Verdeil, Éric, Ghaleb Faour, and Sébastien Velut. *Atlas du Liban: Territoires et société*. Beirut: IFPO/CNRS, 2007.

Volk, Lucia. *Memorials and Martyrs in Modern Lebanon*. Bloomington: Indiana University Press, 2010.

Weizman, Eyal. *Hollow Land: Israel's Architecture of Occupation*. New York: Verso, 2007.

Whitaker, Brian. *Unspeakable Love: Gay and Lesbian Life in the Middle East*. London: Saqi, 2006.

Whyte, William Foote. *Street Corner Society: The Social Structure of an Italian Slum*. Chicago: University of Chicago Press, 1943.

Young, Michael. *The Ghosts of Martyrs Square: An Eyewitness Account of Lebanon's Life Struggle*. New York: Simon & Schuster, 2010.

Index

Note: Page numbers in *italics* indicate images.

www.ingramcontent.com/pod-product-compliance
Ingram Content Group UK Ltd.
Pitfield, Milton Keynes, MK11 3LW, UK
UKHW032028240225
455518UK00001B/111

9 781477 309919